MODERN AMERICAN PROTESTANTISM
AND ITS WORLD

MODERN AMERICAN PROTESTANTISM AND ITS WORLD
Historical Articles on Protestantism in American Religious Life

Edited by Martin E. Marty

Series ISBN 3-598-41530-3

MODERN AMERICAN PROTESTANTISM AND ITS WORLD
Historical Articles on Protestantism in American Religious Life

13. Missions and Ecumenical Expressions

Edited with an Introduction by

Martin E. Marty

The University of Chicago

K · G · Saur
Munich · London · New York · Paris 1993

BV
2070
.M578
1993

Publisher's Note

The articles and chapters which comprise this collection originally appeared in a wide variety of publications and are reproduced here in facsimile from the highest quality offprints and photocopies available. The reader will notice some occasional marginal shading and text-curl common to photocopying from tightly bound volumes. Every attempt has been made to correct or minimize this effect.

Copyright information for articles reproduced in this collection appears at the end of this volume.

Library of Congress Cataloging-in-Publication Data
Missions and ecumenical expressions / edited with an
    introduction by Martin E. Marty.
        p. cm. -- (Modern American Protestantism and its world ; 13)
    Includes bibliographical references and index.
    ISBN 3-598-41544-3 (alk. paper)
    1. Protestant churches--Missions. 2. Ecumenical movement.
I. Marty, Martin E., 1928-   . II. Series.
BV2070.M578 1992
280'.4'0973--dc20   92-4318
                                                    CIP

Die Deutsche Bibliothek - CIP - Einheitsaufnahme

Modern American Protestantism and its world: historical
articles on Protestantism in American religious life / ed. with
an introduction by Martin E. Marty. - Munich ; London ; New York ;
Paris : Saur.
    ISBN 3-598-41530-3
NE: Marty, Martin E. (Hrsg.)
Vol. 13. Missions and ecumenical expressions. - 1993
    ISBN 3-598-41544-3

☉
Printed on acid-free paper/Gedruckt auf säurefreiem Papier

All Rights Strictly Reserved/Alle Rechte vorbehalten
K.G. Saur Verlag GmbH & Co. KG, Munich 1993
A Reed Reference Publishing Company

Printed in the United States of America

Printed/Bound by Edwards Brothers Incorporated, Ann Arbor

ISBN 3-598-41544-3 (vol. 13)
ISBN 3-598-41530-3 (series)

Contents

Series Preface

Protestantism is America's "only national religion and to ignore that fact is to view the country from a false angle." Andre Siegfried, an astute visitor from France, made that observation in 1927. One did not have to be very astute to see America as the French journalist did, for reasons that are beginning to be lost among Americans today.

Wherever one looked, there was Protestantism. It had come with the Anglicans of Virginia and the other southern colonies, which established their Episcopal church and did what they could to suppress Catholics who had settled in Maryland. Protestantism in its Puritan form motivated the Pilgrims and Puritans who settled the New England states and established Congregationalism there. They did what they could to quarantine Rhode Island, because it welcomed people of many faiths--Jews settled in early--but New England was firmly Protestant. As for the middle colonies, where no one church was supported by law, Protestants prevailed.

At the time of the birth of America, there were probably somewhat more than four million people in the colonies. Many estimate that only about 30,000 of these were Catholics and 3,000 were Jews. Native Americans, most of them resistant to Protestantism, were being pushed away; when slave owners started caring about the souls of slaves, they Protestantized them, and black America remains overwhelmingly Protestant.

The birth of America meant the gradual ending of state support for Protestantism. But the power that Protestants lost in the legal realm they recouped in other ways. They formed strong competitive church bodies, headed out to win the West for their religion and ways of life, developed voluntary organizations for reform and good works, and tried to pass laws favoring their outlooks. They developed what I have called a "religious empire."

What about everyone else? A year after Andre Siegfried wrote, Protestant America helped defeat Governor Al Smith's bid for the United States Presidency; Smith's Catholicism offended them, and not until 1960 was a Catholic elected President. Catholicism made up the largest single church for a century, and Catholics had enormous power in northern cities. But Catholic were often not part of the American elite. Jews also were not.

Today it is hard to picture how strong the Protestant hold was on the whole nation. Nowadays we speak of America as "pluralist," not a Protestant society. There are as many Muslims as Episcopalians. The heirs of established Congregationalism are few, while the Asian population grows. Judaism has unimaginably more influence than it did a century ago. Catholics are at home and at ease in all elements of American life, exerting influence where and as they will. What the Protestants of old called "infidelity" and of more recent times called "secularism" has a power they feared but did not really believe could establish itself.

How Protestantism came from its position of near-monopoly to mere hegemony to its place as a set of faiths among other sets of faiths is central to the drama of American religious life, indeed, American life as a whole. Yielding power as it did is an act which normally one would expect would have issued in bloodshed and produced revolutions. Every morning's newspaper and television bring stories of interreligious, intertribal, and intercultural clashes that exact terrible tolls on human life: one thinks of Lebanon, the Asian subcontinent, Northern Ireland, and elsewhere for examples. In America the change was made without loss of life--but not without drama.

The drama of adjustment by Protestants to the world they had made and was now moving beyond them makes up the background to the articles chosen to depict Protestantism's changing place in American life in this series of articles and books.

What is this Protestantism that exercised so much influence and still has to be reckoned with in most dimensions of American life? The Protestant churches represent that element in Western Christianity which is not obedient to the Pope at Rome. That negative definition seems to be as far as one can go in finding something which all Protestants held and hold in common. But Protestantism is also a cultural force of great influence in the culture, as a glance at American history shows.

Protestants, for instance, believed in exalting the individual. They formed churches and other collectives, but they insisted that the conscience and reason of the individual mattered supremely in the plan of God. While Protestantism is not the only source of American individualism, to overlook it would be to misunderstand America. But individualism was by no means a unique stress. The early Protestants came with a sense of "covenant," a claim that God had reached out and, in effect, made an agreement with them. God would favor them if the Americans would be faithful. So citizens of the United States started thinking of themselves as "chosen" people with a "mission" and a "destiny."

Many of the extensions of these themes of chosenness, mission, and destiny helped produced the best and worst times in American life. They have led to moral productivity, as in support of human rights, just as they have led to pride and folly, as when Americans tried to impose their will and ways on other nations.

Protestant themes course through American literature, through the novels of Hawthorne and Melville and more. They are present in economic thought, beginning with a concept of one's "vocation" or "calling" in daily life, in the use of the world's resources. Americans do their debating of vital issues: defense policy, attitudes toward Israel, a welfare society, abortion, and the like, employing themes planted by Protestants.

The Protestant movement, even though it no longer has hegemony, is by no means weak. Taking black and white Protestantism together, the churches of this movement attract the loyalty and active participation of well over a hundred million Americans. They give billions of dollars and hours to the cause, providing places of worship, shelters for the homeless, agencies for involvement in political life, centers for training the young, participating in institutions of human care, keeping contact with people around the globe, and marking the stages of peoples' individual lives. They share "clout," but that does not mean they do not have "clout."

Protestantism has passed through many stages in America. This series concentrates on those that occurred in a period code-named "modern." Making sense of modernity is a full-time job for individuals, for a nation, for the churches, and for the scholars. In this collection, we take the modern period to represent roughly the past century. Decades after the Civil War and toward the end of the century, Americans saw that they were turning urban, industrial, pluralist. Village life, a natural home for Protestants, was turning metropolitan, where Protestants were being overwhelmed by non-Protestant immigrants. Yet, instead of growing weaker and seeing their churches empty, as in the European experience, American Protestants built more and filled the houses of God. If one Protestant movement weakens--as the mainstream seems to have done in recent decades--others, such as black, fundamentalist, evangelical, and pentecostal fill the void and Protestantism finds new ways to prosper.

If Protestants once "ran the show" in an America that no longer is ruled by a single force, they are still not folding their tents, turning their churches into museums, or ceasing in efforts to influence the whole society. For that reason, there is a strong interest in the near-contemporary, the turmoil of the recent past, which helps shape American political and social discourse as the century ends. The articles in these volumes are alert to changes as America comes to a period called "post-modern." These are times when many pay attention, if only eclectically, to traditions. When Americans rummage in their collective attics looking for what they might make use of in a new day, much of what they find has "Protestant" on the label. Understanding Protestantism has become urgent.

In comparison to other movement--Mormonism, "cults," the Asian presence, the New Age, and the like--Protestantism suffers. Because it is so identified with the wallpaper and woodwork of the mental furnished apartment in which Americans live, many take it for granted. It does not seem arcane, exotic, alluring to a public which seeks novelty. Yet that very bonding with the environment which makes Protestantism hard to study is part of the secret of its power. It remains a sort of insider in a pluralist and secular and modern world. To overlook its power and the changes it has experienced in the past century is to miss the point of much of American Life. These articles help a new generation find the point, as a step toward helping them then make up their mind what to do about it.

Introduction

Christianity has always been a missionary religion. While some religions have expanded naturally, Christianity was born with an exclusive view: there was salvation under no other name than that of Jesus Christ. And with that claim went a mandate: go into all the world and preach the Gospel.

After the first three centuries, most of that mission had been tinged with compulsoriness. That is, as Christians extended empire, they either baptized the conquered people, or led a leader to find motives for being baptized and he would turn around and have all his people Christianized. The baptism of King Clovis of the Franks was typical; Boniface chopped down a sacred oak among Germanic peoples and got them to accept the cross; Scandinavian kings converted and took their people with them. There were, of course, eloquent spokespersons for the faith, tireless missionaries who paid little attention to crown--one thinks of Francis Xavier in the sixteenth century who went as far as Japan--but these were exceptions.

The Protestant Reformation of the sixteenth century did little to change the situation. Catholic rulers became Protestant in northern Europe, and their people had to turn Protestant with them. The preaching of Martin Luther and John Calvin does not say much about going into all the world, converting people to fulfill the commands of Christ. Mission meant imperial growth.

Modernity brought change to Protestants and Protestants helped initiate religious changes in modernity. Roughly concurrent with the birth of America, a number of Protestant movements including Continental Pietism and, notably in England, Wesleyan Methodism and Anglican Evangelicalism, were moved by people who preached conversion and who heard far beyond their nation the call to get people to claim Christ. In the 1790s any number of societies to send out missionaries were born. Increases in communication and efficiency of transportation coupled with expansion of the British empire made the context rich; ideology accompanied it.

In the United States, Protestants started missions which followed the pattern of European Christian expansion of the European Empire. In the second and third decades of the nineteenth century young men (and sometimes notable spouses or single women) from Eastern colleges formed an elite of missionaries to the Holy Land, the Sandwich Islands, Burma, India, eventually to China, and even to the Muslim world. Participating in the movement came to be an heroic thing for men and an ennobling thing for women to do. Stories of their vicissitudes and triumphs enlivened Sunday school lessons and provided sermon illustrations. The denominations took pride in their overseas agents, and interdenominational agencies formed.

To some critics of the venture, the missionaries looked like nothing so much as either chaplains to exploiters or legitimators of capitalist ventures. Now it is true that the Protestant missionary expansion of the nineteenth century, the one that missionary historian Kenneth Scott Latourette called "great" because it was great for missions, was associated with the spread of capitalism and imperialism. But a fair accounting of what went on suggests that for all the jingoism and cultural superiority expressed by missionaries, to say nothing of an exclusivism which many find offensive in later times, countless missionaries did effect positive change in the nations they reached.

The reappraisers suggest that change was coming willy-nilly, as technology reached the nations later to be called "developing" or of the Third World. Such change would be merely materialistic, utterly impersonal, militarily and politically and mechanically relentless. The missionaries at least provided alternative ways of dealing with the change. A real affection grew between them and the missionized people. What is more, missionaries performed services among the people to whom they condescended. They built schools, clinics, hospitals, relief centers, and many other kinds of agencies to show that they cared about more and other than merely saving souls. (None of them would have used the word "merely" there, but they might know what I mean in this context!) Their graves in Africa and Oceania are testimonies to their dedication.

Change has come. Since the middle of the twentieth century, the ecumenical movement has deprived Western and especially American mainstream Protestantism of their freedom and choice to be superior. Now there is more interest in interreligious dialogue, in stimulating the development and autonomy of the "independent" churches that used to be called "younger" and, before that, "mission" churches. Appreciation for positive values in other religions has grown. Protestant agencies work to support the schools and clinics they founded, and often to help workers participate in movements of change elsewhere.

The withdrawal of aggressive missionaries from mainstream Protestant sources left a vacuum into which fundamentalists, evangelicals, and pentecostals moved, and they have prospered. There are more missionaries from American Protestantism in the field now than there were in the heyday of mainstream efforts to evangelize the world. But the attention of historians has focused more on the men and women who went forth from the world of the standard-brand Protestants that were normative in the nineteenth and earlier twentieth centuries.

Missionary history has known vicissitudes. Much of the earlier work permeated as it was by denominational agents, was hagiographic, biased, ethnocentric, and denominationally prejudiced. Then came a period of reaction, in which the writing of missionary history meant the search for foolish or guilty parties. Serious historians tended to let the story lie. But diplomatic historians, students of international relations, and the like, have begun to call for more and better history of missions, a call to which authors like those in this volume have begun to respond.

Paul Varg's study of motives in Protestant missions sets the themes, and Charles Forman extends the study of motivations, while Robert McClellan focuses on the experience of China, which held special magic for the missionaries from America. Dorothea Muller's examination of Josiah Strong takes up issues associated with an intense nationalist. A number of essays, including those by Neil Lebhar and Martyn Minns, Daniel J. Adams, and John J. Feeney, Jr., focus on personalities and exemplifications of establishmentarian denominations like Episcopalianism and Presbyterianism.

The second half of the volume deals with the centripetal counterpart to the first half's centrifuge. That is, in the twentieth century the same Christians who dispersed around the world and competed began to return and seek means of finding amity and convergence. This effort, which came to early resolution in the United States in 1908 and 1910, with the Federal Council of Churches and participation in an International Missionary Council, initiated a movement called "ecumenical." It was not in contradiction to but it supplemented the missionary movement, and became the major force in Protestantism through much of the new century. Two essays talk about the Federal and the National Councils; Richard V. Pierard concentrates on evangelist Billy Graham, who straddled the evangelical (and hence often antiecumenical) and ecumenical spheres, while William M. Clements studies the rhetoric of radio ministry, thus concentrating on a pioneering agency that had much to do with both missions and ecumenism.

* * *

Peter D'Agostino and Gil Waldkoenig, successively my research assistants while this project was being conceived and executed, made major contributions to the selecting and editing, and I thank them for their creative and persistent participation.

In order to assure representationality and variety, for the choice of articles in this set of volumes we consulted with dozens of scholars who specialize in American religion. In some cases, several of them nominated the same articles. We wish to acknowledge the cooperation of Gerald H. Anderson, N. Keith Clifford (deceased), Robert Clouse, E. Brooks Holifield, and Dewey D. Wallace, Jr.

MISSIONS AND ECUMENICAL EXPRESSIONS

MOTIVES IN PROTESTANT MISSIONS, 1890-1917*

PAUL A. VARG, *The Ohio State University*

In terms of the number of missionaries, financial contributions, and amount of home front propaganda, the missionary movement reached its peak in the United States in the years from 1890 to 1917. Only during this period did the foreign missions of the Protestant churches enjoy sufficient popular support to warrant use of the term "crusade."

This raises the question as to why Christian missions should have had such a strong appeal to the generation which elected Theodore Roosevelt to the presidency, embarked on a crusade to liberate the Cubans, and later sent its sons to Europe allegedly to defend the moral principles of democracy. Nothing could have been more quixotic than the slogan adopted by the Student Volunteers: "The Evangelization of the World in this Generation." This motto expressed the vision of the thousands of college and seminary students who joined the Student Volunteers. It was also the goal of the hosts of women's missionary societies and the Laymen's Movement, the organization which marshaled the support of more than 100,000 men in the churches in behalf of foreign missions.

The crusade assumed amazing proportions but the degree of self-dedication on the part of young men and women who volunteered to go out as missionaries was even more remarkable. Upon their graduation from Yale, Sherwood Eddy, Henry Luce, and Horace Pitkin went to Union Theological Seminary. Their lives came to have one purpose, the carrying of the gospel to China Sherwood Eddy later recalled:

> From that moment my life was focused upon what seemed to me the greatest work in the world. I too felt I must be a crusader. I was jarred broad awake: my studies meant more, and even athletics had a new meaning. When I would box every afternoon with Pitkin and when we would run our daily mile in the gym or the open air, we would say, "This will carry us another mile in China."[1]

A few years later Pitkin was killed by the Boxers. Before his execution he penned a note to his infant son urging him to take up the burden of the evangelization of China as soon as he came of age.

*Read at the Annual Meeting of the Society, Chicago, December 29, 1953.

MOTIVES IN PROTESTANT MISSIONS, 1890-1917

Why the American people should have accepted the Christianization of far-off lands as one of the most laudable of all human enterprises involves the ever difficult question of motives. It is a question which often eludes those who, like the historian, have to limit their investigation to the aims which have been proclaimed or implied in the written records. Whatever the deeper recesses of the subconscious might reveal or a knowledge of the experiences peculiar to an individual might suggest, these avenues of research are largely closed. Yet, recognizing these limitations, the historian may be able to offer a satisfactory explanation of missionary enthusiasm.

It was in the prevailing spirit of Moody revivalism that the missionary movement found its deepest religious source. The former shoe clerk, Dwight L. Moody, plumbed no new intellectual depths and his theology, to the degree he had any, was no more complex than that he had learned as a boy in Sunday School. Yet, no American of his generation had a larger audience. What he lacked in intellect and deep spiritual insight, he made up for in his unshakable grasp of religious stereotypes and an amazing ability to put into words the religious problems that troubled the average church-goer. Unlike some of his successors Moody never consciously developed a theatrical technique for swaying his audiences, and to his thousands of listeners he seemed the completely consecrated man.

The Moody type of revivalism did not emphasize theology. Instead it exploited the guilt complex and preached justification by faith. What it conceived to be the evils of its day raised no questions about the social order and the solution to all ills it conceived to lie in the redemption of the individual. Stated in religious terms, it had a passion for souls and it was this sense of urgency which served as a major impetus to the foreign missionary crusade.

The converts of the revivals looked upon themselves as vessels of the Holy Spirit, and they experienced a joy that could not be suppressed. In a state of religious rapture, they spoke of having met God on a spiritual mountain top. At the close of an emotional sermon at a religious conference in Maine the presiding officer arose and said: "Our brother has something which I have not received. . . . I must be filled with the Spirit. . . . Now I shall kneel here and stay on my knees till

what God has done for Bro. Steele He shall do for me. Let all who desire it do the same."[2] For three hours the audience of four hundred
knelt in silent prayer. A participant reported that the place became awful
with God's presence.

At the Student Volunteer Conventions a sense of divine presence
prevailed. Sermons stressed the obligation to rule out all selfish ambitions and to live a life dominated by Christ. To become transformed
into Christ's image, this was the goal. All other ambitions were vain
strivings; only in striving for Godlikeness, said a speaker, could one
achieve abundant fulfillment. Bishop William McDowell told the Volunteers that God was standing before them waiting for each of them
to take himself and all his powers and his sense of obligation up into
unconquerable resolution and cry for time and for eternity, for weal or
for woe, *"I will."*[3] A sermon given by Robert E. Speer reflected the
solemnity of the Volunteer conventions.

> . . . I simply ask in this opening hour, quietly, each one alone, to forget
> everybody else, to be just as though Christ and you were alone here in
> this hall together and everything else just silence and emptiness round
> about us. . . . Would that here, during these first moments, we could
> realize that there is the fact—that over against each one of us the Lord
> is standing, the Lord with a thorn-crowned head and the nail-pierced
> hands and the pleading voice of His infinite love calling to us, calling.
> Surely we can almost hear His voice calling to us. How can we hold
> back from that call?[4]

Here was the great drama, a man confronting his creator. "Is it
true, or is it false, that Jesus Christ is the only rightful owner and Lord
of our lives?, asked J. Campbell White, formerly a missionary to India.[5]
Few were in a mood to claim that their own ambitions had a priority
over the divine plan for their lives. Sherwood Eddy pressed home the
point; not give oneself was to be disobedient to the heavenly vision.[6]

In this state of religious excitement a mood of jubilation prevailed.
Here was an experience demanding that the world be given some outward manifestation of the inward joy. And what could be more in ac-
cord with the inner religious ecstasy than volunteering to become a foreign missionary?

In the evangelical churches a large proportion of members had
shared in the convulsive experience of a revivalistic conversion. Now
that missions had become a supreme Christian duty, church-goers could

scarcely refuse to share in the enterprise. Those who failed to do so, said Speer, were either culpably ignorant or their Christianity was "a fictitious thing, a sham, a travesty."[7] In 1898 the Methodist bishop of Kentucky, T. U. Dudley, asked his listeners how, if Jesus "had touched my eyes and now I can see, yes, see the good hope that there is for humanity, see the open door and the Father's house and the welcome of the prodigal, and the feasting, and the joy of the universe because sinners are redeemed, how can I help going, that I may bring those that are blind as I was, that He may touch their eyes?"[8]

The dynamic force underlying the missionary movement was the revivalistic spirit, and revivals took place only among the orthodox. The theological liberals, for the most part, frowned on both revivals and the missionary crusade. It was the conservatives who provided the leadership for the missionary cause. John R. Mott and Robert E. Speer were essentially conservatives in their theology and the same may be said of most of the speakers at Student Volunteer conventions. A few, like Sherwood Eddy and Fletcher S. Brockman, became liberals as the years passed, but their early interest in foreign missions stemmed from their religious conversions in revivals. Neither of them broke any lances in behalf of a liberal theology until after the first World War.

A desire to save the heathen from damnation was the traditional motive of foreign missions. Hudson Taylor, founder of the China Inland Mission, told the convention of Student Volunteers meeting at Detroit in 1894,

> The gospel must be preached to these people in a very short time, for they are passing away. Every day, every day, oh how they sweep over! . . . There is a great Niagara of souls passing into the dark in China. Every day, every week, every month they are passing away! A million a month in China they are dying without God![9]

The argument that the heathen were going to Hell had served as a stimulus to missionary work and it was feared that to surrender it was to rob the missionary enterprise of its chief motive. Why send missionaries to the heathen if they were to be spared damnation anyway? Dr. E. K. Alden, secretary of the American Board of Commissioners for Foreign Missions, required all candidates for the Mission field to affirm their belief in a creed which included the phrase "I believe in the resurrection of the dead, the final separation of the righteous and the wicked, and the life and death everlasting."[10] Alden told one candidate that he should be as sure of the eternal punishment of the unconverted as he was of the existence of God. In 1886 the question of including this requirement occasioned a great debate. In 1893, missionary candidates of the American Board were freed from accepting Alden's creed.

By 1900 ideas of eternal damnation and a fast approaching judgment day were rapidly losing their hold. Contemporary currents of humanitarianism and democratic thought exalted the dignity of man and led to a corresponding decline of the former obsession with sinfulness. Likewise, the idea of hell receded as an ennobled conception of man made eternal damnation incongruous with the new concept of God as a merciful father. Consequently, the notion that a righteous God would send the heathen—who had never heard of the gospel—to hell because they had not accepted it, appeared both unjust and arbitrary in the new climate of opinion.

Under the impact of these new currents of thought the missionaries' proclaimed aim of snatching the heathen from the jaws of hell gave way to a new missionary motive. A professor in the Southern Baptist Theological Seminary observed that "The changed conception of the nature of God and of his relation to the world and to humanity has cooperated with the conception of religious evolution in the race to discredit the notion that men who 'die out of Christ' are doomed to death eternal."[10] Eternal punishment received literally no attention in the missionary literature after the turn of the century. In 1910 a commission reporting to the World Missionary Conference at Edinburgh found that among both volunteers and contributors in the United States few seemed to have been influenced by the thought that the heathen would go to hell.[12] In fact, by 1910 Robert E. Speer, one of the chief spokesmen for missions, charged that the idea that missionaries were motivated by the thought of saving the heathen from damnation was an invention of the scornful stay-at-homes and that missionaries had never been primarily moved by this consideration.[13] Nothing demonstrates more clearly how unpopular the idea had become than this attempt to absolve all past and present advocates of having used this argument.

However, silence on the damnation of the heathen by advocates of missions seems to have been dictated in part by public repugnance rather than any changed notion as to the ultimate destiny of the heathen. While apologizing for the idea, the Southern Baptist theological professor confessed that he could find no satisfactory explanation as to how any other fate could await men who did not attain salvation through the gospel.[14] Good public relations seem to have made necessary a change in the strategy of missionary promotion and apparently the consuming public had developed such an aversion toward damnation that, while they didn't want the Chinese to come to California, neither did they want them to go to hell. Theology and public sentiment seem to have been partly at cross purposes, but theology was also adjusting itself to new currents of thought and few theologians found it difficult to believe that the heathen would be spared damnation.

Despite the fact that the Moody revivals stirred up a new evangelical zeal, the revival spirit did not lead inevitably to a quickening of the foreign missionary impulse. Moody himself manifested little interest in missions. It was the young converts who directed Moody's revival campaigns from the goal of saving America to saving the world. They represented the new generation of Americans who were looking outward. They were the contemporaries of the business man with an eye to foreign markets and of the new statesmen with an irrepressible urge to cast the weight of American influence onto the scales of international power politics.

The missionary movement, the increasing concern of business with foreign markets, the political imperialism of the American government were not unrelated. A bald and sometimes sordid economic and political imperialism certainly was made more palatable by the fact that Americans could clothe these drives in the altruistic terminology of the missionary who spoke of bringing Christianity and the advantages of western civilization to undeveloped areas.

During the earlier decades of the nineteenth century American missionaries sometimes deliberately and consciously promoted American economic and political interests in China. The famous Dr. Peter Parker, the first medical missionary to China, has been acclaimed as the man who opened China at the point of a lancet. Yet no one seems to have been more aware of the inadequacies of this instrument for cutting through the Chinese wilderness of anti-foreignism and prejudice against the barbarian of the outside world than the doctor himself. As Secretary of Legation and later as Commissioner to China he not only made frequent pleas for more adequate naval forces but he urgently advocated that the United States should annex Formosa.[15] Dr. Parker's fellow missionary, S. Wells Williams, in a similar vein praised the work of the British in the Opium War and on one occasion in 1858 confessed that he was afraid "that nothing short of the Society for the Diffusion of Cannon Balls will give them the useful knowledge they now require to realize their own helplessness."[16]

A few missionaries after 1890 followed in the tradition of Parker and Williams in advocating the old gunboat policy. A few asked for a greater display of American strength and on occasions when they faced mob violence asked for protection. At home, that apostle of sweet reasonableness, Lyman Abbott, commented favorably upon armed might and commercial endeavor as allies of the missionary in opening the way for the Anglo-Saxon.[17]

Despite the early attitude of missionaries to China, most of those who went out after 1890 were highly critical of western merchants and frequently of the practices of European governments. Speer's charge that the motives of European governments and of missions were irreconcilable was a widely shared opinion among missionaries. In China antagonism between foreign merchants and missionaries was traditional. The latter held that business men as a group had no sympathy with missionary aims and that their behaviour reflected unfavorably upon Christianity. The business man in China, in turn, often looked upon the missionary as a hopeless zealot. There were exceptions to this feeling of mutual distrust but there can be no question that there was little cooperation between them.

It was on the home front that the missionary crusade received the support of a great many business leaders. The Laymen's Missionary Movement was almost wholly a business man's organization and every important denominational missionary board had a number of prominent business leaders. John T. Underwood, president of the Underwood Typewriter Company, served on the Presbyterian board, C. Edgar Welch, president of the Welch Grape Juice Company, was a member of the Methodist board, J. Edgar Leaycraft, a prominent New York real estate dealer, worked with the American Bible Society, and S. W. Woodward, owner of a large department store in Washington, D. C., was a leader among the Baptists. John R. Mott, head of the Student Volunteers, took pride in his success in raising money among business men.

Missionaries never argued that their work would lead to an expansion of trade but some of their supporters at home saw this as one of the much to be desired bi-products of foreign missions. Charles Denby, former minister to China, in an article for the *Independent,* suggested that missionary leaders should use this argument, for "the statesman, the diplomatist, and the business man look at this work with reference to its influence on commerce and the general prosperity of the world."[18] A prominent woman journalist who had travelled in the Orient and who lectured extensively, Margherita Arlina Hamm, argued that the missionaries' western goods excited attention and created a demand for these things. "From this point of view," the writer said, "every missionary is a salesman for the manufactures of Christendom!"[19] The Reverend Francis E. Clark, president of the United Society of Christian Endeavor, saw among the many advantages of foreign missions the increase of trade and commerce and "the widening of our empire."[20] Theodore Roosevelt called for public support of missions in part because missions would help us commercially.[21] Chester Holcombe, in his early years a missionary to China and later Acting Minister in Peking, called the missionary enterprise in China "unequalled by any other, for the development of our commerce with that vast population."[22] In brief, there was an awareness of the missionary's role as a promoter of trade. Undoubtedly the economic benefits to be derived played some part in the marshaling of public support. Yet, there is no evidence to support any general thesis that the missionary enterprise was merely a tool of the middle class to prepare the way for the exploitation of China.

A study of the motives and aims of the missionary movement makes clear that they were closely related to the currents of nationalism and humanitarianism. The new and far distant horizons came into view at a time when American nationalism was reaching new heights. Facing no immediate challenges from abroad and having, with the exception of the Philippines, no vital interests outside of the western hemisphere, Americans could be altruistic toward the outside world. Consequently, their nationalism expressed itself less in conspicuous spending for armaments than in the vaunting of material wealth, pride in democratic institutions and free public schools, boasts of American technological know-how, and in a general feeling of righteousness.

Nationalism at the turn of the century was parallelled by a rapid rise of humanitarianism. In politics Progressivism gave expression to a widespread desire to improve the living conditions of the working class and to lighten the burdens of the poverty stricken. Jacob Riis, crusading for children's play-grounds in New York, and Jane Addams, working to improve the conditions of immigrants on Chicago's west side, symbolized the movement to uplift the downtrodden.

The missionaries, isolated from their home environment, were slow in adopting a humanitarian emphasis. Most of them continued to look upon both schools and hospitals primarily as avenues to get at the heathen in order to convert them. One missionary told his readers that the hospital ward afforded unexcelled opportunities for preaching, for there "thoughts of the hereafter naturally arise."[23] As late as 1913, Dr. J. Preston Maxwell of the Yungchun hospital cited the rules which should be followed in any Christian hospital. The walls of rooms should be decorated with texts from the Bible, tracts and hymn books should be distributed, and there should be morning and afternoon religious services for all well enough to attend. He recommended a special evangelistic service for Sunday afternoon. At these times the sermon should be directed to making conversions. Maxwell advised against "abstract addresses on either God, or creation, or ethical subjects unless they lead directly and every time to the full presentation of the Saviour for sinners." While there was no element of strength lacking in Dr. Maxwell's convictions, he admitted that it was not easy to sit down with a patient day after day and repeat the same things and teach the same hymns and texts. He observed that it was amazing "the way some patients are able to apparently absorb teaching, and pass it out without assimilating almost anything, and it is certainly discouraging, after 14 days' work, to be told that the Name of the Son of God is 'Satan.' "[24]

The humanitarian emphasis made headway much more rapidly on the home front. Educational and medical work gradually came to be viewed as worthy ends in themselves. Publicity particularly stressed the humanitarian aspects of schools and hospitals while saying almost nothing about them as agencies of conversion.

If one were to choose a landmark in the history of American foreign missions as a dividing point between the old stress on snatching the heathen from the jaws of Hell and the new view of missions as a humanitarian agency, perhaps the publication in 1897 of the Rev. James S. Dennis' two volume work *Christian Missions and Social Progress: A Sociological Study of Foreign Missions* would be the most appropriate.[25] The author had been a missionary in Syria. His book purported to be a sociological study of the role of missions, and much of the tremendous prestige it enjoyed was undoubtedly due to its supposedly scientific character. The book certainly had a scintillating tone of modernity and of authority and it was welcomed by missionary enthusiasts as the definitive statement on missions.

Dennis described missions as a factor in the social regeneration of the world. The aims of foreign missions were to elevate human society, modify traditional evils, and introduce reformatory ideals. Underlying Dennis' approach to missions lay the assumption that Christianity had been the supreme force in the social regeneration of the western world. Christian countries were different, said Dennis, in that while they were not free from evil there was a spirit of protest against all that degraded human personality. Among the heathen dishonesty, thievery, vulgarity, and cruel customs not only prevailed but they were accepted and unchallenged. The task of Christian missions was to introduce a spirit of regeneration and a Christian conscience which would protest against moral laxity and social injustice. This would inevitably lead, in the case of China, to the abolition of the binding of little girls' feet, the granting of equality to women, the sharp censuring of those who were dishonest, and the lifting of life to a higher level. He believed that this spirit of regeneration could only be introduced as individuals were won over to Christianity.

Dennis' study embodying the new view of missions gained him a wide reputation. He was called upon to lecture at several theological seminaries, and many writers on missionary topics acknowledged their indebtedness to him. He was elected to the Presbyterian Board of Foreign Missions and in 1910 was one of its representatives at the World Missionary Conference in Edinburgh. The recognition bestowed upon Dennis was in considerable part a tribute to the social view of missions.

The new view had many spokesmen after 1900. Speer declared: "The world needs to be saved from want and disease and injustice and inequality and impurity and lust and hopelessness and fear, . . ."[26] During the days of the Spanish-American War, John R. Mott asked "Where is the war?" and then proceeded to define it as a war against social evils around the globe.[27] In 1900 the best known of all missionary writers on China, Arthur H. Smith, told his American readers that Christianity could improve the position of the girl in the family, show Chinese parents how to train as well as how to govern their children, improve education, create an intellectual atmosphere in the home, abolish polygamy and concubinage, purify and sweeten the home, and promote patriotism.[28] The former president of Ohio Wesleyan University, Bishop J. W. Bashford, asked how Christians, when they saw "the unevangelized peoples of the earth . . . living in poverty and disease and ignorance and sin" could refrain from offering them "the key which will open to them the divine storehouse."[29] By 1915, one missionary leader on the home front looked back on the change in missionary emphases and noted:

> One of the most marked changes taking place in the foreign mission propaganda during the last century has been the shift of emphasis from the individual to society. The social aspect of Christianity was not given due recognition at home or abroad a generation ago. It is not strange therefore that while the missionaries were promoting great, sweeping social movements, international in character and fundamental in reach, they did not recognize them as such, but continued there as we did here to put supreme emphasis upon individual conversion.[30]

It is clear that Dennis, Speer, Mott, and the other leaders of the missionary movement were advocates of a program whereby conversion of the heathen was gradually becoming a means to an end, namely an improved society.

That a new emphasis more in harmony with current American humanitarianism had replaced the traditional concern with rescuing the heathen from damnation is clear. Yet, while the final aim had been readjusted to the climate of opinion in the United States, the means had remained the same. The goal of social regeneration was to be reached by conversion of individuals to Christianity. In this respect the new missionary program was true to tradition. It involved no sharp break with the past to the degree that the Social Gospel did at home.

Speer, who did more to formulate the new program and to win it adherents than anyone else, argued strongly against seeking to introduce western institutions. To him, the backwardness of heathendom was not so much a product of heathen institutions as it was due to the absence of a Christian spirit within these institutions. His prescription called for changing Chinese society by changing individual men.[31]

This approach had a tepid quality from the point of view of those who wanted a new social order. They had come to the conclusion that there could be no significant improvement in China until the institutions and customs which shaped men to be slaves of disease, ignorance, and exploitation were replaced. But there were very few missionaries who went this far in their thinking about the social evils they encountered. Not until 1912 did any missionary or any advocate of missions espouse any all-out social reform program. In that year a missionary in China, the Reverend H. K. Wright, wrote apologetically that there was no contradiction between the Scriptural view of individual salvation and of social salvation. He thought that the social views found in the Bible led to religious work in behalf of social and economic amelioration and regeneration and sometimes of revolution. Too much missionary work in education and missions, he observed, had been "a mere exhibition of Christianity, or a clinic in which mental objections to it could be removed." Missionaries had acquiesced in a social system which made coolies possible, "beings beside whose position that of the American slaves was enviable." Or, if any note was taken of these miserable souls, missionaries had usually said, " 'Be ye warmed and fed with the Gospel,' not stopping to consider that Christianity is for beings in their position a simply impossible thing." Wright thought that China must change, that missionaries must help in providing leadership, and that they would do well to examine the proposals of the Christian Socialists.[32]

Missionaries who held such aims for the missionary movement were certainly rare and among active supporters of missions at home there is no record that any held such views. This does not alter the fact that the missionary program was humanitarian in emphasis and it was this humanitarian emphasis which explains in considerable part why it enjoyed such a large measure of public support. It explains why some men outside of the church endorsed foreign missions.

Edward Alsworth Ross, the eminent sociologist, found much to praise in missionary work after a trip to China. He wrote of the influence of mission schools on the new government educational system, of the advance of female education, and of the influence of missionary translations of the great books of western learning. Ross thought that the achievements of the missionary were not to be counted in the number of Christian converts but in the changed attitude toward opium-smoking, foot-binding, concubinage, slavery, "squeeze," torture, and the subjection of women.[33] He observed that what the missionary was teaching was not so much the gospel but western ideas of what was right and wrong. Another sociologist, Franklin Henry Giddings, spoke of the Christian missionary enterprise as devoting itself to the diffusion of knowledge, to the improvement of conditions, and to the upbuilding of character and considered it one of the most important factors in uniting the classes and the races of men in a spiritual humanity.[34] That the humanitarian motive struck a responsive chord in large parts of the population is also attested to by the many endorsements of American presidents and diplomats.

The social aims of the missionary movement reflected the current humanitarianism, faith in progress, and social reform. Another equally significant transition accompanied this development. When missionaries first went to China from the United States, individual heathen were the focal point rather than China as a nation. Once the missionary program envisaged the regeneration of Chinese society, there developed an interest in the future of China as a country. The salvation of individual Chinese was now linked to the progress of the nation, its political reform, and most important, to the question of what kind of a China would eventually emerge. That China was changing was clear, and to the highly nationalistic Americans who viewed China through paternal eyes there was no little uneasiness concerning China's future. That she would be powerful, no one doubted. Whether the new China would be a force for peace, democracy, and world brotherhood or a yellow dragon employing technology and her vast human resources to destroy western civilization was considered an open question.

The question of China's future role made possible the dramatizing of the missionary enterprise as the agency determining the fate not only of isolated individuals but of a whole nation. A picture of four hundred million Chinese caught in the throes of revolutionary change excited the most prosaic of imaginations. Observing the changes in China after 1900 one writer described what was happening as "a political revolution, a moral advance, an intellectual renaissance, a religious reformation, and a nineteenth century of scientific and industrial development all combined."[35]

Missionary leaders anxiously asked what was to be the final outcome as China rushed headlong through the many stages of historical development which had transformed the western world since the decline of feudalism in the thirteenth century. Marshall Broomhall, a representative of the China Inland Mission, asked the question which was uppermost in the minds of westerners: "Shall Asia experience merely an Intellectual Renaissance or a Spiritual Reformation? Shall the East merely conform to Western scientific principles or be transformed by the renewing of the Holy Spirit?"[36] John R. Mott, leader of the Student Volunteers, described the non-Christian nations as plastic and changing. These nations, he wrote, were examining the west to see what had made it rich and powerful. Should these people fail to see that religion "is the most fundamental thing in our civilization" the result would be moral disaster. This, then, said Mott, was the decisive hour.[37]

Thousands of church-going folk now turned their eyes to the struggle going on in the great China arena. The fetters of ancient thralldom were being sundered by missionaries, commerce, and the forces of the modern world. Would the awakened Chinese dragon emerge from his long sleep only to threaten the world or would he employ his immense powers to further the realization of the western ideals of universal brotherhood and the welfare of mankind? In a book entitled *Our Share in China and What We Are Doing With It*, George J. Bond, a China missionary, held that the "yellow peril" could be avoided if the Christian church did its duty. He wrote: "China is moving indeed, and as Napoleon truly said, she will move the world. But how?"[38] The Methodist bishop, Charles Henry Fowler, reduced the problem to terms calculated to wrest the most indifferent from apathy. The bishop told his listeners:

> Her very numbers is God's promise of perpetuity. The Yellow Race will remain the menace of the world. It lies on the shore of Asia, a huge club, only waiting to be picked up by some Hercules. China is the world's problem for the twentieth century. Who will seize this club? . . .
> It is a Bear standing on the trail. His posture does not change his nature. If Russia appropriates and assimilates China, we are face to face with the most powerful Empire ever known among men. The world problem is this: Shall Russia be allowed to absorb China? This problem is full of dragon's teeth, teeth enough to seed down the world with century-long strifes.[39]

Nor was this opinion confined to the churches. Captain Alfred T. Mahan, noted historian of the influence of sea power in history, took the position that the western world had a common interest in bringing the Asian peoples within the compass of the family of Christian states; "not by fetters and bonds imposed from without, but by regeneration promoted from within." He warned of danger should China become westernized technologically without accepting the mental and moral forces "which have generated, and which in large measure govern, our political action."[40] Mahan praised the work of the missionaries because he believed they were inculcating the guiding moral principles of the West. Theodore Roosevelt, haunted by many fears, called for support of the missionaries because their work tended to avert revolutionary disturbances and to lead China into a position of power for peace and righteousness.[41] A similar view was expressed by a sociologist who held that it was the Bible more than blood that united the English race and that it would unite China with the English race in bonds more deep than those of any political convention.[42] Americans generally looked forward with confidence to China becoming a democratic nation guided by Christian ideals and closely allied with the United States and they believed that this would be largely a product of the missionaries, those non-commissioned ambassadors of the great American republic.

The missionary movement was thus linked to the strong nationalism of Americans which expressed itself in the belief that China would follow them in the paths of righteousness and become, in turn, a guiding star for humanity at large as it sought the way into the land of Canaan with its promise of brotherhood and the life abundant. The alignment of missions with national self-interest invited support from people who otherwise would have been indifferent. China was not viewed as any immediate threat but there was a deep feeling that sometime in the distant future she would either be a firm and valuable friend or a difficult enemy. Certainly hope outweighed fear. The danger seemed remote and there was never any real alarm. The vision of a friendly and democratic China converted to Christianity provided a stronger motive than any lurking fear of a remote future when a powerful and hostile China might be thrown into the balance against the United States.

This rapid survey seems to warrant the conclusion that the greatest source of strength of the missionary movement as it was related to

China lay in the fact that its program was in harmony with current fashions of thought and popular attitudes in the United States. Its strongest religious source was the Moody revivals. That the fervor of this movement should have transferred itself to an interest in missions is to be explained in terms of the new nationalism in the United States which expressed itself in an interest in world affairs. That the aims of the program should be stated in terms of humanitarianism was assured by the climate of opinion at home.

1. Sherwood Eddy, *Pathfinders of the World Missionary Crusade* (New York: Abingdon-Cokesbury Press, 1945), p. 50.
2. William M. Beahm, *Factors in the Development of the Student Volunteer Movement for Foreign Missions* (Unpublished Ph. D. dissertation, Divinity School University of Chicago, 1941), p. 16.
3. *Students and the Present Missionary Crisis. Addresses Delivered Before the Sixth International Convention of the Student Volunteer Movement for Foreign Missions, Rochester, New York, December 29, 1909, to January 2, 1910* (New York: Student Volunteer Movement for Foreign Missions, 1910), p. 197. Hereafter cited as *Report of the Student Volunteer Convention of 1910*.
4. *Students and the Modern Missionary Crusade: Addresses Delivered Before the Fifth International Convention of the Student Volunteer Movement for Foreign Missions* (New York: Student Volunteer Movement, 1906), p. 15. Hereafter cited as *Report of the Student Volunteer Convention of 1906*.
5. *Ibid.*, p. 29.
6. *Report of the Student Volunteer Convention of 1910*, p. 507.
7. Robert E. Speer, *Missionary Principles and Practice. A Discussion of Christian Missions and of Some Criticisms upon Them* (New York: Fleming H. Revell Company, 1902), p. 19.
8. *The Student Missionary Appeal. Addresses at the Third International Convention of the Student Volunteer Movement for Foreign Missions* (New York: Student Volunteer Movement, 1898), p. 151.
9. *The Student Missionary Enterprise. Addresses and Discussions of the Second International Convention of the Student Volunteer Movement for Foreign Missions* (New York: Fleming H. Revell Co., 1894), p. 48.
10. Lyman Abbott, *Reminiscences* (Boston: Houghton Mifflin Co., 1915), p. 477. For a discussion of this controversy see David Swift, "Conservative Versus Progressive Orthodoxy in Latter 19th Century Congregationalism," *Church History*, XVI, March, 1947, pp. 22-31.
11. William Owen Carver, *Missions and Modern Thought* (New York: The Macmillan Company, 1910), pp. 13-14.
12. *World Missionary Conference, 1910. Report of Commission VI. The Home Base of Missions* (New York: Fleming H. Revell Company, 1910), pp. 133-134.
13. Robert E. Speer, *Christianity and the Nations* (New York: Fleming H. Revell Company, 1910), p. 33.
14. Carver, *op. cit.*, p. 14.
15. Senate Document, 2nd Session, 35th. Congress, p. 1208.
16. *The Life and Letters of Samuel Wells Williams*, ed. Frederick Wells Williams (New York: G. P. Putnam's Sons, 1889), p. 257.
17. Lyman Abbott, *The Rights of Man, A Study in Twentieth Century Problems* (Boston: Houghton, Mifflin and Company, 1901), p. 273.
18. Charles Denby, "The Influence of Mission Work on Commerce," *The Independent*, December 12, 1901, p. 2960.
19. Margherita Arlina Hamm, "The Secular Value of Foreign Missions," *The Independent*, April 26, 1900, p. 1001.
20. Francis E. Clark, "Do Foreign Missions Pay?" *The North American Review*, March, 1898, p. 280.
21. Theodore Roosevelt, "The Awakening of China," *The Outlook*, November 28, 1908, p. 666.
22. Chester Holcombe, "The Missionary Enterprise in China," *Atlantic Monthly*, September, 1906, p. 354.

23. George J. Bond, *Our Share in China and What We Are Doing with It* (Toronto: The Missionary Society of the Methodist Church, 1909), p. 62.

24. J. Preston Maxwell, "How Best to Obtain and Conserve Results in the Evangelistic Work amongst Hospital Patients," *The Chinese Recorder*, May, 1913, p. 283.

25. James S. Dennis, *Christian Missions and Social Progress. A Sociological Study of Foreign Missions* (New York: Fleming H. Revell Company).

26. Robert E. Speer, *Christianity and the Nations* (New York: Fleming H. Revell Company, 1910), p. 29.

27. John R. Mott, "What of the War?" *The Student Missionary Appeal Addresses at the Third International Convention of the Student Volunteer Movement for Foreign Missions* (Cleveland, 1898), p. 274.

28. Arthur H. Smith, *Village Life in China A Study in Sociology* (New York: Fleming H. Revell Company, 1899), pp. 342-345.

29. J. W. Bashford, *God's Missionary Plan for the World* (New York: Eaton and Mains, 1907), pp. 44-45.

30. James L. Barton, "The Modern Missionary," *Harvard Theological Review*, January, 1915, p. 6.

31. Speer wrote: "The West and Western nations, which owe all their good to Christianity, are under a heavy debt to the rest of the world, which it is not the function of the Christian church to discharge. It is the function of the Christian Church to inspire the Christian nations to do justice and to give help to the non-Christian nations, but there are many great and truly Christian services with which the foreign missionary enterprise is not charged. They are to be rendered through other forms of international relationship." *Christianity and the Nations*, p. 57.

32. H. K. Wright, "The Social Message and Christian Missions," *The Chinese Recorder*, March, 1912, pp. 147-155.

33. Edward Alsworth Ross, *The Changing Chinese. The Conflict of Oriental and Western Cultures in China* (New York: The Century Company, 1911), p. 245.

34. Franklin Henry Giddings, *The Principles of Sociology* (New York: The Macmillan Company, 1928), p. 360.

35. S. Earl Taylor and Halford E. Luccock, *The Christian Crusade for World Democracy* (New York: The Methodist Book Concern, 1918), p. 64.

36. Marshall Broomhall, *Present Day Conditions in China* (New York: Fleming H. Revell Company, 1908), pp. 1-2.

37. John R. Mott, *The Decisive Hour of Christian Missions* (New York: The Student Volunteer Movement for Foreign Missions, 1911), p. 34.

38. George J. Bond, *Our Share in China and What We Are Doing with It*, p. 27.

39. Charles Henry Fowler, *Missionary Addresses* (Cincinnati: Jennings and Graham, 1906), pp. 44-45.

40. Alfred T. Mahan, "Effects of Asiatic Conditions Upon International Policies," *North American Review*, November, 1900, p. 615.

41. Theodore Roosevelt, "The Awakening of China," *The Outlook*, November 28, 1908, p. 666.

42. Henry William Rankin, "Political Values of the American Missionary," *The American Journal of Sociology*, XIII, Sept. 1907, p. 172.

Missionary Influence on American Attitudes
Toward China at the Turn of This Century

ROBERT F. MCCLELLAN

For many years of America's existence China has been low on the priority list of national concerns. Now she has emerged as one of the most serious problems facing this nation. However, the increase in the need to relate to China has not been matched by a corresponding increase in an understanding of American attitudes toward China. The Chinese have been viewed as an inferior people characterized by strange and even barbaric cultural habits. In recent years feelings of condescension and even contempt have been readily apparent in America's relations with the Orient. It has been suggested that the atomic bomb would not have been dispatched so readily if its destination had been a city in Europe rather than one in Asia. The idea of a preventive war against China has also been advanced. As technology and tensions accelerate the need for understanding increases.

At the end of the nineteenth century when national perspectives were expanding, Christian ideas had a formative influence on the development of American attitudes toward China. The role played by missionaries and other ministers in gathering and distributing information about the Chinese was extremely important in a time when little was known about the Far East. Returning missionaries brought back lantern slides and ancedotes to instruct congregations curious about the place and the people who had been an object of their prayers and contributions. Mission society publications like the *Baptist Review*, the *Missionary Herald*, and the *Methodist Review*, provided a continuous supply of news and features about Chinese life.

A less obvious though equally important way in which the Christian point of view influenced attitudes toward China was through the cultural impact of the Protestant ethic upon American society. The confluence of Protestant Christianity and American business and the resulting effect upon cultural patterns of thought and activity has

Mr. McClellan is assistant professor of history in Northern Michigan University, Marquette, Michigan.

been described before. However, the extent to which Christian thought especially with regard to missionary work among the Chinese has had a formative influence upon the shaping of national attitudes toward China has not been made clear. The evaluation of Chinese character offered by religious workers in the field and by those in charge of administering the mission program was a basic point of reference for attitudes developed by others less familiar with the Chinese.

One of the results, therefore, of missionary activity in China was that Americans drew heavily upon an interpretation of Chinese life derived from the experience of missionaries. There were hundreds of diplomatic and business people involved in China but there were thousands of Christian workers. The reports of United States consuls made the pages of newspapers or periodicals less frequently than did the experiences of missionaries. Furthermore the arrival or departure of a mission worker had an impact on the town and the local congregation which not infrequently surpassed any reaction to events in Washington. If one recalls the overt dependence on moral and religious criteria for evaluating human life by businessmen and politicians alike perhaps it is not an exaggeration to suggest that the influence of the missionary point of view on American attitudes toward China represented another kind of imperialism—the imperialism of righteousness.

One of the greatest needs for the mission worker as well as the minister at home with regard to the missionary effort was to justify the expense in life and money of an evangelism reaching halfway around the world. Since the first requirement for a conversion experience was the presence of a sufficiently depraved subject, missionaries frequently described the moral condition of the Chinese in the blackest possible terms. One missionary who lacked confidence in his own words relied upon a description of the Chinese in Samuel Wells Williams' *Middle Kingdom.* "The Chinese are vile and polluted in a shocking degree; their conversation is full of filthy expressions, and their lives of impure acts. . . . The universal practice of lying and dishonest dealings; the unblushing lewdness of old and young; harsh cruelty towards prisoners by officers . . . all form a full unchecked torrent of human depravity (and) . . . moral degradation of which an excessive statement can scarcely be made. . . ."[1]

1. John R. Hykes, "The Importance of Winning China for Christ," *Missionary Review,* 5 (February, 1892), 83.

This view of the Chinese was characteristic of the majority of missionary publications during the years at the turn of the century, and it is this attitude which has had a powerful impact on American ideas about the Orient. Because it was felt that the Chinese were debased and immoral many missionaries were unable to appreciate either the Chinese personally, at least until converted, or their civilization. In their description of Chinese life missionaries often emphasized the superstitious beliefs, strange customs, abnormal vices and immorality of the Chinese people. The missionary whether he realized it or not was effectively developing an image of the Chinese as a pagan barbaric people.

For example, Jefferson Davis, a congregational minister in China who witnessed the execution of a Chinese criminal, was appalled at the brutality which accompanied the act and insisted in his description that such behavior was indicative of the debased nature of the Chinese character.[2] Readers of his account gained the impression that the Chinese were at about the same level of development as the American Indian when the first settlers arrived. Missionary accounts of the custom of foot-binding appalled American readers as did descriptions of the ability of the Chinese to endure pain on the battlefield. One clergyman reported that while waiting for his train at Port Arthur he saw a Chinese coolie raise himself up on the sharp edges of an open barrel and with his chin tucked into his knees promptly fall asleep while another observed with amazement a serious operation on a wounded Chinese performed without benefit of ether.[3] From the point of view of many missionaries the Chinese appeared to be a barbarous and uncivilized people greatly in need of the humanizing effects of the Christian gospel.

Unfavorable descriptions of the Chinese were not confined solely to missionaries in the field. The large population of Chinese on the West coast and the communities of Chinese in several larger cities provided opportunities for observation by clergymen who worked among them. The stories told by these men were the same as those of their more widely travelled colleagues. A common theme of both domestic and foreign missionaries was that the Chinese were a corrupted race whose only hope for salvation lay in the efforts of religious workers who with God's help would introduce them to the teachings of Jesus Christ.

2. Jefferson A. Davis, "A Chinese Crucifixion," *Independent*, 47 (October 24, 1895), 1424.
3. Julian Ralph, "Side Notes from the Asiatic War," *Harpers Weekly*, 39 (May 11, 1895), 448.

Mission work among the Chinese people in the United States was thought to be important not only for the sake of the Chinese but because of the supposed danger to the American way of life created by the presence of a debased minority. Lyman Abbott, who by any standards would have passed in his day as an enlightened liberal clergyman, characterized the Chinese as a "persistently servile and alien population" whose presence endangered the moral safety of the country.[4] As editor of the influential and independent *Outlook,* his opinion was especially potent among professional people whose attitudes were important in shaping popular opinion.

The notion that the Chinese had the capacity to corrupt the morals of those who experienced even the briefest contact with them was so strong that some people questioned the value of any attempt to convert them.[5] For a few years a minor controversy raged among directors of religious education over whether or not Caucasian girls should be allowed to teach Chinese in the missionary Sunday schools. It was reported that in some instances these girls had married their Chinese students and the question was posed whether it was worth the "corruption" of white girls in order to save the soul of a "heathen."[6]

When the argument for the depravity of the Chinese was put so strongly it tended to some extent to defeat itself. A Baptist minister, for example, in an article written in 1890 for the *Baptist Quarterly Review* argued that the Chinese should not even be allowed to enter the country because they represented such a moral peril to our civilization.[7] Implicit in his conclusion was the notion that the depravity of the Chinese was too powerful even for the forces of Christianity. This was the thought expressed by a longtime mission worker on the West coast, Frederick Masters, who commented that the Chinese were "irredeemably and irretrievably bad and vile, as a rule, and all efforts to Christianize them only makes them greater hypocrites than ever."[8] Evidently the Chinese were so debased as to be beyond the reach even of the healing power of the gospel.

4. "The New Chinese Exclusion Act," *Outlook,* 70 (January 18, 1902), 153.
5. "Teaching the Chinese," *Public Opinion,* 12 (February 20, 1892), 504.
6. *Ibid.*
7. Addison Parker, "The Exclusion of the Chinese," *Baptist Quarterly Review,* 12 (October, 1892), 622.
8. Frederick J. Masters, "Can a Chinaman Became a Christian?", *Californian,* 2 (October, 1892), 622.

Sunday school children could hardly have been expected to understand the subtlties of the theological and moral arguments concerning the debased character of the Chinese, but they could easily grasp the image presented to them by one enterprising minister. A story was told by a Protestant clergyman in Pittsburgh about a Sunday school program where lantern slides were used to illustrate a talk on foreign missions. At one point a slide was shown which portrayed a Chinese reposing on a couch and in subsequent slides huge rats were seen to appear from the corners of the room. When the Chinese opened his mouth they plunged down his throat. The children of course were delighted and the sequence was so popular that the minister was forced to curtail the biblical features of the program in order that the children might feast their eyes on the rat-eating Chinese.[9] While the children may have been confused about the relevance of the "rat-eating chinaman" to the missionary program one of their first impressions of the Chinese was certain not to fade.

In retrospect it appears that many missionaries were highly selective in their descriptions of Chinese life and that the information which was presented was designed to place the Chinese in the most unfavorable light. The intent of these missionaries was understandable enough and was not inspired by meanness of motivation. Yet by suppressing the favorable aspects of Chinese life and emphasising the undesirable ones they fashioned a distorted and unfavorable view. By emphasising the cruelty, the strange customs, and the crowded cities they reinforced the sense of Western superiority and Eastern inferiority. It is true that there was much that was unfortunate in Chinese life, though every society has had its weak as well as its strong points. But by selecting the more unfortunate aspects of Chinese life it was possible to cast China in the mold of a barbaric, heathenish people incapable of measuring up to Western standards and unable to help themselves except with Western assistance.

The sharply unfavorable interpretation of the Chinese offered by many missionaries at home and abroad was moderated to some extent by the descriptions of converts to the Christian faith. Every missionary had stories to relate about the loyalty and courage of converted Chinese who faced severe tests in witnessing to their new found faith. For these Christians the missionaries had unstinting praise and in many instances a deep affection born out of common trials at the hands of hostile nonbelievers.

9. E. R. Donehoo, "John Chinaman," *Charities Review*, 7 (January, 1898), 914.

At first glance the favorable descriptions of the converted Chinese might appear to balance the unfavorable descriptions of the unregenerate. Yet this was not really the case. Even though the depraved Chinese could become a new man through a conversion experience, he remained a captive of the missionary's perception of him and consequently failed to emerge as an individual in his own right. Just as the debased nature of the Chinese had been distorted in order to justify a need for evangelization so the fruits of that effort were also exaggerated for the same reasons. The Chinese had undergone little fundamental change because of his religious experience, and even though the missionary's portrayal of him changed markedly, the description of the converted Chinese was no more accurate than the description of the degenerate Chinese.

One of the best summarizations of the missionary's evaluation of the Chinese was offered by William C. Pond who had spent more than a dozen years in China. "If the testimony is to be taken on both sides, it simply amounts to this; the Chinese, as a nation, are not so bad as to be past help, and not so good that they cannot be made better. In short, like every nation, China needs the gospel of our Lord and Saviour."[10]

Pond was a dedicated minister who gave many years of his life in the exhausting and sometimes dangerous work in rural China. It is gratuitous to question his deep concern for the human beings to whom he sought to bring what he conceived of as a better life. Yet it is still true that in spite of the best intentions even his most favorable descriptions of the Chinese were heavily laden with a heavy-handed paternalism. Even the best qualified missionaries like Pond were unable to rid themselves of the assumptions of Western superiority which colored their attitudes toward the Chinese.

It is understandable that the missionary's attitude toward China was similar to the American attitude toward anything foreign. The egocentrism of American nationalism which was so strikingly expressed in the country around the turn of the century was certainly not unique among nations. But it is unfortunate that popular attitudes toward an entire people were so deeply impregnated in the fibres of the American experience. The missionaries cannot be held solely re-

10. William C. Pond, "The Los Angeles Chinese Mission," *American Missionary*, 51 (May, 1897), 161-2.

sponsible for this, but they contributed heavily to the formation of an image of the Chinese which was sadly deficient in its representation of the important human qualities.

One missionary in the field for example analysed the human characteristics of the Chinese for the *Sewanee Review*.[11] After living several years in China he was convinced that it was inaccurate to describe the Chinese as lacking "common humanity" because they are more cruel and value human life to a lesser degree. Rather, he said, what is lacking from their character is common Christianity. With conversion and the ingestion of the Christian value of life the Chinese could be transformed into the sort of creature to which the Western world would ascribe the term "human being." Perhaps this is a more favorable portrayal of the Chinese, yet if it was true that the oriental heathen could only be made human through Christianity the alarming conclusion must have been that the vast majority of Chinese would remain inhuman, because even the most wildly optimistic missionary estimates claimed a conversion rate of no greater than one in ten.[12]

The missionaries themselves were probably not conscious of the paternalistic note struck by their descriptions of the Chinese. And it was true that there were many instances in which relationships between Caucasion and Oriental were built upon sincere and mutual trust and respect. During the Boxer Revolt in 1900 many missionaries, their families, and other religious personnel connected with the mission either lost their lives or were forced to flee. Yet one of the most striking aspects of the events of that year were the numerous stories told by missionaries of the support which their Chinese converts gave them in a time of severe stress.[13] Often at the risk of their own lives and in the face of extreme pressure from their families and friends, Chinese Christians sided with the missionaries and did all that they could to protect their lives and property.

Yet, in spite of the real affection and common respect between the missionaries and their converts it is impossible to diverge significantly from the point of view expressed by John Hykes. After a

---

11. Partridge, "Our Mission in China," *The Sewanee Review*, 1 (November, 1892), 74-89.
12. William Ashmore, "High-Water Mark in Foreign Missions," *The Independent*, 44 (January 21, 1892), 18.
13. See religious publications such as *Missionary Review, American Missionary, Sewanee Review, Methodist Review, Catholic World, Missionary Herald* and *Baptist Missionary Magazine* for the years 1880-1910.

short time in the field he wrote an article for the *Missionary Review* in which he urged other clergy and lay workers to consider the challenge offered by the opportunity in China.[14] After recounting some of the difficulties of the task which lay ahead he insisted that the job of converting China was not a hopeless one if enough resources could be brought to bear. It is his final point which is interesting. He suggested emphatically that unless the Chinese were converted the potentially great nation of the East would be doomed to continue in its dismal heathen ways until it was overcome by the enlightened Christian powers of the West. Thus in the final analysis the humanization of the Chinese could come only through the experience of Christian conversion.

The attitude of Christians concerned with the Chinese in the United States varies little from that of the workers in the mission field except that there tended to be more antagonism locally. Chinese converts in New York, San Francisco, and towns on the West coast were lauded by the missionaries who worked among them but the condescension and outright antagonism which lay at the root of the attitudes of these workers was thinly veiled. The head of the mission at Santa Cruz, for example, after a fire in 1894 had destroyed the Chinese settlement there wrote, "of course I feel very sorry for our mission brethren, but I am glad Chinatown is in ashes. We were all getting sick from the impure air. Some of the boys had been sick for months on account, I think, of the filth surrounding our mission rooms, and I believe it was the Lord's will that it should burn."[15]

In this same letter addressed to William C. Pond, who was in charge of the ministry to the Chinese on the West coast, the young woman from Santa Cruz praised the Chinese who had been converted at the mission. She noted how conversion had actually made the faces of these heathen brighter and their eyes more sparkling.[16] At Stockton California when the mission there celebrated the first anniversary of its founding, John C. Holbrook who was the guest speaker noted with surprise the volume and quality of the singing. He remarked that he had not expected ever to hear Chinese barbarians singing so well.[17] Holbrook had visited Chinese missions at San Diego,

---

14. John R. Hykes, "The Importance of Winning China for Christ," *Missionary Review*, 5 (February, 1892), 82-91.
15. William C. Pond, "The Chinese," *American Missionary*, 48 (July, 1894), 269.
16. *Ibid.*
17. John C. Holbrook, "Chinese Mission Anniversary," *American Missionary*, 45 (March, 1891), 108.

Riverside, Los Angeles, Santa Barbara, and Ventura as well, and at all of these places he was impressed at the striking difference in appearance and attitude between the converts and their heathen fellows elsewhere.

Testimony in support of the qualities of Chinese converts was offered from another missionary who had seen action in China and was able to present comparisons between the domestic and the foreign product. The integrity of the converted Chinese in California could not be questioned he thought. Ninety per cent of the converts remained true to their profession of faith and he even knew of one man, Lum Foon, who became so enthusiastic about Christianity that he returned to China as a missionary in order to bring the good news to his fellow countrymen.[18] Another Chinese, Lem Chung, who became a Christian after his arrival in Sacramento, was one of the mainstays of the mission there and even wrote for the *American Missionary*.[19] These and other Chinese were praised for their enthusiastic support of the missionary endeavor in California.

If the testimony of the missionaries is examined closely the extent to which their evaluation of the Chinese reflected a deprecating analysis of their character is striking. With rare exceptions even when the good qualities of the convert were being described the assumption of inferiority was apparent. Despite private relationships based upon genuine affection and understanding, public statements even by those who spoke favorably were implicitly condescending. If the converted Chinese were no longer to be viewed as subhuman it was nevertheless clear that they were an inferior people whose condition precluded all remedies except one: the application of large doses of the healing and strengthening medicines of the Christian gospel at the hands of American missionaries. Because there was so little general contact with the Chinese, information about them was often filtered through the interpretations of missionaries at home and in China. Consequently for the vast majority of people in this country at the turn of the century who had any awareness of a Chinese, whether he was loathed or tolerated, he remained still a "chinaman."

18. Frederick J. Masters, ''Chinese Mission in San Francisco,'' *Missionary Review*, 5 (July, 1892), 546-7.
19. Lem Chung, ''Anniversary of Our Sacramento Mission,'' *American Missionary*, 45 (June, 1891), 234-37.

American attitudes toward the Chinese were shaped by more than just the experiences of the missionaries. They were, after all, a product of a culture as well as of a theology. Therefore, popular concepts of the Chinese at the turn of the century were developed in part as a response to the demand of a rapidly evolving economic system for the development of a rationale which could reconcile the increased emphasis on material well-being with the traditional articulation of the philosophy of American life. Most Americans during these years never saw a Chinese at close range nor did they acquire to a significant extent any degree of understanding of them. Consequently, the popular attitude toward the Chinese was shaped in large part by the urgent desire at home to explain both the impact of rapid economic change on American life and the implications of an expanded national role in world affairs.

One of the features of national life at the end of the nineteenth century and the beginning of the twentieth was the relationship between Protestantism and business. The soldiers of the cross and the soldiers of the gun in foreign lands often shared common goals as did the cleric and the businessman at home. Max Weber, Richard Tawney, and others have outlined the dimensions of the Protestant ethic and described its impact on American culture. The role of the Protestant church in the development of a cultural-theological dogma was both formative and supportive. Therefore, the impact of the point of view of many missionaries on attitudes toward the Chinese can be understood in part only within the broader framework of the Protestant ethic.

The closeness of the relationship between Protestantism and business is obvious when we identify some of the leading exponents of the cult of success through leading the good life. Henry Ward Beecher, Lyman Abbott, William Lawrence, Horatio Alger, and others were as familiar to the congregations of the faithful who worshipped God as they were to those who worshipped mammon. It is fruitless to debate the issue of who allied with whom, but there is enough evidence to suggest the existence of an alliance between business and Protestantism in American society at that time. The compact may have been initiated by the religious who wished to glorify the success of business leaders, predominantly Protestant, as an example of how to succeed through clean living, or it may have been originated by a commercial world which sought moral justification for its practices. The sermons of Andrew Carneige come easily to mind. But whatever the sequence it was a happy friendship and one which helps to explain the relationship between missionaries and merchants in China as well as between Protestantism and business at home.

It is apparent that the bonds which joined portions of the Christian community and the business community were fashioned out of the basic needs of each. For Christian evangelism the existence of a pagan people was as important as the opportunity for new markets was to a developing capitalistic economy. If it could be established, as it was in part through the example of Horatio Alger, that success in religion and success in business were not only compatible but interdependent, then China and the Chinese could be presented as a joint opportunity for commercial and Christian evangelism. It was necessary to describe the Chinese as pagan in order to justify the missionary enterprise and as uncivilized in order to justify commercial exploitation. On this basis it was possible for American businessmen to preach the need for the development of the China market as a God-directed activity reflecting the responsibility of the superior race for an inferior one. The profit in dollars and self-righteous satisfaction was immense, but the cost in misunderstanding has yet to be paid in full.

The notion that the China market was as vital to the economic good health of the nation as the missionary endeavor was to its good conscience was clearly stated by Brooks Adams. In *The Law of Civilization and Decay* he explained how every human community was directed by the force of "cosmic energy."[20] As societies became more civilized they tended to dissipate their store of energy as they sought greater security. Gradually the source of energy was expended until man in his most civilized state lost his desire to improve himself and sought only to protest his position. Brooks Adams saw only a grim future ahead for Western Europe and especially for the United States which he thought had stopped moving forward and was now using its remaining energy to preserve its present level of attainment.

It was on the basis of these assumptions that Brooks Adams argued in *America's Economic Supremacy* that the greatest opportunity for the revitalization of the nation existed in China.[21] If, in the

20. Brooks Adams, *The Law of Civilization and Decay* (New York, 1895).
21. Brooks Adams, *America's Economic Supremacy* (New York, 1900).

past, civilizations had regained lost vigor through a barbaric infusion, then Adams argued that China could prove to be a source of such energy. If the United States could absorb the vitality still remaining in Chinese civilization it would be possible to delay the process of disintegration. China occupied a vital place in the future of America because the exploitation of her markets would mean the revitalization of American manufacturing and trade. Thus he says, "the Chinese question must, therefore, be accepted as the great problem of the future, as a problem from which there can be no escape."[22] The United States will be forced of necessity ". . . to enter upon the development of eastern Asia, and . . . reduce it to a part of our economic system."[23]

Since it was agreed that China lacked the power to regenerate herself either spiritually or economically the burden of accomplishing these tasks fell upon the United States. In many ways it was a happy opportunity because it offered a chance for Christian evangelists to respond to the call of their Lord to "go . . . and teach all nations, baptizing them in the name of the Father, and of the Son, and of the Holy Ghost."[24] At the same time it offered a nation bursting with the energy of capitalistic nationalism an opportunity and a rationale. The forces of commerce did not need to concede that theirs was a lesser call because it had already been established that the angels were on the side of American expansion, and that together, soldier, merchant, and minister would evangelize, civilize, and uplift the Chinese and possibly even the world. It is understandable that the true nature of the Chinese was submerged beneath succeeding waves of American ethnocentrism.

The formation of the popular image of China was heavily influenced by the activities of missionaries at home and abroad and by the prevailing notion that the interests of Christian evangelism were well served by cultural and commercial expansion in the Far East. Supported by a climate of opinion which interpreted the opportunities for expansion presented to the nation at the turn of the century as the result of divine providence and the reaction to those opportunities as

22. *Ibid.*, p. 194.
23. *Ibid.*
24. Matthew 28:19.

the result of divine guidance, the church was not slow to justify its attitude toward the Chinese. The overriding need of clergy and informed laymen alike was to view the Chinese from a perspective which supported the interpretation of their responsibility to evangelize the world. The result was a picture of the Chinese which bore little resemblance to the realities of their life either in China or the United States.

Very little real understanding of the Chinese was achieved because to a considerable degree the attitude toward China was formed out of the needs of American culture. It was based upon the belief in a divine mission and shaped by the concept of a barbaric heathenish people who in reality lived within a tradition of civilization more ancient than that of the West. China was viewed as an unprecedented opportunity for commercial and spiritual evangelism with little willingness to face the difficulties caused by geographical distance and cultural difference. Undergirding all thinking about the Chinese was the assumption that China as a nation and as a people represented a unique opportunity to establish the American claim to cultural, economic, and moral leadership in the world.

Evangelization and Civilization: Protestant Missionary Motivation in the Imperialist Era*

Introduction
William R. Hutchison

This symposium constitutes one stage in a longer-range collaborative study of "Missionary Ideologies in the Imperialist Era, 1880–1920." The prospectus for this larger study (in which some twenty scholars, at present, are engaged) contained language that may help in clarifying the authors' objectives in the initial papers presented here:

> The aim will be to provide description and comparison, both of the stated purposes of the missionary movement in this period and of the presuppositions and motivations informing the enterprise. The project will focus principally, though not exclusively, on Protestant examples.
>
> Investigators will be asked especially to consider the attitudes of missionary spokesmen toward the colonialism of the era, and to analyze the ways in which both spokesmen and missionaries may have operated as collaborators or as critics of imperial expansionism. More particularly, we shall inquire about the extent to which missionaries in this period considered themselves responsible for the spread of "Christian civilization"; and how such civilizing obligations were reconciled with the primary goal of evangelization, which in some eras had been thought to preclude any direct preoccupation with civilizing activities.
>
> We hope that, in pursuing these central questions, investigators will take note of variations in ideology, not just among the several "sending" cultures, but between missionary spokesmen or supporters at home and their workers in the various missionary fields. We also expect, of course, that the writers will discuss the more striking changes that occurred over time, particularly where these changes

constituted responses to criticism at home or, more important, to pressures and changed conditions in the "receiving" societies.

Finally, although we have thought it best to limit our focus to the 1880–1920 time period, we shall encourage writers to refer, as much as is necessary and appropriate, to preceding and subsequent phases of the foreign-mission movement.

At least three of the self-limitations stated or implied in that description deserve some elaboration: they speak to definitional problems that arise in any research on missions, especially if it adopts a determinedly comparative methodology.

The first such limitation involves our concentration on Protestant missions. In what Professor Walls likes to call the high imperial era, a study of missions that omits the French might be considered "*Hamlet* without Hamlet"—or at least as *The Three Musketeers* without d'Artagnan. To be sure, we have commissioned several papers on Catholic missions for the Missionary Ideologies project. Yet, despite misgivings, we have found it wisest to concentrate on comparisons within Protestantism. The analyses of Catholic missions will serve as "controls"; we do not pretend that they will offer an adequate number or range of Catholic comparative examples.

We have, second, agreed to concentrate on ideas; and on those systems of ideas for which, *faute de mieux*, we are using the term "ideologies." This means that although we shall frequently discuss implementation or behavior—what actually happened in the mission fields—we are trying principally to gain clarity about what it was the Western churches or societies thought and asserted. We consider it sufficiently ambitious, in this first step toward larger-scale comparative analyses, to lay out and compare the stated rationales of the movement during one crucial period.

The third limitation, our virtually exclusive concentration on *Western* conceptions of the missionary enterprise, also raises serious questions with which the committee planning this project has

William R. Hutchison is Charles Warren Professor of American Religious History at Harvard University.

struggled extensively. One need not rehearse all the arguments; our decision was that we should not claim, fundamentally, to be examining the missionary movement through any but Western eyes, perceptions, and categories.

It is at this point that the project is most clearly a prolegomenon, a kind of staging area. One acknowledges this not out of modesty, but precisely to make the point that a subsequent comparative analysis, fashioned from *non*-Western perspectives, will be the main story—or at least should be chapter two in any further development of this field.

The difficulty, of course, is that one can easily see arguments for making the non-Western perceptions chapter one. Catherine Albanese, in her new history of American religion, seeks to combat the "mainstream" bias in traditional scholarship by examining the nonmainstream religions first; by treating first the "manyness" of American religion, and only then the "oneness."[1] Investigators of mission history might in the same way reverse the usual order of things and gather non-Western perceptions first, thus decreasing the chances that the scholarly agenda will be further confined in its traditional Western categories.

For European and American scholars to "organize" non-Western perspectives is, however, equally problematic—scarcely a remedy for the scholarly Eurocentrism identified (if also exaggerated) by Edward Said or, before that, by Mssrs. Gallagher and Robinson.[2] We chose, therefore, to focus quite consciously on Euro-American ideology, and to make it clear that we appreciate the dangers inherent in that decision.

Having described three of the more difficult choices made in designing this project, I should add a final word about the ambitious overall intentions that made such stringent delimitations necessary. One reason comparative history is such a "young" or unexplored discipline—after all these centuries—is that genuine comparative analysis (as opposed, for example, to mere "side-by-side" cataloguing of national or societal histories) is enormously demanding even after one has managed to control for a large number of the relevant variables. Confronted, in the missionary phenomenon, with an ususual array of cultural and other factors—a veritable cornucopia of apples, oranges, and stranger fruit—one naturally strives for the time-honored (and result-honored) diffidence of the restricted historical monograph.

But why attack the subject in this ambitious "comparative" manner in the first place? Is that not, given the primitive condition of the scholarship on particular sending and receiving societies,[3] rather like running the train before building the tracks?

Perhaps. But there are even stronger arguments for striving from the start toward comparative judgments. One such argument is that any history—even of national or other "single" entities—that is not consciously comparative dooms itself to being unconsciously so. Raymond Grew, who argued that proposition in an article for the *American Historical Review,* quoted another social scientist's strange-but-true observation that "thinking without comparison is unthinkable."[4]

Also strange but true, I believe, is the insistence that rigorous comparison is especially needed in certain disciplines, such as church history and missionary history, that one might have thought were essentially and automatically comparative. Fields like church history, dealing as they do with fundamentally cross-cultural phenomena, tend to be altogether too complacent in assuming that their traditional assumptions about (for example) national or regional peculiarities are reliable, when actually these assumptions are peculiarly in need of tightly controlled comparative assessment.

This paper is one of four that, together with Professor Hutchison's introductory and concluding remarks, have been adapted from a panel presentation—organized and moderated by Professor Hutchison—at the Washington, D.C. meetings of the American Society of Church History in December 1980. The authors acknowledge with appreciation the support of the Lilly Endowment.

Recent experience with the study of imperialism, moreover, suggests that comparison must be pursued from the outset, and not just at some later point; that train-running and track-laying had better proceed together. The Gallagher/Robinson proposal, which highlighted the importance of "native" responses in the transition from informal to formal (or classic) imperialism, generated a highly productive debate. But it also prompted considerable wheel-spinning that—as hindsight tells us—could have been avoided had the original proposal not referred so exclusively to one colonial power (Great Britain) and one colonized area (Africa).

Our assumption in the Ideologies project, therefore, has been that a comparative methodology is not merely helpful, but primary and quite fundamental. I think that even the following small sample—showing Anglo-American activism as it diverged from quietist Continental models, yet also showing Scandinavian departures from the Germans, and the British living in a different world from that of the Americans—confirms the importance of nuanced comparative analysis if we are to refine our generalizations about missions and imperialism.

Notes

1. Albanese, *America: Religions and Religion* (Belmont, Calif.: Wadsworth, 1981).
2. Edward W. Said, *Orientalism* (New York: Pantheon Books, 1978); John Gallagher and Ronald Robinson, "The Imperialism of Free Trade," *Economic History Review*, 2nd series, 6 (1953): 1–15.
3. "Primitive" is an apt term especially for mission *ideology*. Torben Christensen, in a letter accompanying the paper printed here, remarked that "no scholarly work has ever been done on Danish missions, not to mention the problem of evangelization and civilization." And Pierce Beaver's retort, when he was asked in the 1960s to "reinterpret" American thought on missions, is still all too appropriate: "The task . . . is not reinterpretation. First interpretation has not yet been achieved" (Jerald C. Brauer, ed., *Reinterpretation in American Church History* [Chicago: Univ. of Chicago Press, 1968], p. 113).
4. Grew, "The Case for Comparing Histories," *American Historical Review* 85 (October 1980): 768n.

II. The Americans

Charles W. Forman

Confidence and optimism were the marks of American life as the nineteenth century gave way to the twentieth. The spirit of the times was expansive, vigorous, and, in one of its favorite words, "forward-looking." This was the "age of energy," a time for great enterprises. America, which had always had a sense of mission, from its beginnings as an "errand in the wilderness" to its later commitment to a "manifest destiny," was now ready to step out onto the world stage, carrying some of the moral fervor that had marked its earlier life.

Foreign missions matched the national mood. They were a mighty enterprise calling for energy and optimism. "The whole horizon is aflame," wrote Arthur T. Pierson, the man who did the most to stir up missionary enthusiasm in the late nineteenth century. John R. Mott took up the same theme when he became the major voice for missions at the beginning of the twentieth century. He could always see a "rising spiritual tide" and perceive that "the influence of Jesus Christ was never so widespread and so penetrating and so transforming" as it was in his day. The readiness to take on the whole world was evidenced in the watchword of the Student Volunteer Movement for Foreign Missions: "The Evangelization of the World in this Generation." Missions were a way of making a worldwide impact in a benevolent fashion. All the presidents of the country in the early twentieth century—McKinley, Roosevelt, Taft, and Wilson—spoke in praise of foreign missions; not, as a rule, because missions advanced American interests but because they represented a "national altruism," a "contribution to the . . . moral forces of the world."[1]

America became in those days the leading nation in the sending out of Protestant missionaries. Prior to 1880 missions had been maintained by relatively small and specially dedicated groups of

Charles W. Forman is Professor of Missions at Yale Divinity School.

believers, but now they blossomed into a major interest of the churches and a significant interest of the nation. The number of American foreign missionaries, which stood at 934 in 1890, reached nearly 5,000 a decade later and over 9,000 in 1915. In support of those workers large movements were organized not only in the churches but in the nation generally. The Student Volunteer Movement was begun in 1886 to recruit missionaries, and in its first winter of work on the college campuses its two agents won 2,000 volunteers. Twenty years later the Laymen's Missionary Movement was organized. Over 100,000 men, mostly business-men, were involved in the prayer meetings, conferences, and study groups of this organization in support of foreign missions. Some church officials, impressed by its size and the fact that it was en-tirely lay-organized and lay-led, declared: "this movement is the most epoch-making that has occurred in the Christian world since the Protestant Reformation."[2]

America was enchanted with sheer bigness and here too for-eign missions corresponded to the ethos of the land. The United States showed the world what dimensions a missionary conference could assume. At the midpoint of the period under consideration, in 1900, there came the great Ecumenical Missionary Conference in New York. London may have seen its great mission gatherings in Exeter Hall in earlier years, but this conference attracted so many people that no one hall could accommodate them. Carnegie Hall was jammed just for the women's sessions. Churches around the city were filled with working parties on particular topics. Between 170,000 and 200,000 people were in attendance, making this the largest missions gathering that has ever taken place. President Wil-liam McKinley opened the conference and ex-President Benjamin Harrison presided over its major sessions.[3]

Business efficiency and planning were another mark of the American culture at that time and also characterized foreign mis-sions. Arthur T. Pierson and John R. Mott wrote repeatedly of the values of overall, worldwide organization and planning. It was the desire for organizational efficiency that led to the incorporation of missions into ecclesiastical structures. A study of the way in which foreign missions became an official church responsibility in this country, rather than remaining in the hands of independent missionary societies as they did in Europe, shows that the major factor behind that change was not a profound theological conviction that the church exists for mission, but the pressures of practical administrative efficiency and organizational control. Foreigners, it would seem, were both impressed and amused by this American proclivity. The head of the British delegation at the New York Ecumenical Conference said: "We thank you for the careful preparation you have made. American business habits and alertness of intelligence and keenness for statistics and hunger for information have almost overpowered us during the last two years."[4]

In some respects this enthusiasm for size and organizational efficiency met its nemesis at the end of the period here considered. The Interchurch World Movement, launched in February 1919, was to have been an extravaganza of coordinated interdenominational, nationwide propaganda and money raising for foreign missions, appealing to the general public as well as to church people. But it was so big and involved so many interrelated plans and had to be so unspecific in its appeals that it soon floundered and then quickly collapsed.

With an outlook closely parallel to the general national mood, foreign missions could easily fall into line with national efforts for imperialist expansion. This occurred at the time of the Spanish-American War and the acquisition of the Philippine Islands. The rapid growth of missions began a decade before that war and its attendant imperialist fervor, so the growth can hardly be seen as the result of imperialist interests. But when the imperial expansion came missionaries generally did not oppose it. Certain well-known church leaders opposed the acquisition of the Philippines, but missionaries and mission boards were not numbered among them.[5] Rather, mission organizations lent strength to the imperialist position by hastening to send their envoys to those islands. Some of their missionaries proved to be vocal advocates of American rule of the Philippines. Bishop James M. Thoburn, head of the Methodist church in India and Southeast Asia, and Homer Stuntz, the dominant figure in the initial years of Methodist work in the Philippines, were the most notable of these. Stuntz hailed the opportunity for missions "to cooperate with the State in shedding the light of Christian civilization." Thoburn even urged the sending of American warships to the China coast. In China at the same time the American Congregational mission called on America to annex the former Spanish islands of Micronesia. Most missionary statements were more qualified than these, condemning the idea of sheer imperial aggrandizement, but leaving the door open to imperial domination for the sake of stability and social services. Robert E. Speer, the chief leader of Presbyterian missions, supported the American intervention in the Philippines for its liberating and civilizing effects, but also declared that missions were not concerned "to turn independent states into dependencies upon European or American governments."[6]

In general American missions, outside the Philippines, were not dedicated to the advancement of American interests—political or commercial. Even in the Philippines, once American rule had been established, missionaries spent more time challenging the government to adhere to the high purposes that they had assigned to it than they did in praising its accomplishments.[7] The increase of American commerce and exports was not part of the missionary agenda, though a number of apologists in the United States spoke of the commercially advantageous by-products of missions.[8] A study of the statements of purpose made by missionary candidates in this period reveals no interest in the expansion of American power or commerce, but only an interest in religious objectives. And an analysis of the leaders of the Laymen's Missionary Movement, which, as an organization of businessmen, would be most likely to attract people with commercial motives, shows that none of the men was involved in commercial ventures that could be served by the expanding of missions.

Business interests in fact came in for negative comment from missionaries and mission leaders. Some important missionaries,

like Hiram Bingham, Jr., in Micronesia, were opposed to the growing commercialism of American life, and most American missionaries in China after 1890 were critical of Western merchants.
Distrust between missionaries and businessmen was common in
the field though unknown at home.[9]

Apart from political and commercial concerns, however,
American missions did maintain considerable interest in the spread
of American culture. Often this was implicit rather than explicit.
The emphasis on efficiency and businesslike methods, for example, was simply assumed in the work the missionaries did, and it
necessarily carried influence in the direction of rationalization and
modernization of the way of life of other countries. Methods of
agricultural work in the newly developing agricultural missions or
of medical work in the well-established medical missions had a
certain secularized character, which was also assumed and which
inevitably had what may be called a secularizing impact on the
more pervasively religious societies that many missionaries confronted. The individualism inherent in the way in which they presented their faith and called for individual conversions also
implied a cultural transformation wherever they went.

In other matters the desire for cultural change was fully explicit. More than in previous times, mission thought and mission
propaganda devoted itself to the cultural benefits that came with
the missionaries. The greatest expression of this kind of interest
was the three-volume work, *Christian Missions and Social Progress,*
published between 1897 and 1906 by the Presbyterian missionary
James S. Dennis. A number of other authors worked along the
same vein.[10]

The attitude evidenced in such writings was not a blanket endorsement of American culture, nor a desire for the spread of every American trait. The mission advocates stressed only a limited
number of cultural advantages that, it was presumed, Americans
had to offer. An improvement in the position of women was always first and foremost. The limitations placed on women in other
societies and programs for their liberation and education were spo-

ken of continually, especially by the women missionaries and women mission leaders. These women, incidentally, were not looking merely for a duplication of current Western standards; they were involved in frequent confrontations with Western limitations on women's roles.[11]

A Western type of education and Western medical science were the other two cultural features that were uniformly recommended by the missions. The advocacy of any other types of education or medicine would have been regarded as anachronistic by them, and doubtless also by the leading elements in the non-Western societies of that time. The government of Japan, for example, was pressing forward with the same kind of Western education that the missionaries were offering and some of its work, especially in the applied sciences, was unexcelled anywhere in the world. American missions, in fact, were more ambivalent about Western education than were the leading elites of the non-Western lands. They feared the impact of Western schools and universities when divorced from their religious roots. This fear infected much of the missions' reaction to Westernization. Both Mott and Speer spoke of it. "The greatest obstacle to the world wide spread of the Christian religion," wrote Mott, "is the un-Christian impact of our Western civilization." And Speer said that the connection with the West was a handicap to Christ.[12]

Aside from women's rights, education, and medicine, the possible cultural impact of missions attracted little attention from the mission forces. At the Ecumenical Missionary Conference in New York only one session out of forty dealt with such cultural impacts. Of the eighty-five missionaries who spoke about their work in foreign lands only six mentioned Western improvements other than those three, while eight missionaries spoke negatively of Western influences.[13]

Some members of the mission force were ready to recognize the achievements and values of non-Western cultures. This readiness increased toward the end of the period and was most evident in an intellectual center like Yenching University, begun in 1915. The American founders of that missionary institution felt that they must learn from the Chinese what the special contributions of Chinese culture might be to Christian understanding. Among some mission-minded leaders of the American churches the appreciation of other cultures extended even to the religions of those cultures, which were seen as having great value. Yet it was still believed that the noblest aspirations of other faiths would find their fulfillment only in Christ.[14]

A more liberal way of thinking about religion was evidently creeping into missions. Among the thousands of new recruits brought in by the Student Volunteer Movement were men and women less closely identified with the conservative inner circles of church life than their predecessors, who for the most part had been recruited directly by the churches. The Presbyterian missions in India, for example, which prior to 1890 had received practically all their men from two conservative Presbyterian seminaries—Princeton and Western—began in that year to receive their first graduates from the liberal Union Seminary in New York.[15] It became common after 1900 for mission leaders to recognize the possibility of salvation for non-Christians, though around 1890 a bruising battle had had to be fought over this question in Congregational mission circles.

The growth of liberalism in missions carried the seeds of later dissension and disruption. Serious divisions in the American missionary movement did not come until after 1920, but their origins lay in the nascent liberalism of this period and the first reactions thereto. A. J. Gordon, staunch conservative leader and mission advocate, condemned both biblical criticism and Continental theology, and advocated Bible distribution in preference to other, more secular forms of missionary activity. Pre-millennialism became widespread among missionaries; its influence worked against liberalism and proved a source of later conflict. The pre-millenialists opposed efforts for structural changes in society, since Christ was coming before any great change could take place.[16]

Though much has been said here about the cultural interests of the missionaries, it needs to be recognized before reaching a conclusion that their principal motive—whether they were pre- or post-millenialist, liberal or conservative—was not "civilizing" but "evangelizing." This has already been implied in the reference to the complete absence of "civilizing" aims in the application statements of missionary candidates. It has also been recognized in the fact, noted above, that only six of the eighty-five missionary speakers at the Ecumenical Conference mentioned cultural values other than education, medicine, and women's rights. In the conference session dealing with the aim of missions none of the speakers mentioned cultural aims, but all spoke of presenting Christ, converting men, and establishing churches. Even the chief protagonist of the cultural achievements of missions, James Dennis, explained that social change was a by-product of the missionaries' work; the main purpose was to teach the gospel. Robert E. Speer repeatedly took the same stand.[17]

The religious purpose was stated far more in terms of converting individuals than of developing churches. Speer and Mott, indeed, spoke of the importance of building national churches with an indigenous life of their own, but this was an emphasis in their thought that developed mostly toward the end of the period. In general the emphasis on the indigenous church, which had been paramount in the thinking of Rufus Anderson, the principal American spokesman in the mid-nineteenth century, was little in evidence at the end of the century. It appeared as central only in the writing of one American theorist, the Lutheran Edward Pfeiffer; and he, it must be admitted, derived his ideas from Germany rather than from his American context. The great aim of American missions was evidently not to develop churches any more than it was to spread American culture.[18]

The great aim was, as Speer put it, to plant "the life of Christ in the hearts of men."[19] This was central and must be recognized as such, despite the fact that civilizing motifs accompanied the evangelizing motives.

Notes

1. Pierson and Mott quoted in Charles W. Forman, "A History of Foreign Mission Theory," R. Pierce Beaver, ed., *American Missions in Bicentennial Perspective* (South Pasadena, Calif.: William Carey Library, 1977), pp. 81, 91; Paul Varg, *Missionaries, Chinese and Diplomats* (Princeton, N.J.: Princeton Univ. Press, 1958), pp. 79–81; *Ecumenical Missionary Conference . . . in Carnegie Hall,* 2 vols. (New York: American Tract Society), 1:39–40. Roosevelt did mention the possible advancement of American trade through the influence of foreign missions, but this comment was not typical of the presidential pronouncements (Varg, *Missionaries,* p. 74).

2. Valentin H. Rabe, *The Home Base of American China Missions, 1880–1920* (Cambridge, Mass.: Harvard Univ. Press, 1978), p. 26; W. Richey Hogg, "The Role of American Protestantism in World Missions," in Beaver, *Bicentennial,* pp. 369, 376.

3. W. Richey Hogg, *Ecumenical Foundations* (New York: Harper & Brothers, 1952), p. 45.

4. *Ecumenical Conference,* 1:31; Earl MacCormac, "The Transition from Voluntary Missionary Societies . . . among the American Congregationalists, Presbyterians and Methodists," unpublished Ph.D. dissertation, Yale Univ., 1960.

5. Fred H. Harrington, "The Anti-Imperialist Movement in the United States, 1898–1900," *Mississippi Valley Historical Review* 22 (September 1935): 211–23; Winthrop S. Hudson, "Protestant Clergy Debate the Nation's Vocation, 1898–1899," *Church History* 42 (1973): 110–18.

6. Kenton J. Clymer, "Religion and American Imperialism: Methodist Missionaries in the Philippine Islands, 1899–1913," *Pacific Historical Review* 49 (1980): 29–50; H. C. Stuntz, "The Open Door in Hawaii and the Philippines," in Charles H. Fahs et al., eds., *The Open Door* (New York: Methodist Episcopal Church, 1903), p. 139; Kenneth M. MacKenzie, *The Robe and the Sword* (Washington, D.C.: Public Affairs Press, 1961), p. 11; Varg, *Missionaries,* p. 83; Forman, "History of Foreign Mission Theory," pp. 85–86; H. McKennie Goodpasture, "Robert E. Speer's Legacy," *Occasional Bulletin of Missionary Research* 2 (1978): 41; Robert E. Speer, *Missionary Principles and Practice* (New York: Fleming H. Revell, 1902), pp. 28–29.

7. Clymer, "Religion and American Imperialism," pp. 37–50.

8. MacKenzie, *The Robe and the Sword,* pp. 14–15; David Healy, *U.S. Expansionism* (Madison: Univ. of Wisconsin Press, 1970), pp. 136, 142; Paul Varg, "Motives in Protestant Missions, 1890–1917," *Church History* 23

(1954): 74. Of the ten "apologists" referred to in these sources, only one was clearly involved in mission work, while the identity of one other is uncertain.

9. Varg, "Motives," p. 73; Charles Millar, "A Temperate Note on 'Holy and Unholy Spirits,' " *Journal of Pacific History* 14 (1979): 230–32.

10. Stephen C. Knapp, "Mission and Modernization," in Beaver, ed., *Bicentennial*, pp. 146–209; James S. Dennis, *Christian Missions and Social Progress*, 3 vols. (New York: Fleming H. Revell Co., 1897–1906); Arthur M. Schlesinger, Jr., "The Missionary Enterprise and Imperialism," in John K. Fairbank, ed., *The Missionary Enterprise in China and America* (Cambridge, Mass.: Harvard Univ. Press, 1974), pp. 336–73.

11. R. Pierce Beaver, *All Loves Excelling* (Grand Rapids, Mich.: Wm. B. Eerdmans Publishing Co., 1968).

12. *Ecumenical Conference*, 1: 511; John R. Mott, *The Present World Situation* (New York: Student Volunteer Movement for Foreign Missions, 1914), p. 120; *Conference on Cooperation and the Promotion of Unity in Foreign Missionary Work* (New York: Foreign Missions Conference, 1914), pp. 102, 111.

13. *Ecumenical Conference*, 1: 347–78.

14. Varg, *Missionaries*, pp. 106–11; C. Howard Hopkins, *John R. Mott* (Grand Rapids, Mich.: Wm. B. Eerdmans Publishing Co., 1979), p. 154; Jessie Lutz, ed., *Christian Missions in China: Evangelists of What?* (Boston: Heath, 1965), pp. 13–14; Philip West, *Yenching University and Sino-Western Relations, 1916–1952* (Cambridge, Mass.: Harvard Univ. Press, 1976), pp. 39, 49; Forman, "History of Foreign Mission Theory," pp. 85–87; Sushil Pathak, *American Missionaries and Hinduism* (Delhi: Munshiram Manoharlal, 1967), pp. 220–28.

15. Rabe, *Home Base*, pp. 90–93; John Webster, *The Christian Community and Change in 19th Century North India* (Delhi: The Macmillan Co. of India, 1976), pp. 32–36, 98–101.

16. A. J. Gordon, *The Holy Spirit in Missions* (New York: Fleming H. Revell, 1893), pp. 201–33; Timothy Weber, *Living in the Shadow of the Second Coming* (New York: Oxford Univ. Press, 1979), pp. 65–81. Arthur Pierson refused to speak at the Parliament of Religions because of its liberal basis. Delavan Pierson, *Arthur T. Pierson* (New York: Fleming H. Revell, 1912), p. 303.

17. *Ecumenical Conference*, 1: 67–77; Dennis, *Christian Missions*, 2: 32–33; Speer *Principles*, pp. 34–35, 37; Goodpasture, "Speer's Legacy," pp. 38, 41.

18. Forman, "History of Foreign Mission Theory," p. 92; Edward Pfeiffer *Mission Studies* (Columbus, Ohio: Lutheran Book Concern, 1908).

19. Quoted in Goodpasture, "Speer's Legacy," p. 38.

Josiah Strong and American Nationalism: A Reevaluation

Dorothea R. Muller

J OSIAH Strong, whose career as a Congregationalist minister spanned the period 1869-1916, was recognized as a pioneer social reformer who devoted his efforts to awakening the church and the nation to the challenge of the city. Strong had witnessed the tremendous economic growth of the nation following the Civil War, experienced the enthusiasm and optimism of the settlement of the West as a missionary in Cheyenne, anticipated the nation's limitless potential as a home missionary in the Ohio Valley in the 1880s, and developed an ardent spirit of nationalism. His fervor was a part of the larger resurgence of nationalism in the United States in the last decades of the nineteenth century. Strong's contemporaries characterized his book *Our Country: Its Possible Future and Its Present Crisis* as having been "the Uncle Tom's Cabin" of social reform and referred to the movement for applied Christianity which he sought to inspire. At the time of his death in 1916, Strong won praise as "a great seer" who escaped national parochialism and who "had seen this process of world unification through interdependence long before the wisdom of mere politics had gotten its eyes open."[1]

Historians, however, termed Strong's *Our Country* "a post-Appomattox expression of manifest destiny," jingoistic, and "prophetic of imperial expansionism."[2] The volume, because of its tremendous circulation of

Dorothea Muller is associate professor of history in the C. W. Post College of Long Island University. The author gratefully acknowledges a fellowship from the American Association of University Women which facilitated the preparation of this article.

[1] Editorial, *Outlook*, CXIII (May 10, 1916), 56; *American Institute of Social Service: Report of the Work of the American Institute of Social Service for the Year, 1916-1917. Bulletin, Vol. II, No. 1* (New York, 1917), 12; James H. Ecob, "Interdependence and Internationalism," *Gospel of the Kingdom*, IX (March 1917), 97.

[2] Ralph Henry Gabriel, *The Course of American Democratic Thought: An Intellectual History Since 1815* (New York, 1940), 343; Henry F. May, *Protestant Churches and Industrial America* (New York, 1949), 114.

176,000 copies by 1916, is considered to have been an influence "in nurturing the imperialistic urge" in the nation in the 1890s.[3] Strong is cited together with John Fiske, John W. Burgess, Albert J. Beveridge, and Alfred T. Mahan as an advocate of Anglo-Saxon imperialism based on the Darwinian idea of competition among nations and races ensuring survival of the fittest and, if necessary, involving the dispossessing of weaker peoples. Thus Strong is declared to have maintained that "the Anglo-Saxon was destined by God and evolution to rule the world."[4]

Did Strong's use of the concepts of Anglo-Saxon superiority, competition among races, and survival of the fittest mean that he was expressing an aggressive nationalism? Strong explained that the "all-conquering Anglo-Saxon" to whom he referred was armed with the "aggressive traits" of unequalled energy and indomitable perseverance, was "powerful" in resources of population and wealth, and was vital in possessing the highest civilizaton based on spiritual (not ritualistic) Christianity and civil liberty. The race, through its missionaries, traders, adventurers, and settlers possessing such characteristics, would carry its civilization to other peoples in Mexico, Central and South America, Africa, and beyond, making its civilization that of the world "until in a very true and important sense it has Anglo-Saxonized mankind." Strong emphasized that this was "no war of extermination." He declared the contest "not one of arms, but of vitality and of civilization."[5] When addressing a convention of the Christian Endeavor Society in July 1892 on "Our Country for Christ," he asserted that

[3] Richard Hofstadter, William Miller, and Daniel Aaron, *The United States: The History of A Republic* (Englewood Cliffs, 1957), 551, 572. See also Julius W. Pratt, *Expansionists of 1898: The Acquisition of Hawaii and the Spanish Islands* (Baltimore, 1936), 19.

[4] Henry Bamford Parkes, *The United States of America: A History* (New York, 1953), 490. See also Pratt, *Expansionists of 1898*, 5-6; Julius W. Pratt, *America's Colonial Experiment* (New York, 1950), 25; Merle Curti, *The Growth of American Thought* (New York, 1943), 670-72; Richard Hofstadter, *Social Darwinism in American Thought: 1860-1915* (Philadelphia, 1944), 153-54; Harvey Wish, *Society and Thought in Modern America: Volume II. A Social and Intellectual History of the American People From 1865* (New York, 1952), 389-90; Edward McNall Burns, *The American Idea of Mission: Concepts of National Purpose and Destiny* (New Brunswick, 1957), 207-08, 217; Clifton E. Olmstead, *History of Religion in the United States* (Englewood Cliffs, 1960), 501; Richard W. Van Alstyne, *The American Empire: Its Historical Pattern and Evolution* (London, 1960), 22-24; Walter LaFeber, *The New Empire: An Interpretation of American Overseas Expansion, 1860-1898* (Ithaca, 1963), 72, 79-80; Foster Rhea Dulles, *America's Rise to World Power: 1898-1954* (New York, 1954), 30-31. Dulles later stated, in *The Imperial Years* (New York, 1956), 34, that "Strong himself was not yet thinking, in 1885, of political power or overseas expansion . . . and he saw his countrymen in the van of a great movement which would extend Christianity and democratic principles through precept and teaching."

[5] Josiah Strong, *Our Country: Its Possible Future and Its Present Crisis* (New York, 1885), 175-77; Josiah Strong, *The New Era or The Coming Kingdom* (New York, 1893), 79-81.

"travel, commerce, the missionary" were carrying the language and the civilization of the "restless Anglo-Saxon" around the globe just "as the Greek carried his language and civilization around the Mediterranean."[6] Extension of political authority was not the instrument or the result of competition among races and nations. In *The New Era or The Coming Kingdom* in 1893 he explained the nature of the "extension" of the Anglo-Saxon race and civilization he was describing:

True, she [England] has empire which she holds by force and which she might lose by force, but North America, South Africa, and Australia are hers by a different tenure. She has conquered these lands by giving to them her sons and daughters, her free institutions, her noble civilization. England might be sunk in the sea and these vast areas would remain her glory, loyal to the essential principles which she has given to them.[7]

Extension of political authority over other peoples was not necessary to influence their civilization. Strong's often quoted statement that the Anglo-Saxon race "having developed peculiarly aggressive traits calculated to impress its institutions upon mankind, will spread itself over the earth" was not a call for the advance of American political power overseas but a statement of a generally accepted view of the migrating tendency of the race.[8] Phrases such as "occupy the land," "possess the land," "new fields of conquest," and "world-conquering power" were typical of the militant language of the home missionary. Strong, thoroughly familiar with this rhetoric, had prepared *Our Country* at the request of the American Home Missionary Society to arouse interest in and support for home missions. At the annual meetings of the Society in the 1880s, which Strong attended and in which he participated, papers were presented discussing many of the themes of *Our Country* and were later quoted by Strong in his volume.[9] Indeed, Strong's motive, message, and method in *Our Country* was that of a missionary. He envisioned evangelizing the world through the persuasive power of example and practice of Christian civilization carried by its peo-

---

[6] New York *Times*, July 10, 1892.

[7] Strong, *New Era*, 68.

[8] Strong, *Our Country*, 175. The passage most often quoted as evidence of Strong's expansionist views was his reworking of a similar passage which appeared in the 1858 edition of the home missionary tract, *Our Country*, which he was revising. See [Anon.], *Our Country, No. 2 A Plea for Home Missions* (New York, 1858), 19, 13.

[9] For phrases used by home missionaries and themes stressed at the annual meetings, see *Home Missionary*, LIII (Jan. 1881), 213; LIV (Jan. 1882), 243; LVI (Jan. 1884), 350; LVII (July 1884), 128; LVIII (Sept. 1885), 174, 192; LX (Dec. 1887), 330. Strong presented papers on immigration and on the West. *Ibid.*, LVI (Aug. 1883), 153-56; LVII (Aug. 1884), 138-40. For a discussion by Strong of the home-missions background of his ideas in *Our Country*, see *Union Signal*, July 9, 1891. See also Jurgen Herbst, ed., Josiah Strong, *Our Country* (Cambridge, 1963), ix-xix.

ple to all parts of the world as they traveled or migrated—but not by the extension of American political power or force.

Reviews of *Our Country* pointed out that the volume aroused a sense of pride in the nation's institutions, development, and possible future. It is significant, however, that the patriotism aroused apparently was directed toward "saving" American institutions. The *Advance* commented, "The book ought to be in the hands of every patriot in the land as a thesaurus of important material facts and as an incentive to stand on higher grounds of civic and religious duty."[10] One home missionary in the Dakota area wrote, "I hope our wealthy men will read it, and see that they cannot put their money to better use than in home missionary work. It surpasses any novel in interest to any one who cares for his country as a patriot, and for the world as a Christian."[11] In the many references to *Our Country* in the 1880s and the 1890s in the *Home Missionary*, organ of the American Home Missionary Society, no interest in overseas areas was expressed. Instead, it noted Strong's discussion of the various perils to the church and to the nation as well as his radical ideas on Christian stewardship. In 1891, at the time of increasing interest in strategic areas overseas, the second edition of *Our Country* was still considered "a hand-book of home missions." Comment on this edition ignored the chapter on the Anglo-Saxon and the world's future but called attention to the new chapter dealing with the critical issue of the public schools.[12]

Although an increasing interest in expansion was evident in the religious and secular press during the period 1886-1900, *Our Country* was not cited in editorials or articles on foreign affairs. For example, the New York *Times* frequently referred to Strong's applied Christianity, but it did not mention his works in any discussion of expansionist sentiment.[13] The only references to *Our Country* in either the *Century* or the *Forum* were in connection with labor issues.[14] Neither the proexpansionist *Review of Reviews*

[10] *Advance*, XXI (March 18, 1886), 166.

[11] *Home Missionary*, LVIII (April 1886), 419. See also *Christian Union*, XXXIV (Aug. 19, 1886), 22-23.

[12] *Home Missionary*, LIX (Nov. 1886), 275; LX (Jan. 1888), 361-63; LXI (April 1889), 534; LXIV (Nov. 1891), 363; LXVI (July 1893), 116. Strong's chapter, "Money and the Kingdom," was often quoted by advocates of home and foreign missions. See, for example, *Christian Advocate*, LXI (Sept. 16, 1886), 589; *Congregationalist and Christian World*, CI (May 11, 1916), 630; John R. Mott, *Addresses and Papers of John R. Mott. Volume One: The Student Volunteer Movement for Foreign Missions* (New York, 1947), 65, 311.

[13] New York *Times*, Oct. 16, 1886; Feb. 27, 1887; Jan. 14, Dec. 8, 1889; July 10, 1892; Dec. 16, 1896; July 5, Dec. 13, 1897; April 23, June 11, 1898.

[14] Editorial, *Century Magazine*, XXXII (June 1886), 319; C. M. Morse, "The Church and the Working Man," *Forum*, VI (Feb. 1889), 653. The periodicals which have been checked for reviews of *Our Country* or references to the volume in editorials or articles are *Home Missionary* (1886-1903), *Andover Review* (1884-1893), *Christian Union* (1886,

nor the antiexpansionist *Nation* cited Strong on foreign affairs in the 1890s. In 1893, however, the *Review of Reviews* asserted that *Our Country* had placed Strong "in the front rank of reformers" who held the church responsible for the solution of social problems and had "aroused an interest and quickened a sense of patriotic responsibility in circles far wider than those limited by ecclesiastical lines."[15]

Among those clergymen acknowledging the influence of *Our Country* were William Reed Huntington, rector of Grace Church, New York City, and Graham Taylor, founder of the Chicago Commons settlement. Huntington called it "that marvelous little book" with a note of crisis. Taylor wrote in June 1886 that Strong's "powerful little book" spirited him with "a more earnest desire to spend and be spent" for his "Fatherland" and his "faith." In 1895, when a wave of jingoism was rising in the nation, Taylor classified *Our Country* among those books which inspired interest in social issues and recommended both *Our Country* and *The New Era* in his bibliography, *Books For Beginners in the Study of Christian Sociology and Social Economics*.[16] Both Huntington and Taylor were outspoken anti-imperialists at the turn of the century. Contemporaries referred to *Our Country* not as a call for militant nationalism or expansion, but as a plea for home missions and for religious as well as social reform.

Historians have not only made unfounded assumptions concerning the influence of *Our Country* but also have read imperialistic meanings into Strong's chapter on "The Anglo-Saxon and the World's Future," ignoring completely the nature of his religious philosophy. Strong's philosophy of nationalism did not begin with Darwinism, as some have asserted, but with a two-fold conviction that Christian individuals and nations had a primary obligation to fulfill the missionary charge of world evangelization and that in the late nineteenth century Americans as Christians had a special obligation and opportunity to fulfill this charge. Just as his means more and more

1890-1892), *Outlook* (1893, 1898-1901), *Christian Advocate* (1886, 1891, 1893, 1897-1901), *Homiletic Review* (1886, 1891, 1893, 1898-1901), *Independent* (1886-1901), *Open Court* (1887-1907), *Forum* (1886-1902), *Nation* (1886-1901), *North American Review* (1886-1900), *Harper's New Monthly Magazine* (1885-1900), *Review of Reviews* (1891-1893, 1898-1901), *Political Science Quarterly* (1886-1901), *Century: Illustrated Monthly Magazine* (1886-1887, 1891-1893, 1898-1901).

[15] *Review of Reviews*, VIII (Sept. 1893), 353.

[16] John Wallace Suter, *Life and Letters of William Reed Huntington, A Champion of Unity* (New York, 1925), 290, 299; Graham Taylor, *Books for Beginners In the Study of Christian Sociology and Social Economics* (Boston, 1895), 3; Taylor, *Syllabus in Biblical Sociology* (Chicago, 1900), 28; Taylor, Diary, June 4, 1886, Graham Taylor Collection (Newberry Library). See also Louise C. Wade, *Graham Taylor: Pioneer For Social Justice, 1851-1938* (Chicago, 1964), 96-97. *The Commons*, II (June 1897), 9, 15, denounced Theodore Roosevelt's jingoistic statements and in the same issue praised Strong's *New Era*, "Which many settlement workers had come to regard as fundamental."

stressed the evangelizing mission and the social gospel, his ends were not only the kingdom of heaven but the kingdom ideal—the achievement of the kingdom of God on earth through the universal application of the principles of service, sacrifice, and love. In *Our Country* Strong declared that all followers of Christ, regardless of occupation, "have but one business in the world; viz., the extending of Christ's Kingdom." The mission to advance the kingdom ideal also came to include the application of Christian ethics to international life. In 1909, when many Americans considered control of the Philippines a liability to the nation, Strong stressed that the missionary duty of unselfish service placed the nation under an obligation to complete its program of self-government and social reform in the islands.[17] Believing, as did most Protestant clergymen of his generation, that God worked through men and nations, Strong saw providential meaning in the fact that the two ideas in which he believed—spiritual Christianity and civil liberty—had done most for human progress and were the basis of Anglo-Saxon civilization. He concluded that all English-speaking peoples, but especially Americans, possessing these "two greatest blessings," had an obligation and an unprecedented opportunity to elevate the human race by carrying these concepts to the rest of the world. Not only the superiority of the nation's institutions but also its material resources, wealth, and growing population clearly demonstrated its "peculiar" responsibility as a Christian nation to fulfill the evangelical charge.[18]

Strong's identification of the nation's providential role to advance the kingdom with missionary expansion and the extension of Anglo-Saxon civilization was typical of the concept embraced by most Protestant clergymen in the 1880s and 1890s, particularly the home missionary.[19] By 1891, however, Strong had extended his view beyond that of many of his colleagues by interpreting the nation's Christian mission in the context of a social-gospel, kingdom philosophy. He now defined the kingdom of God on earth as a world-society that was to be perfected materially as well as spiritually and that was to be realized by the implementation of a world-life—

[17] Strong, *Our Country*, 195; Josiah Strong, "The Social Laws of Jesus," *Gospel of the Kingdom*, I (July 1909), 73-74; Gabriel, *American Democratic Thought*, 344. Strong, "The Outlook for Practical Religion in the Decade," *Independent*, XLIII (Jan. 1, 1891), 9, stated that "few of us know enough" to accept or reject the Darwinian hypothesis "intelligently."

[18] Strong, *Our Country*, 161, 181-82.

[19] On the concept of mission held by Protestant clergymen during this period, see John Edwin Smylie, "Protestant Clergymen and America's World Role 1865-1900: A Study of Christianity, Nationality, and International Relations" (doctoral dissertation, Princeton Theological Seminary, 1959), 58-59, 101-17, 154-58, 191. Smylie does say that Strong "unabashedly preached Anglo-Saxon racism" with "spread-eagleism" fervor.

recognizing the emerging interdependence of man. In 1893 in *The New Era* he explained that "saving" the world meant bringing about the kingdom through applying at home and abroad the concepts of social Christianity. His concept of the kingdom ideal led him to reaffirm the providential significance of Anglo-Saxon civilization because it was unique in coordinating a higher development of the individual and a more powerful, far-reaching organization of society than any civilization past or present. Anglo-Saxon civilization, therefore, was "more favorable than any other to the spread of those principles whose universal triumph" was necessary for the destined perfection of the world. To Strong it seemed to be "especially commissioned," "pre-eminently fitted, and therefore chosen of God, to prepare the way for the full coming of His kingdom on the earth."[20]

Although Strong believed in the superiority of Anglo-Saxon civilization, he was not self-righteous in maintaining that it was above criticism. He saw the nation's mission threatened not only by the corruption of its civilization at home but also by the distortion of its mission through the character and methods of Anglo-Saxons in dealing with other peoples. Declaring that Anglo-Saxons were not "righteous overmuch," he warned, "They will have to answer for many sins against weaker races and against the weaker of their own race. They produce as worldly, as gross, as selfish and beastly men and women as do any other people. . . ." Expressing a typical missionary complaint, he deplored "the pioneer wave of our civilization" for carrying with it a greater destructive force than enobling power, "more scum than salt."[21] "If we had a Christian enthusiasm for mankind," he explained, "we should be preparing them [Negroes and Chinese] by the thousand to go as missionaries to their brethren. But instead we are debauching Africa with our New England rum, and outraging China by our brutal legislation."[22] He supported the proposal of an African leader, whose friendship he had known since the days of the Parliament of Religion of 1893, for a council of the friends of Africa to protect the underdeveloped races of the world from the vices of civilization.[23] In 1900 he criticized those nations which would use the murder of a missionary as a pretext for seizing the territory of less advanced nations. In later years he ridiculed the use of the term "white man's burden" by Europeans to justify their partitioning of China

[20] Strong, "Outlook for Practical Religion," 9; *New Era*, 69, 81, 354.

[21] Strong, *New Era*, 54-55; *Our Country*, 177, 115.

[22] Josiah Strong, *Expansion Under New World-Conditions* (New York, 1900), 296-99; *New Era*, 356.

[23] Josiah Strong, "Introduction," Prince Momolu Massaquoi, "Africa's Appeal to Christendom," *Century Magazine*, LXIX (April 1905), 927-28. Although Strong had written the introduction in 1896, the article was not published until 1905.

and Africa for economic exploitation and applauded Japan's success over Russia in 1904, calling it "a victory of every dark race in the world, for the white man had bullied them all."[24] Anglo-Saxon civilization was not synonymous with the kingdom of God on earth. On the contrary, Strong emphasized that Anglo-Saxon civilization itself needed to be brought under the laws of the kingdom, a never-ending process as conditions changed from generation to generation.[25] Indeed, Strong's pride in the nation's institutions and civilization was significantly humbled by his awareness of the urgent need of "saving" both its people and its institutions.

To Strong, Anglo-Saxon supremacy did not imply racial hostility. "When we get near enough to a man to see in him the likeness of Christ," he wrote in 1893, "whether he be white or black, red or yellow, we must needs love him."[26] Competition, ensuring adaptation and thus survival of the fittest among races, nations, and economic groups, was, he believed, a necessary step in the evolution toward a cooperative world-society—the method of creating an integrated society based on differences. Survival of the fittest did not mean the reduction of all mankind to a single Anglo-Saxon race. "In my judgment," he maintained, "the reduction of all races to a single type would not be possible, even if it were desirable; and again, it would not be desirable, even if it were possible."[27] Thus, while Anglo-Saxon civilization was to prevail in the world because of the vitality of the race and because of the superiority of its religious and political ideas, "the marked variations of races, with their different needs, different adaptations, and different kinds of skill" would still remain, providing the basis for the development of an integrated social and economic commerce and continue as an essential part of a world-life. To attempt to achieve the kingdom ideal through an identity of custom, of religion, of race, he emphasized, "would be so far from a world-life that it would not even be the first step toward it."[28] He characterized the Chinese as a "wonderfully vital" people who

[24] Strong, *Expansion*, 226; Josiah Strong, *Our World: The New World-Life* (New York, 1913), 160.
[25] Strong, *Our Country*, 178, 214; *New Era*, 81, 133-34. For the conclusion that advocates of the social-gospel, kingdom philosophy considered the kingdom to be synonymous with American civilization, see H. Richard Niebuhr, *The Kingdom of God in America* (Hamden, 1956), 179, 183; Sidney F. Mead, "American Protestantism Since the Civil War. I. From Denominationalism to Americanism," *Journal of Religion*, XXXVI (Jan. 1956), 13-14; Gabriel, *American Democratic Thought*, 344.
[26] Strong, *New Era*, 77-78, 315. For criticism of Strong on the ground that he failed to assert that the Anglo-Saxon race would supplant all other races, see John B. Robins, *Christ and Our Country or, A Hopeful View of Christianity in the Present Day* (Nashville, Tenn., 1892), 75.
[27] Strong, *World-Life*, 168, 173-75, 17.
[28] Strong, *Expansion*, 217, 224, 41; Josiah Strong, "A New World Tendency," *Social Ser-*

were destined to influence greatly "the social, intellectual and spiritual life of the nations" and to provide "a permanent and prominent element in the world's life" as long as they remained "a virile stock."[29] His concept, Strong asserted, emphasized the value of the basic differences among the various races, for these differences supplemented and served one another. The philosophy of the kingdom created "an enthusiasm for humanity" rooted in the brotherhood of man under the fatherhood of God, which, Strong wrote, saved one "from race antipathy and from all spirit of cast.... from fanaticism and prejudice."[30]

In *Our Country* Strong's plea had been for world evangelization.[31] From 1891 on, as his religious philosophy became centered in social Christianity, the kingdom ideal, and an integrated international society, he enlarged his concept of the nation's mission. Indeed, service to world-life and the kingdom ideal became the unmistakable theme, purpose, and spirit of his nationalism. He was among the first of the social-gospel school to teach that the principle of unselfish service ought to be applied to world relations. It was not until the late 1890s that Lyman Abbott, Washington Gladden, and Richard T. Ely asserted world responsibilities as part of the kingdom philosophy.[32]

Strong was also among the few to stress that the development of an interdependent society was co-relative with the realization of the kingdom. He explained a world-life not only as a goal of the kingdom philosophy but also as a condition currently being created and made a practical necessity by economic developments in the last half of the nineteenth century. In *Our Country* he noted the impact on the world of the revolution in transportation and communication. In 1891 and again in 1893 he asserted that the industrial and commercial revolutions had made "the whole world a neighborhood and every man a neighbor."[33] He concluded that increasing internationalization of life was an inevitable step toward the realization of a world-ideal, which, when spiritualized and vitalized by the social gospel,

vice, VII (Jan. 1903), 1-4; Josiah Strong, "The Increasing Oneness of the World," *Gospel of the Kingdom*, I (Dec. 1908), 17; Josiah Strong, "The Race Question," *ibid.* (Aug. 1909), 81.

[29] Strong, *Expansion*, 109-10, 124.

[30] Strong, *New Era*, 350, 352; Josiah Strong, *Our World: The New World-Religion* (New York, 1915), 387, 81. Hans Kohn, *American Nationalism: An Interpretative Essay* (New York, 1957), 160, asserts that Strong was "in no way a racialist in a narrow or exclusive sense."

[31] Strong, *Our Country*, 218.

[32] Lyman Abbott, *Christianity and Social Problems* (Boston, 1896), 19, 24-25; Washington Gladden, *Our Nation and Her Neighbors* (Columbus, 1898), 30-36; Richard T. Ely, *The Social Law of Service* (New York, 1896), 89, 138-39; Graham Taylor, *Religion in Social Action* (New York, 1913), 99.

[33] Strong, *Our Country*, 14; *New Era*, 345.

would be the kingdom. Closer economic and social relations among nations would eventually cause men and nations to take an interest in others from self-concern and self-interest. He maintained, however, that economic relations among nations would become "simply intolerable unless they are *right* relations, adjusted in harmony with the laws of the kingdom of God," and urged that a higher motive than self-interest or "enlightened selfishness" be adopted by individuals and nations as the basis for world interest. He called for Christian concern, "an interest in others for *their* sakes" which was measured "not by the rule of justice . . . but by the rule of sacrifice."[34] "Surely," he declared, "with a growing sense of the brotherhood of man, and a restored vision of the coming Kingdom, and with such opportunities and facilities for blessing mankind as were never before offered . . . this generation in America *ought* to exult in its transcendent opportunities for service."[35] The kingdom philosophy would inspire an "enthusiasm for humanity" which would make men as ready "to toil and to sacrifice for generations far removed in time as for nations far removed in space."[36]

During the years of a growing, aggressive, expansionist spirit in the nation, Strong taught an unselfish nationalism that was an integral part of an internationalism that was rooted in social Christianity, expressed in terms of world duties providentially prepared by the growing economic interdependence among nations. He declared in 1893: "He does most to Christianize the world and to hasten the coming of the Kingdom who does most to make thoroughly Christian the United States. I do not imagine that an Anglo-Saxon is any dearer to God than a Mongolian or an African. My plea is not, Save America for America's sake, but, Save America for the world's sake."[37] Strong disagreed with the advocates of "the large policy" in the 1890s who urged the nation to "look outward" toward the Pacific and the Caribbean for basically commercial and strategic reasons; he urged the nation to adopt an attitude rooted in Christian brotherhood and the dependence of "different classes, nations, and races . . . on each other."[38] In 1897 and 1898, when discussing the problems of the city, Strong stressed that

[34] Strong, *New Era*, 345, 347.
[35] *Ibid.*, 353-54.
[36] *Ibid.*, 359.
[37] *Ibid.*, 80; *Expansion*, 213. See also Amory Bradford, "America for the Sake of the World," *Home Missionary*, LXX (July 1897), 37.
[38] Strong, *New Era*, 352. In 1896 and 1897 Strong, as secretary of the Evangelical Alliance for the United States, directed the efforts of the Alliance toward securing a permanent treaty of arbitration between the United States and Great Britain. In 1898, 1901, and 1903 he addressed the Lake Mohonk Conference on International Arbitration on the effect of world-life on international arbitration.

twentieth-century Christianity ought to recognize and teach duty to neighborhood, town, state, country, and the world, for "to neglect these duties is to sin against God."[39] Strong's concept of mission, however, did not stress the traditions and institutions of the past; it required a radical change in both the spirit and purpose of nationalism and of the nation's institutions if it were to be fulfilled.[40]

When he entered the debate on overseas expansion and foreign policy in the fall of 1900 with his volume, *Expansion Under New World-Conditions*, he maintained that any discussion of the nation's role in world affairs must recognize that changes in commerce, industry, communications, and transportation had made the world a neighborhood and that the teachings of the kingdom made "my neighbor my brother."[41] The nation must adopt a new policy which recognized and implemented the new interdependence and followed the principles of the kingdom. The failure of many Americans to appreciate the revolutionary changes in the world's development, he asserted, was the basic cause of their well-intentioned but misguided judgment of the international issues of 1900. The nation must understand that under new conditions "the farthest-sighted wisdom, the highest statesmanship, the purest patriotism" was unselfish service to world-life.[42] World-life had enlarged the duties of nations as well as limited their rights. Service to world-life, he declared, now included the encouragement and the protection of civil and religious liberty, self-government, health, and international peace and order. These obligations could be fulfilled either through efforts to enlighten and instruct a nation, or, if prompt action were needed, through the benevolent use of force—international police duty.

He advised that world duties would cost the nation "effort, perplexity, sacrifice . . . a good deal of treasure and some blood." The "policy of political isolation" of the past which "left other nations to police the world, while we rub our hands in holy glee that they have never been fouled in the dirty politics of the world . . . and make all the money possible out of the peace for which other nations pay" was "contemptible."[43] Strong believed that under the political organization of the world in 1900 the nation might be required to act alone in pursuit of world interests, as in Cuba and

---

[39] Josiah Strong, *The Twentieth Century City* (New York, 1898), 138, 119.
[40] Burns, *American Idea of Mission*, viii-ix, argues that the idea of mission was conservative.
[41] Strong, *Expansion*, 215, 235. Neither the press nor the personal papers of contemporaries indicate Strong's position on the Philippines in 1898 or 1899. *Social Service*, the publication of Strong's League for Social Service, did not discuss the Philippines; it simply printed the publisher's advertisement of *Expansion* in its Nov. 1900 issue.
[42] Strong, *Expansion*, 273-75, 260-61.
[43] *Ibid.*, 274-75, 251, 240-46, 282. See also Gladden, *Our Nation and Her Neighbors*, 35.

the Philippines, or in concert with other major powers, as in China. By 1913 he advocated a world federation of nations as the means of providing "a sufficient force on sea and land to do the world's police duty."[44]

The issue in the Philippine debate in 1900, Strong maintained, was neither the legal or constitutional authority of the United States in the islands nor the nation's tradition of consent of the governed, but the effect of immediate independence on the Filipinos themselves and on a world-order determined by the capacity of peoples for self-government. Citing reports of observers in the Philippines and noting especially the views of President Jacob G. Schurman of Cornell University and Bishop Henry C. Potter of New York, both of whom had opposed annexation and then, after visiting the islands, supported continued control by the United States, he concluded that to give the Philippine people independence in 1900 "would wrong the world in general and themselves in particular." Interdependence among nations had limited the right of any people to "a lawless independence." Individuals had to be taught the principles and the methods of self-government before they could exercise the "right."[45] He warned the nation, however, that neither "national ambition" nor "commercial considerations" but unselfish service ought to be the purpose of its Philippine policy if the corruption of the American political system predicted by the antiexpansionists was to be prevented. He insisted, "We want no tribute-bearing colonies."[46] As did other social-gospel ministers who supported expansion into the Philippines, Strong maintained that the action of the United States differed from Old World imperialism because of the nation's altruistic motive and goal.[47]

Although Strong supported continued American control of the Philippines in 1900, he had evidently questioned the administration's policy in the islands in 1899; in December 1899 he was invited to attend a private meeting in New York together with a group of well-known anti-imperialists to discuss the possible formation of a third party.[48] A difference between Strong and the aggressive, nationalistic expansionists of 1900 was

[44] Strong, World-Life, 51.
[45] Strong, Expansion, 288-89. For earlier statements of the same concept of self-government see Our Country, 53; New Era, 330; Twentieth Century City, 91.
[46] Strong, Expansion, 261, 295; Josiah Strong, "The Preacher in Relation to the New Expansion," Homiletic Review, XLII (Dec. 1901), 491.
[47] Strong, Expansion, 273. The temporary nature of annexation was also stressed by Washington Gladden and Lyman Abbott. See Gladden, Sermon, Dec. 18, 1898, Washington Gladden Papers, Box 41, No. 11 (Ohio Historical Society Library, Columbus); New York Times, Nov. 25, 1898; Jan. 27, 1899.
[48] Edwin Burritt to Carl Schurz, Dec. 18, 30, 1899, Carl Schurz Papers (Manuscript Division, Library of Congress). Among those invited to the meeting were Richard W.

noted by Huntington, an anti-imperialist and a member of the advisory council of Strong's League for Social Service. In October 1900 he knew "in advance" that he would like Strong's book on expansion "just because" it was Strong's and confided that what he particularly dreaded was the transformation of "our country" by "the Jingo party . . . whether Democrats or Republicans, who covet England's colonial system" and advocate "grabbing what we can when we can."[49] After 1900 Strong criticized the imperialist policy of European nations, the United States' policy of naval expansion, and the policy of private companies overseas.[50] When he emphasized world-life and world duties as the determining factors in the Philippine question, he was not rationalizing an imperialist view but discussing the issue in terms of the principles of his long-held kingdom philosophy. He saw the Philippines as providing an opportunity and an obligation for service. In advocating continued control of the islands by the United States in 1900, Strong was not proposing a general policy of overseas expansion; rather, he was accepting "expansion" as the only means feasible, under the particular circumstances of 1900 in the islands and among the world powers, of fulfilling world responsibility.

At the same time that Strong taught service and the kingdom as the goal of national life and the guide for determining national policy, he advised that economic, political, and geographic factors must also realistically be considered in shaping foreign policy. He cautioned that while the nation must "never forget . . . ideals and never cease to struggle toward them," it must "never forget actualities" and that it is "compelled to deal with them."[51] In seeking to obey the laws of service and sacrifice, a nation could not sacrifice national life itself since the nation was the very instrument

Gilder, Charles H. Parkhurst, Henry C. Potter, and Robert F. Cutting, who were also members of the advisory council of the League for Social Service. By Dec. 30, 1899, neither Strong nor the other members of the League had answered the invitation. However, Cutting later served as treasurer and Parkhurst as a vice-president of the New York Anti-Imperialist League. An examination of the correspondence and papers of Richard W. Gilder, William R. Huntington, Henry Van Dyke, Edward W. Ordway, William Bourke Cockran, Bolton Hall, Edwin L. Godkin, Franklin H. Giddings, and Abram S. Hewitt, who were New York anti-imperialists and/or invited to the meeting, did not provide any information about Strong and the anti-imperialists. The papers of Albert Shaw, expansionist and also member of the Committee of Direction of Strong's League did not reveal any information on expansion. On the New York meeting, see R. F. Pettigrew, *Imperial Washington: The Story of American Public Life from 1870 to 1920* (Chicago, 1922), 321; Fred H. Harrington, "The Anti-Imperialist Movement in the United States, 1898-1900," *Mississippi Valley Historical Review*, XXII (Sept. 1935), 225-26.

[49] William R. Huntington to Strong, Oct. 1900, William R. Huntington Papers (Episcopal Theological School Library, Cambridge).

[50] Strong, *World-Life*, 114, 139; *Gospel of the Kingdom*, I (July 1909), 80; VII (April 1915), 64; (May 1915), 75.

[51] Strong, *Expansion*, 283, 10; *New Era*, 74.

through which world interests were to be served.[52] But while vital national interests were to be considered in determining national policy, Strong stressed that the validity of national interests was determined by the relationship between those interests and service to world interests. His conclusions concerning the nation's economic and strategic needs were based on the views of men whom he considered authorities. He repeated the statements of Carroll D. Wright and Franklin H. Giddings that the nation needed overseas markets for its surplus goods, that the Philippines were the gateway to the markets of Asia, and that the Pacific was to be the area of a future struggle for influence between Russia and the United States.[53] Quoting Alfred T. Mahan, Strong reiterated the thesis that it was both commercially and strategically advantageous for the nation to possess Hawaii and islands in the Caribbean "through righteous means." He also supported an open door policy in Asia and Africa, not territorial acquisition, as the solution for the nation's need for world markets.[54] Although Strong thus accepted in 1900 the arguments and the steps necessary for commercial expansion advanced by many of the expansionists of the 1890s, he differed significantly in that he de-emphasized their goals. The Christian Socialist magazine, *The Social Gospel*, which had criticized the expansionist views of Senator Albert J. Beveridge and Brooks Adams as "unmitigated, sordid commercialism," advised its readers against "vigorously disapproving, unread," Strong's *Expansion* because of any summary of its economic and strategic arguments; for, the review stressed, an outline of the book could not convey the author's faith in and "assumption of" the principles of Christian altruism.[55]

Henry Cabot Lodge, Beveridge, and other expansionists asserted, as did Strong, that duty and destiny required the United States to retain the Philippine Islands. Lodge qualified his concept of duty, however, for he as-

[52] Strong, "Preacher in Relation to the New Expansion," 491.

[53] Strong, *Expansion*, 159-60, 196-99, 79-80, 133-34, 185-86. He stressed, however, that the failure to solve the economic and moral problem of distribution had resulted in a "surplus." Seeking to avoid a conflict with Russia by "Westernizing" Russia, the League for Social Service by Sept. 1899 had members and foreign correspondents in Russia; by 1915 an institute of social service had been established. See *Social Engineering*, I (Sept. 1899), 6, 12; New York *Times*, Sept. 19, 1915.

[54] In 1900 Strong, rather than advocating a program of colonial expansion, apparently accepted Mahan's commercial-strategic bases concept of empire. On Mahan's concept of empire, see Walter LaFeber, "A Note on the 'Mercantilistic Imperialism' of Alfred Thayer Mahan," *Mississippi Valley Historical Review*, XLVIII (March 1962), 674-85, and *New Empire*, 85-101.

[55] *Social Gospel*, II (June 1899), 14-16; III (March 1900), 16; (Nov. 1900), 29-30; see also *Literary Digest*, XXI (Oct. 20, 1900), 454-55; *Outlook*, LXVII (Jan. 26, 1901), 227-29; *Christian Advocate*, LXXVI (Oct. 3, 1901), 1589. The antiexpansionist New York *Evening Post*, Oct. 11, 1900, considered the book to be a statement of the economic argument for expansion.

sured the nation, "Whatever duty to others might seem to demand, I should pause long before supporting any policy if there were the slightest suspicion that it was not for the benefit of the people of the United States."[56] Strong declared that national interest and national duty were determined by world needs, for

world life is something greater than national life, and world good, therefore, is something higher than national good, and must take precedence of it if they conflict. Local, and even national, interests must be sacrificed, if need be, to universal interests. Or rather, world interests will prove to be the best criterion by which to judge of national interests, and it will ultimately be seen that he serves his country best who serves the world best, because the well-being of the member is found to depend on the health or well-being of the life of which it is a part.[57]

Thus, Strong's concern for world interests made national interest something other than self-interest or enlightened self-interest. He maintained that the standard of unselfish service was not impracticable, unrealistic, and visionary but the only possible standard for a Christian nation.[58] In 1901 he asserted that it was "the high function of the pulpit so to Christianize the national conscience that the supreme aim of our government shall not be national aggrandizement, but the noblest ministry to the new world-life."[59] He later accused "the individualistic church" of having "not simply excused national selfishness" but of having "elevated it to the rank of a virtue and baptized it patriotism."[60] A world federation of nations should be established, he advised, to set standards for "arbitration, world patents, sanitary regulations for ports, industrial interests, and the control of world monopolies," and thus become an instrument through which the nation could protect national interests and serve world interests.[61]

Although an international outlook was an integral part of Strong's philosophy, he directed his efforts and writings primarily toward city evangelization and social reform during the period 1885-1900. As secretary of the Evangelical Alliance for the United States, he organized interdenominational conferences on applied Christianity in 1887, 1889, and 1893.[62] The

[56] *Cong. Record*, 56 Cong., 1 Sess., 2627 (March 7, 1900).
[57] Strong, *Expansion*, 269-70, 273; "Book Review," *Social Service*, III (May 1901), 160.
[58] Strong, *New Era*, 234; *World-Religion*, 216, 479.
[59] Strong, "Preacher in Relation to the New Expansion," 494.
[60] Strong, *World-Religion*, 511.
[61] Strong, *World-Life*, 50; Josiah Strong, "After the War, What," *Gospel of the Kingdom*, VII (Jan. 1915), 11-16.
[62] Aaron Ignatius Abell, *The Urban Impact on American Protestantism: 1865-1900* (Cambridge, 1943), 90-92; Charles Howard Hopkins, *The Rise of the Social Gospel in American Protestantism: 1865-1900* (New Haven, 1940), 112-16. See also Dorothea R. Muller, "Josiah Strong and the Social Gospel: A Christian's Response to the Challenge of the City," *Journal of the Presbyterian Historical Society*, 39 (Sept. 1961), 150-75.

culmination of his thinking and activities in the 1890s was a plan for church leadership of the social reform movement. He outlined the scheme in a series of articles in 1897 and the next year expanded it in his book, *The Twentieth Century City*. The book was declared to be "a ringing appeal to all men to begin now the new and better time, the era of man's brotherhood and God's Fatherhood."[63] Before the annual meeting of the Congregational Home Missionary Society in June 1898, he discussed the challenge of "The Twentieth Century City," referring only indirectly to the war with Spain.[64] During the summer and fall of 1898, he organized and sought support for his own agency, the League for Social Service, to continue his work of educating the church and the nation in the principles of applied Christianity. The League was intended to serve church leaders and reformers at home as well as those in other lands. By September 1899 "branch offices" were established in London and Edinburgh, and support came from members in France, Germany, Italy, Russia, Sweden, Mexico, New Zealand, Japan, and China. Strong hoped that a chain of institutes established around the world would result in "leveling international barriers, cultivating international peace and security, and hastening the final organization of the world into the Kingdom of God."[65] By 1916 cooperating agencies had been established or planned in fifteen countries.[66] The League was only one of many plans—among others were international scholarships for the education of foreign students in the United States and a lay missionary movement of technicians, business and professional men and women—which Strong proposed and sought to carry out in the next decade.

Obviously, historians have misread and misinterpreted Josiah Strong's works and role in American history. *Our Country* was significant to Strong for the sole reason that he believed an Anglo-Saxon nation had a providential opportunity and obligation to hasten the coming of the kingdom through evangelizing the world and implementing world-life. Applied Christianity and the kingdom philosophy provided the spirit, the motive, and the method of achieving the nation's mission. Strong taught a unique nationalism inspired by the principles of a social Christianity. Strong's philosophy made nationalism an instrument for serving internationalism.[67]

[63] *Christian Advocate*, LXXIII (May 19, 1898), 822.

[64] *Home Missionary*, LXXI (July 1898), 39-42.

[65] Editorial, *Social Service*, XI (Jan. 1905), 13; *Social Engineering*, I (Sept. 1889), 6, 14.

[66] New York *Times*, Sept. 19, 1915; James H. Ecob, "Dr. Strong and the War," *Gospel of the Kingdom*, X (April 1918), 106.

[67] His ideas on interdependence among peoples and nations were quoted in and made the basis of an Ohio minister's pamphlet on "worldism" in the early 1900s. James William Van Kirk, *Worldism: The Rainbow, A World Flag For Universal Peace* (Youngstown, [1912?]).

Strong's nationalism, viewed in the context of his religious philosophy and life's work, was not that of an expansionist or imperialist clothing a doctrine of power-politics "in talk of providence, duty, destiny," nor were his "moral judgments . . . elaborate rationales for a blatant ethnocentrism."[68] World evangelization, the kingdom, and world-life were to be realized not by territorial expansion and world empire but by the trader, the traveler, the missionary, and agencies like the League for Social Service. Strong was neither a prophet of imperialism in 1885 nor an advocate of the "large policy" in the 1890s. And he did not encourage the growing expansionist interest in acquiring Samoa, Hawaii, or Cuba in any of his articles, books, or activities. He supported continued control of the Philippines by the United States in 1900 not as the first step in the course of empire but as a step toward responsible internationalism through the only method feasible under the circumstances. In 1916 Abbott characterized Strong as "a patriot to his heart's core" and "for the past thirty years our foremost missionary by voice and pen at home and abroad" of the patriotic ideal of "not devotion to our country only, but rather to our country for the world."[69] Strong himself stated that he had been thinking in world terms since the days of *Our Country*. "It is a matter of common knowledge," wrote Strong's colleague, James Ecob, "that Dr. Strong was one of the foremost pioneers in arousing the nations to the necessity of a New Internationalism."[70]

[68] Robert R. Roberts, "Economic and Political Ideas Expressed in the Early Social Gospel Movement, 1875-1900" (doctoral dissertation, University of Chicago, 1952), 159, 173.
[69] Editorial, *Outlook*, CXIII (May 10, 1916), 56.
[70] Strong, *New World-Life*, vii; Ecob, "Dr. Strong and the War," 106.

Why Did The Yankees Go Home?
A Study of Episcopal Missions:
1953-1977

Neil Lebhar and Martyn Minns

The decade of the seventies is a decisive one for Episcopal missions. There has been a continual decline since the sixties in both the number of appointed missionaries sent out by the Episcopal Church and the percentage of money appropriated for overseas ministry. Yet there has also been greater cooperation by the National Church with overseas churches and a resurgence of interest in voluntary missionary societies. Two such societies, the Episcopal South American Mission Society, and the Episcopal Church Missionary Community are actively attempting to revive missionary interest within the Episcopal church.

If missionary activity is to be renewed, the last two decades of Episcopal missionary work must be understood. The reasons behind the decline in the number of missionaries must be analyzed. The positive fruit from the indigenization of national churches and from the increased cooperation within the Anglican Communion must be noted and affirmed.

This study does not pretend to be a complete analysis of all the positive and negative aspects of the missionary efforts of the Episcopal Church from 1953 to 1977. The study is restricted to analyzing the deployment of appointed missionaries sent overseas by the Episcopal church and the amount of money used for world missions. Some of the contributing factors behind the recent decline in missionary support will then be briefly discussed.

ANALYSIS

1. Financial Summary:

The percentage amount of money available for overseas work reached its maximum in 1968. Since that time it has fallen substantially. The percentage

Mr. Lebhar is assistant minister at St. James Church, New London, Connecticut. Mr. Minns is assistant minister at St. Paul's Church, Darien, Connecticut.—*Editor's note.*

GRAPH 1

Financial Analysis of Episcopal Church
compared with total USA religious giving

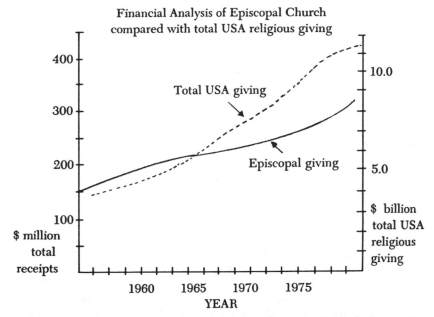

GRAPH 1

Financial Analysis of Episcopal Church
compared with total USA religious giving

allocated to the General Church Program Budget by General Convention
has fallen from 5.7% to 4.2%. Also, the percentage of the budget allocated
to overseas work has diminished from 45% to 35%. However, the most
significant change has been in the total giving of the Episcopal church.

Overall: The Episcopal church has not kept up with the rest of the USA
in religious giving.[1] Graph 1 and Table 1 show that until 1965 the Episcopal
church gave a fairly steady 4.4% of the toal amount of money given for
religious purposes in the USA but from then on there has been a decline
to about 3.0%. This decline is clearly related to the drop in membership
(Table 2) which peaked in 1966 at 3.44 million and has declined steadily
to 2.86 million in 1975. However, the remaining members have also failed
to keep up with the rest of the USA in giving.

[1]The source of the data on total USA giving is the American Association of Fund
Raising Council, *Giving USA*, annual editions, 1958–1976. Episcopal church giving is obtained from the compilation of the Parochial Reports on total receipts from
income and capital reported in the General Convention Journals, 1953–1976. The
Presiding Bishop's Fund, the United Thank Offering and other extra-parochial gifts
and grants are not included.

TABLE 1

Financial Analysis of Episcopal Church
General Church Program Budget

Year	$ million total budget	$ million Overseas Department	% *Overseas Dept.* Total Program Budget
1953	5.806	2.151	37
1955	5.838	2.297	39
1958	7.050	2.596	37
1959	8.060	3.139	39
1960	8.996	3.248	36
1961	9.820	3.381	34
1962	10.505	3.964	38
1963	11.497	4.294	37
1964	12.104	4.581	38
1965	12.777	5.437	43
1966	13.379	5.668	42
1967	13.923	5.899	42
1968	14.654	6.615	45
1971	11.808°	4.542°	38
1974	13.561	4.681	35
1977	14.000°°	?	?

° 'minimum commitment budget'
°° approximate figure

National Budget: The total receipts from income and capital, as reported in the General Convention Journals, were compared with the Program Budget that was approved at those Conventions to investigate whether there has been any change in commitment to national church programs. Table 2 shows that from 1953 until 1974 the percentage of the receipts that was allocated to General Church Programs has fluctuated between 4.2% and 5.7%. There does not appear to be any significant trend except that 1971–1977 do appear to suggest the beginning of a declining commitment to General Church Programs with a percentage drop of 1.5%. The data for 1977 is not readily available and so no definitive statement can be made about the current implication of this.

Overseas budget: Most of the money that can be identified as supporting Episcopal missions overseas does so through the Overseas Department of the National Church.[2] The budget is voted on at each General Convention

[2]This department has undergone a variety of name changes during the period covered. Its present function is included in the Department for National and World Mission of the Executive Council of the Episcopal church. The funding includes: the support of the Coalition of Overseas Dioceses of PECUSA; the response to Partners in Mission commitments in the Anglican Communion; and to the wider Episcopal fellowship and to ecumenical commitments.

TABLE 2

Financial Analysis of Episcopal Church
compared with total USA religious giving

Year	# million Episcopal Church members	$ million total receipts	$ billion total USA religious giving	% Episcopal / total USA
1953	2.662	115.8		
1954	2.758	129.1		
1955	2.853	124.2		
1956	2.965	138.5		
1957	3.035	150.5	3.4	4.4
1958	3.103	160.7	3.6	4.5
1959	3.175	170.7	3.9	4.4
1960	3.244	181.3	4.2	4.3
1961	3.296	196.8	4.4	4.5
1962	3.307	201.9	4.7	4.3
1963	3.304	207.9	4.9	4.2
1964	3.413	221.4	5.2	4.3
1965	3.429	232.5	5.5	4.2
1966	3.440	236.0	6.5	3.6
1967	3.434	254.8°	6.8	3.7
1968	3.385	256.8	7.4	3.5
1969	3.331	262.5	7.5	3.5
1970	3.254	277.2	8.2	3.4
1971	3.118	277.0	9.3	3.0
1972	3.063	293.2	9.8	3.0
1973	2.928	308.8	10.3	3.0
1974	2.907	326.0	10.8	3.0
1975	2.858	351.0		

° appears as 298.8 in Convention Journal but after investigation by the authors it was concluded that there was a $44 million error in the amount reported for the Diocese of Western New York.

Note: Data applies to Episcopal Church Provinces 1–8 only

and the distribution between the various recipients is agreed upon by the Coalition of Overseas Bishops. Table 3 shows that during the period 1953–1977 the percentage of the General Church Program devoted to overseas work varied between 34% and 45%. In 1961–1968 there was a significant increase from 34% to 45% but since that time there has been a drop to about 35%. The data for 1977 is not readily available and so no definite statement can be made about present trends.

2. Personnel Summary:

The number of appointed missionaries of the Episcopal Church has shown a dramatic drop since 1970 (Graph 2). Alaska and Hawaii were both considered missionary fields at the beginning of the period under study. Yet only a small portion of the decline may be attributed to them becoming full dioceses.

TABLE 3

Financial Analysis of Episcopal Church
Total Receipts compared with General Church Program Budget

Year	$ million Total Receipts	$ million Program Budget	% Total / Program
1953	115.8	5.806	5.0
1955	124.2	5.838	4.7
1958	160.7	7.050	4.4
1959	170.7	8.060	4.7
1960	181.3	8.996	5.0
1961	196.8	9.820	5.0
1962	201.9	10.505	5.2
1963	207.9	11.497	5.5
1964	221.4	12.104	5.5
1965	232.5	12.777	5.5
1966	236.0	13.379	5.7
1967	254.8	13.923	5.5
1968	256.8	14.654	5.7
1971	277.0	11.808*	4.3
1974	326.0	13.561	4.2
1977	?	14.000**	?

* minimum commitment budget'
** approximate figure

GRAPH 2
Appointed Missionaries of Episcopal Church

GRAPH 2

Appointed Missionaries
of Episcopal Church

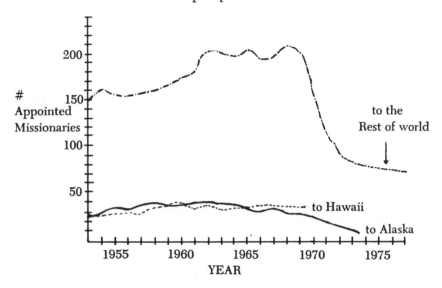

Appointed Missionaries: The data in Table 4 shows that the peak of approximately 200 appointed missionaries occurred during the period 1962–1965. Since that time there has been a rapid decline to the 1977 total of 71 missionaries. The wives of missionaries are also listed in the table because for many years they were considered as having a unique status, which was defined in the "Handbook of the Overseas Department" as follows: "The Wife of a Missionary is regarded as being in every sense a Missionary, though her Missionary Status is derived from and is dependent upon, that of her husband."[3] This view has been questioned in more recent years and so this study will focus only on the appointed missionaries.

Roster Analysis: In order to provide more detailed information on overseas missionary deployment the actual rosters for 1971–1977 were analyzed. Table 5 indicates the placement of the individual missionaries and shows that the reduction in numbers was spread fairly evenly throughout all the

---

[3]The latest appearance of this statement is in the January 1, 1970, list of Appointed Missionaries of the Episcopal Church serving in Overseas Jurisdictions.

TABLE 4

Appointed Missionaries

Year	Alaska		Hawaii		Rest of World		Total	
	A	W	A	W	A	W	A	W

note: A= Appointed Missionary and W= his wife

Year	A	W	A	W	A	W	A	W
1953	23	13	25	21	147	76	195	110
1954	26	14	25	21	160	83	211	118
1955	32	17	28	23	156	85	216	125
1956	31	17	28	22	153	90	212	129
1957	37	19	25	21	158	96	220	136
1958	35	23	31	27	159	101	225	151
1959	34	23	33	28	163	96	230	150
1960	34	25	34	29	171	107	239	161
1961	33	25	31	28	177	115	241	168
1962	36	26	32	28	201	128	269	182
1963	32	26	29	25	199	128	260	179
1964	30	25	33	32	196	133	261	190
1965	32	26	33	32	202	134	267	192
1966	28	26	32	32	189	128	249	186
1967	31	29	32	32	196	136	259	197
1968	25	24	31	28	207	142	263	194
1969	25	°	32	°	199	°	256	°
1970	20	19	–	–	154	116	174	135
1971	16	15	–	–	105	79	121	94
1972	12	11	–	–	88	66	100	77
1973	9	9	–	–	81	62	90	71
1974	–	–	–	–	°	°	°	°
1975	–	–	–	–	73	56	73	56
1976	–	–	–	–	75	57	75	57
1977	–	–	–	–	71	53	71	53

° data unavailable

fields. Table 6 is an analysis of the types of missionaries appointed by the Episcopal Church and shows that more than 16% of the total in 1971 were Bishops. Because the number of Bishops has remained quite stable this has increased to almost 27% of the total in 1977. Reductions have been fairly evenly divided between the numbers of priests and lay people.

In an effort to understand further the deployment of individual missionaries the changes from one year to the next are analyzed in Table 7. As might be expected the largest number remain fairly stable but there is a

TABLE 5

1971–1977 Roster Analysis
Field Placement

note: Data for 1974 is missing because a roster was not developed for that year.

Location	1971 A	1971 W	1972 A	1972 W	1973 A	1973 W	1975 A	1975 W	1976 A	1976 W	1977 A	1977 W
Alaska	16	15	12	11	9	9	–	–	–	–	–	–
Argentina	2	1	1	–	1	–	1	–	1	–	1	–
Botswanna	–	–	–	–	1	1	1	1	–	–	2	2
Brazil	6	4	3	2	3	2	3	2	2	1	2	1
Colombia	1	1	1	1	2	2	2	2	2	2	2	2
Costa Rica	2	2	2	2	2	2	2	2	1	1	1	1
Damarland	1	1	–	–	–	–	–	–	–	–	–	–
Dom. Republic	5	5	2	2	2	2	3	3	3	3	2	2
Ecuador	2	2	2	2	3	3	1	1	3	2	1	1
El Salvador	2	1	2	2	1	1	1	1	1	1	2	2
Guam	1	1	2	2	1	1	1	1	1	1	1	1
Guatemala	2	1	2	1	2	2	1	1	1	1	1	1
Haiti	1	1	1	1	1	1	1	1	1	1	2	1
Honduras	2	2	1	1	3	1	3	1	4	3	5	2
Hong Kong	2	2	2	2	2	2	2	2	1	1	1	1
India	1	1	1	1	–	–	–	–	–	–	–	–
Iran	1	1	1	1	1	1	1	1	1	1	1	1
Jamaica	1	1	1	1	1	1	1	1	1	1	1	1
Japan	10	6	9	5	8	4	7	4	7	4	7	4
Jerusalem	1	1	2	2	1	1	2	2	1	1	1	1
Kenya	1	–	1	–	–	–	–	–	–	–	1	–
Korea	1	–	1	–	1	–	1	–	1	–	1	–
Liberia	9	7	7	6	7	6	7	6	6	4	2	2
Malawi	–	–	1	–	–	–	–	–	1	–	–	–
Melanesia	–	–	–	–	–	–	–	–	–	–	1	–
Mexico	5	4	5	4	5	4	4	3	6	5	5	4
Nepal	1	–	–	–	–	–	–	–	–	–	–	–
Nicaragua	2	2	2	1	2	1	2	1	3	2	3	2
Okinawa	1	1	–	–	–	–	–	–	–	–	–	–
Panama	7	6	5	5	3	3	3	3	3	3	3	3
Philippines	17	11	13	8	14	9	14	9	12	8	13	9
Polynesia	3	3	2	2	2	2	–	–	–	–	–	–
Province IX °	1	1	1	1	1	1	1	1	1	1	1	1
Puerto Rico	1	1	1	1	1	1	1	1	1	1	1	1

TABLE 5 continued

Location	1971		1972		1973		1975		1976		1977	
	A	W	A	W	A	W	A	W	A	W	A	W
Russia	–	–	1	1	–	–	–	–	–	–	–	–
Sudan	1	1	1	1	–	–	–	–	–	–	–	–
Singapore	–	–	–	–	1	1	1	1	1	1	–	–
Taiwan	2	1	2	2	2	2	2	2	2	2	2	2
Tanzania	1	1	1	1	1	1	–	–	2	2	2	2
Uganda	3	3	3	3	1	1	–	–	–	–	–	–
Virgin Islands	6	4	6	4	5	3	4	3	3	3	2	2
Zambia	1	–	1	–	–	–	–	–	1	–	–	–
Zululand	1	1	1	–	1	1	1	1	2	2	1	1
Malaysia	–	–	–	–	–	–	–	–	–	–	1	1
TOTAL	121	94	100	77	90	71	73	56	75	57	71	53
Alaska	16	15	12	11	9	9	–	–	–	–	–	–
Rest of World	105	79	88	66	81	62	73	56	75	57	71	53

* Province IX includes countries in Central and South America

TABLE 6

1971–1977 Roster Analysis
Missionary Categories

	1971	1972	1973	1975	1976	1977
Bishops	20	20	19	19	19	19
Priests	75	60	56	40	42	39
Laity *	26	20	15	14	14	13
Total	121	100	90	73	75	71

* Includes functions such as doctors and teachers.

substantial number of missionaries who are terminated each year. This includes those missionaries who change to local support but it is still indicative of a declining missionary activity. Another sign of this is the minimal
involvement in new missionary fields. One encouraging aspect of the data
is the number of new missionaries sent out to existing fields each year (for
example, ten were sent in 1977).

TABLE 7

1971–1977 Roster Analysis
Missionary Deployment

	1972	1973	1975	1976	1977
No position change	84	76	66	59	55
Study leave or furlough	2	5	5	2	–
Return from leave	2	–	1	1	–
Termination or change to local support	33	21	9	11	19
Redeployed in existing fields	1	3	–	–	2
Redeployed in new fields	–	1	–	–	2
New missionaries in existing fields	10	4	1	12	10
New missionaries in new fields	1	1	–	1	2
Total	133	111	82	86	90
Active	100	90	73	75	71

CONTRIBUTING FACTORS

The decline in numbers of Episcopal missionaries in the late sixties and early seventies resulted from many causes. By their very nature, the causes have a cumulative effect, and therefore their relative individual influences cannot be measured with assurance. Four of the main influences which contributed to the decrease in the number of missionaries will be briefly examined: 1) the nature of missionary support; 2) the changes in missionary strategy; 3) the newer theological presuppositions; and 4) the recent cultural issues both within the USA and abroad.

1. *The Nature of Missionary Support*:

With the emergence of the National Council in 1919 and the subsequent Nationwide Campaign, the Episcopal Church in the 1920's experienced a remarkable resurgence in missionary outreach.[4] At the same time, the national church assumed greater responsibility for the sending of missionaries through the Church Missions House.[5] The pattern used by the National

---

[4]Allen J. Green, "Episcopal Missionary Giving," 1920–1955," *Episcopal Overseas Mission Review*, Vol. I, No. 3 (Whitsuntide, 1956) p. 8.
[5]*Ibid.*

Church to send out missionaries has continued until the present day. As explained by David Birney, the Associate for Overseas Personnel and Scholarships of the Department of National and World Mission:

> How we define a missionary from the point of view of this building (Episcopal Church Center) . . . (is one who has) gone through the appointment procedure and . . . (has) been officially appointed by the Presiding Bishop backed by the vote of the Executive Council to go out as an official missionary of the Episcopal Church, USA. Now there are many who go out on their own . . . . In no way would we say that these people are not missionaries. They are not appointed missionaries of the Episcopal Church, and it's that word "appointed" that's the key.[6]

The advantages of the appointment procedure through the Executive Council are numerous. The appointee and his or her family have been interviewed, psychologically and medically examined, and trained for the assignment. Careful matching of missionary to mission role is accomplished. Financial support is raised through various sources so that the monetary security of the appointee is well assured. Most importantly, a weighing of who needs a missionary most is possible.

Yet there are two reasons why this procedure inhibits the number of missionaries sent out. First of all, a missionary who is everyone's responsibility, as an appointee of the National Church, rapidly may become the subject of no one's interest. As David Birney admits, "It's awfully hard to get a Church this size involved in eight to ten people" who are sent out each year. Even though each appointee has an interview with the Diocesan Press Service, few "dioceses in the United States will take it from the . . . service and put it in their own local newspaper."[7]

As a result of a lack of communication, some sent out feel cut off from home. The Overseas Review Committee noted this feeling in the 1973 report to the General Convention:

> A sense of isolation and loss of relationship had occurred between American missionary personnel overseas and the Church which had commissioned them. They felt forgotten and even betrayed by a Church which seemed to them to have lost any conviction about spreading Christ's word to other than mainland areas.[8]

Thus one problem of the National Church appointment procedure is the

---

[6]From our taped interview with the Reverend David Birney on February 24, 1978, and his subsequent written comments. Mr. Birney is a former missionary to Uganda and Botswana.

[7]David Birney.

[8]Review of 1970 Interim Report from the Overseas Review Committee Appendix to the 1973 *Journal of General Convention*, p. 683.

tendency for the whole Church to be unaware of Episcopal missionary activity. Another problem, closely related, is the low priority of missionary giving to appointed missionaries who are not known by local parishes.[9] The problem of low giving was noted by Allen Green as early as 1956:

> Only 3.8 pennies from each (communicant's) . . . dollar managed to trickle past his rector and vestry as they drew up the parish budget; past the appropriations machinery of his diocese and into . . . (the National Church's) General Missions Fund.[10]

This small percentage of Episcopal money going to the National Church's missionary program dropped after 1956.[11] The problem was complicated in the sixties by an overall decrease in giving to the National Church when inflation is taken into account. The decrease in giving to the National Church was caused by several factors of which only two can be noted. First of all, general membership in the Episcopal Church has been declining since 1967 (see Table 2).[12] Secondly, Episcopalians began to give proportionately less to their General Church Program budget after 1968 (see Table 3). Some trace this lower giving for the National Church budget to the Church's involvement in mission to the inner-city, in the black organizations, and so forth, i.e., the General Convention Special Programs. As the money to the National Church declined, David Birney believes that the Church Center "had to cut every program right down to the bone, and one of the things that went . . . was the number of missionaries we were able to have overseas."[13]

2. *The Change in Missionary Strategy:*
The second major contributing factor to the decline in Episcopal missionaries is the change in missionary strategy that has resulted from the Mutual Responsibility and Interdependence movement (MRI) and the current Partners in Mission Program (PIM). The major missionary thrust through the fifties was to see the Episcopal church, USA, as the sending church and the rest of the world as a receiving mission field. Since the early sixties this view has been revised radically, with calls for partnership between national churches and for the indigenization of mission churches.

The trend for greater cooperation within the Anglican Communion was

[9]Some parishes and dioceses have responded to this problem by directly contributing to the support of individual appointees in addition to their giving through the General Church budget.
[10]Green, *op. cit.,* p. 6.
[11]"Most domestic dioceses spend so much on maintaining structures that neither money nor commitment is left over for Mission," World Mission Appendix to 1976 *Journal of General Convention,* p. AA 234.
[12]The reasons for the decrease in membership are numerous and await evaluation in a future study.
[13]David Birney.

already evident in the 1961 report of the Committee of Conference on Overseas Missions to the General Convention. Among the several recommendations of the Committee, the following deserve special note:

> The Episcopal Church (should) make plans . . . .
>> To permit overseas Missionary Districts fully to participate in the life of existing and adjacent Anglican provinces . . .
>
>> To strengthen working relations with autonomous provinces . . .
>
>> To encourage the steady development of autonomy, and local authority, and responsibility, in existing Missionary Districts . . .
>
> Whenever work is to be begun in a new country by the Episcopal Church, . . .
>> the personnel, support and planning should be shared with other Churches of the Anglican Communion and . . .
>
>> it be the policy of this church to plan and work with other communions toward the ultimate establishment of an autonomous united Church within the area.[14]

As a result of these recommendations and the later summons of MRI in 1964 a new strategy in missions began.[15] The Episcopal church was to make "no more unilateral decisions" about missions.[16] There came to be continuing consultations between Anglican churches and dioceses, especially through the present Partners in Mission Consultations.[17] In these meetings, Churches corporately decided what their priorities were, and what needs for missionaries existed.[18] At the same time autonomy for missionary churches became a clear goal,[19] with each church aiming for "self-government, self-support, and self-propagation."[20] This stress on autonomy meant that missionary churches were encouraged to develop their own support and and leadership. One implication of this move towards autonomy is that a large-scale missionary presence might no longer be needed, and that the responsibility for mission became the responsibility of each church in every

[14]1961 *Journal of General Convention*, p. 763–5.

[15]"Report of the Presiding Bishop's Committee on Mutual Responsibility to the General Convention," 1964 *Journal of General Convention*, Appendix 26, esp. pp. 722–727.

[16]Overseas Review Committee Report, 1973 *Journal of General Convention*, p. 682.

[17]See Joint Commission on World Mission Appendix in 1976 *Journal of General Convention*, especially p. AA 232f, wherein a consultation is described.

[18]David Birney.

[19]Commitee on Overseas Mission Report, 1970 *Journal of General Convention*, p. 568.

[20]Overseas Review Committee Report, *op. cit.*, p. 682.

land, working in partnership with sister churches throughout the Anglican Communion.[21]

One example of this move towards indigenization is a new form of missionary outreach which has developed more fully—the training of nationals in the USA or in educational institutions abroad to minister in their own churches overseas. As David Birney said:

> Because of the work that many of our missionaries have done in the past, local leadership is increasing . . . . Through scholarship funds . . . we bring the people from overseas to be trained here. They then return and often assume positions formerly held by the missionaries.

While autonomy and indigenization are highly desirable, there exists the realization that some mission churches will need money and personnel for the "foreseeable future."[22] Hence "self-support must . . . remain a *goal* and a *policy* rather than condition of relationship."[23]

3. *Newer Theological Presuppositions*:

It is impossible to identify one theology of mission in the Episcopal Church. Each party within the church contends for its own view of what mission properly means. Yet the decline in missionary giving does reflect theological trends within the church which can occasionally be discerned.

The greatest trend is toward relativism, in which the Christian faith is viewed as one of many ways toward God. Robert H. Grant noticed the effects of this in the church during his furlough from the Japanese mission field:

> My missionary endeavours are supported to a degree as long as I show profit in social improvement, economic relief, intellectual development, ... But my assertion that the justification of missions is the growth of Christian conviction is met with the same politely appreciative smiles, such as the 12-year-old daughter of the house receives after she renders . . . Maiden's Prayer . . . on the piano.[24]

The theological view that Christianity is only one type of legitimate faith may well be held by only a minority. Nevertheless, the stress on social action versus evangelism is evident in the 1973 Overseas Review Committee

---

[21]It is estimated that through the Bloc Grant system by which this Church makes grants to Overseas Dioceses that between 1,000-1,400 persons around the world (Bishops, clergy, and lay workers) receive the support required for them to be actively engaged in mission in and from their own lands.

[22]Committee on Overseas Missions Report, *op. cit.*, p. 573, where Ecuador is given as an example.

[23]*Ibid.*

[24]"Creeping Buddhism in American Churches," *Episcopal Overseas Missions Review*, VII 1 (Michaelmas, 1961) p. 8.

Report. The report suggests new patterns of missionary work including 'Mission Fronts: Hunger is a mission front; so are overpopulation, refugees, health care and a host of other forces."[25] While evangelism and personal commitment to Christ are mentioned in the report, they are on a par with the social action ministries.

The emphasis on economic, social and political involvement in mission also springs from the tendency to equate liberation from oppression in all forms with the gospel itself. Stephen Neill reports that "some would go so far as to say that humanization is evangelism; in a situation of oppression there is no other form of preaching the gospel."[26]

It cannot be proved that the trends toward relativism and toward liberation theology have directly contributed to the decline in missionaries sent out by the Episcopal church. Yet the existence of these newer theologies surely demonstrates that the Episcopal Church has no clear theology of mission, and this lack of clarity in and of itself would hinder a more effective missionary outreach.

4. *Recent Cultural Issues in the USA and Abroad*:

During and after the sixties, the USA became more aware of the problems at home, especially civil rights. Much of the energy that might well have gone into missionary efforts was understandably redirected toward the struggle for racial equality.

Even so, in the early sixties there was an idealism about the constructive role the USA could play in the international scene, as evident in Kennedy's call for involvement in the Peace Corps.[27] At the same time, this idealism was reflected in increased numbers of Episcopal missionaries. Yet later on in the decade, the anti-Vietnam War struggle sapped American energy and motivation for involvement overseas. As noted in the 1970 *Journal of General Convention*, there is "a clearly discernible neo-isolationism in the Church, all too much a reflection of the same spirit in our country's foreign relations."[28]

While such "neo-isolation" was developing in the USA, there was an increase in attempts at independence by many Third World countries, in order to throw off the vestiges of colonial rule. This anti-colonial attitude is strongest in Africa where "the call for a moratorium (on missions) is most

[25]*Op. cit.*, p. 691.

[26]*Salvation Tomorrow* (London, 1976), p. 83. Neill is especially considering the Bangkok Assembly of the Department of Evangelism and World Mission of the WCC (1973) and the Fifth Assembly of the WCC in Nairobi (1975). Neill ultimately concludes "that evangelism must accompany and not follow every step in the process of political and economic liberation," p. 97.

[27]William E. Leuchtenburg, *A Troubled Feast* (Boston, 1973) emphasizes the role of the Kennedy administration in helping young people turn their energies toward public affairs like the civil rights movement and the Peace Corps. p. 130.

[28]Committee on Overseas Report, *op. cit.*, p. 567.

loudly and clamorously expressed."[29] This anti-colonialism was also observed by the Committee on Overseas Missions through their task force of visitors to Anglican missions around the world.[30]

A related factor was the tendency of some newly independent Third World governments to consider their churches' connections with overseas missions agencies as threats to national security. In some countries missionary involvement had to be limited to protect the national church from repression. Thus the "neo-isolation" of the USA lessened domestic motivation to send missionaries at the same time that countries overseas were questioning their need for missionaries at all.

CONCLUSION

The missionary imperative for the church: "Go therefore and make disciples of all nations . . . ." has not been revoked. This study shows that we are faced with a tremendous challenge and many questions if we are to reverse the presently declining response by the Episcopal church.

How can the missionary-sending process be restructured to create greater enthusiasm?

How can church-planting take place within the limitations and opportunities of the Partners in Mission process?

What is an adequate theology of missions?

Can we combine evangelism, missions and social concerns?

How does the Church get beyond cultural neo-isolationism?

There are so simple answers. Yet some new directions in Episcopal missions are exciting. The Department of National and World Mission has been authorized by the 1976 General Convention to start a Volunteers for Mission program. There is also a close working relationship by which the Episcopal church Center aides new voluntary societies in placing their missionaries.

Despite these encouraging signs, there is one major problem. The present strategy seems to assume that the whole world is covered by churches of the Anglican Communion.[31] There is no plan for Episcopal missionaries to be sent out to start new churches for the over 2.5 billion people[32] not in close proximity to any Christian church.[33] At present only "twenty-five or

---

[29]Neill, op. cit., p. 47, again reacting to Bangkok Assembly of WCC in 1973.

[30]Op. cit., p. 567, sec. 3.

[31]Howard A. Johnson, Global Odyssey (New York, 1963) illustrates this viewpoint. Even the inside covers have maps which suggest almost worldwide coverage.

[32]The Episcopal Church Missionary Community has brought a renewed emphasis to the fact that there are 2.7 billion non-Christians in the world through its newsletters and other publications.

[33]David Birney said that "at this particular time in history we don't have the structure to do (church planting by appointed missionaries)."

thirty"[34] missionaries are requested by our Partners in Mission, none of whom are used directly in church-planting. However, some are used to train Nationals for this work.

Yet the major obstacle to Episcopal mission is not poor strategy, but the apathy of the Episcopal church towards mission in general. This is made evident by the recruitment difficulties for already-established Anglican posts.

As David Birney has said:

> Until the clergy and laity of this Church are once again committed to and given a vision of the world mission of this Church, in partnership with other Churches, I don't think we will begin to realize the great potential in human and material resources with which this Church has been blessed by God.

[34]David Birney.

Daniel J. Adams

After having served as Professor of Theology at Taiwan Theological College, Dr. Adams now is a theological education missionary in Korea, under the auspices of the Presbyterian Church in the US.

The Biblical Basis for Mission, 1930-1980

I. Introduction

PRESBYTERIANS IN AMERICA have long been a biblical and missionary people, and throughout their history the Presbyterian churches have appealed to Scripture as an authority for mission. Both the United Presbyterian Church in the USA (UPCUSA) and the Presbyterian Church in the United States (PCUS) have cited numerous biblical texts in mission statements over the years.[1] In this study we shall examine these mission statements from 1930 to the present in an attempt to determine which factors have contributed to differences in biblical interpretation in both the past and present, and which of these factors may be a source of conflict in the future.

Presbyterian statements concerning biblical authority for mission are best understood in light of three historical developments. The first of these is the PCUSA Old School/New School division which existed from 1837 to 1870. The Old School was characterized by orthodox theology and a church-centered mission program; the New School took a broadened theological stance coupled with a nondenominational approach to mission. The second of these developments is the Princeton Theology, associated with such names as Archibald Alexander, Benjamin B. Warfield, and Charles Hodge. The Princeton Theology was orthodox, especially in its views concerning Scripture, and was firm in its commitment to church discipline and Presbyterian polity. Both the PCUSA and the PCUS were affected by these two developments.[2]

A third development, unique to the PCUS, is the doctrine of the spirituality of the church, which was prominent from 1861 until 1935 and which continues to exert considerable influence.

Journal of Presbyterian History, 59:2 (Summer 1981)

According to this view the mission of the church "was limited to evangelism and to the fostering of an individual or family morality. Given by divine commission, its task was conceived to be, in the strictest sense of the word, spiritual, that is, evangelistic and pietistic."[3] Mission was understood, therefore, primarily in terms of evangelism.

These three historical developments combined to give form and direction to the first one hundred years of Presbyterian missions. The missionary enterprise was characterized by theological orthodoxy, an emphasis upon evangelism, and personal piety. Social concerns such as education and medicine were seen as a means to an end, that end being evangelism. There was tension, however, between those who held to a church-centered mission and those who favored serving under independent boards.

II. The Point of Change

The year 1930 was a point of change for Presbyterian missions. The first change was theological. As new theologies from Europe began to influence the American church, questions arose concerning the adequacy of the Princeton Theology. The end result was a reorganization of Princeton Seminary and the acceptance of theological pluralism within the church. Many prominent Presbyterian ministers, including some members of the new Princeton Seminary board, signed the Auburn Affirmation, a document that called for a more liberal theology and expressly denied the inerrancy of Scripture.[4] Among those Princeton faculty who stood for the orthodox view was J. Gresham Machen. Machen strongly opposed both theological pluralism in the church and the reorganization of Princeton Seminary.[5] A bitter controversy developed with the result that Machen and those who sympathized with his position withdrew from Princeton and formed Westminster Theological Seminary.[6]

This theological controversy carried over into missions and in 1933 Machen and others formed the Independent Board for Presbyterian Missions "to promote truly biblical and truly Presbyterian mission work."[7] At this point an interesting tension developed within the Princeton Theology. On the one hand Machen and his followers were orthodox in theology, yet they were liberal in church polity, even to the point of forming an independent mission board in open defiance of the General Assembly. The result of this action was the suspension of Machen and his followers from the ministry by the 1936 PCUSA General Assembly. This was an important turning point in mission policy and its effects were still being felt in the church as late as 1975.

Another change was a shift in mission emphasis from evangelism to humanitarian social concern. A number of denominations joined together—the PCUSA among them—to reevaluate the mission program after one hundred years. A lay committee was appointed to carry out this task and in 1932 and 1933 they published their findings. Popularly known as the Laymen's Report, it consisted of a reassessment of the foreign mission enterprise along with suggestions for change in both theory and practice. The findings of the Laymen's Report were summarized in the book *Re-Thinking Missions*.

To begin with very little was said concerning Scripture. Only one text was cited from Matthew 6:10 and Luke 11:2: "The goal to which this way leads may be variously described, most perfectly perhaps in the single phrase, Thy kingdom come. This is, and has always been the true aim of Christian missions."[8] The Kingdom of God was understood primarily in terms of the Social Gospel and the Christian faith was seen as one manifestation of universal religion.[9] Needless to say there was a great deal of concern among those who believed mission to be evangelism to the non-Christian world. Furthermore *Re-Thinking Missions* asserted that three changes had taken place in the overall missionary situation: an altered theological outlook (most conservatives were neither ready nor willing to concede that such an altered outlook had in fact taken place); the emergence of a basic world culture (this was particularly difficult for many in the PCUS to accept); and the rise of nationalism in the East (this posed a direct challenge to American ethnocentrism and nationalism). While many Presbyterians questioned the theological assumptions underlying the Laymen's Report, there was little doubt in anyone's mind that a turning point had been reached and that Presbyterian missions could not return to the past.

III. The Period of Foreign Missions

"And he said to them, 'Go into all the world and preach the gospel to the whole creation'" (Mark 16:15). The Great Commission served as the biblical basis for mission in both the PCUSA and the PCUS. The two fundamental shifts in theology and mission emphasis, however, brought about the need for a corresponding shift in hermeneutic and both denominations responded by holding mission consultations in 1931.

The Chattanooga Mission Conference was a call to the PCUS for a deepened spiritual life coupled with a clearer realization of the world's need. Foreign missions was the glory of the church and in 1926 the denomination of less than half a million members supported over five hundred missionaries in twelve countries. The depression took its toll, however, and by 1930 it was apparent that financial contributions were down and that overseas personnel would have to be drastically reduced.[10] These were changes the conference could not ignore.

The Chattanooga Conference reiterated the PCUS commitment to the Great Commission and declared that while the world had changed, the Christian Gospel remained unchanged. While making this affirmation, Commission I—"Missionary Message and Obligation (Christianity and the non-Christian Religions)"— asserted that interpretations of the Gospel may change as may church statements, emphases, and approaches to mission.[11] The need for adaptability was stressed but within that context an attempt was made to state essential Christian doctrines. This was done through an appeal to Scripture. Doctrines and biblical passages cited include the following:

1. God—Eph. 2:2; Rev. 1:8; 2 Chr. 2:6
2. Christ and Him Crucified—1 Cor. 2:2
3. Christ Revealing the Father—Jn. 14:8-9; Heb. 1:3
4. The Divine Christ—Mt. 16:15
5. The Human Christ—Jn. 1:14; 1 Tim. 2:5; Heb. 2:17-18, 4:14-16
6. Christ Crucified—Rom. 5:6; 1 Cor. 15:3; 2 Cor. 5:21; 1 Pet. 3:18; 2 Pet. 2:24; 1 Jn. 2:2
7. Our Risen Lord—Rom. 1:4; 1 Cor. 15:17-18, 20; Rev. 1:18
8. The Holy Spirit—Jn. 14:6, 26, 16:18; Acts 1:8

Throughout it was clearly stated that salvation could be found only in Jesus Christ and not through any of the non-Christian religions.

The Chattanooga Conference did, however, broaden the concept of salvation to include various forms of social action. Numerous biblical passages were cited: Mt. 9:35, 10:8, 11:3, 5, 25:34-40, 28:18-20; and Lk. 4:18. The Sermon on the Mount, the Golden Rule, the Royal Law of Love, and the parables of the Good Samaritan, the Rich Man and Lazarus, and the Rich Fool were all given as examples of the ethical and social teaching of the Bible. In the words of Commission I: "These form an essential part of the missionary message and the missionary program."[12] Specific reference was made to the race problem as both a domestic and international issue. This broadened understanding of the Gospel was, however, particular in nature: "The Gospel of Jesus Christ, including his social teachings, is the only remedy in all the world for these social ills. . . . It is not so with non-Christian religions." [13] Although Commission I included the social dimension in its definition of salvation the other commissions did not follow suit and the official position of the PCUS did not undergo any radical change at that time. However, the winds of change were in the air.

The Lakeville (Connecticut) Conference was called by the PCUSA as a follow-up to an earlier mission conference held at Princeton in 1920. Its purpose was to re-examine the mission of the church in light of the development of national consciousness abroad and to redefine the nature of the Gospel in relation to social action. In a manner similar to that of Commission I of the Chattanooga Conference, the delegates at Lakeville emphasized "that the ministry of healing, the work of teaching, social service, and the service of the printed page are examples of the spirit of the Master and part of His ministry. They are in themselves part of the full gospel message and not mere keys to unlock doors, mere means of approach or baits to catch men for the Church." [14] Few biblical passages were quoted to support this position; rather, the authority of Scripture was assumed.

Speaking directly to the issue of rising national consciousness abroad, Group III—"The Younger Churches and How Mission Work is Best Related to Them"—raised a question concerning comity agreements with overseas churches. They said: "Care should be taken that neither church nor mission should assume an exclusive responsibility which is manifestly beyond its ability effectively to fulfill. Christ's word, 'Go ye into all the world and preach the Gospel to every creature,' was given to all of His disciples." [15] Here Mark 16:15 was interpreted in such a way that a question was raised concerning the traditional view that mission is from the Christian West to the non-Christian world. This usage of Scripture would seem to illustrate Presbyterian concern for ecumenical mission.

With the publication of the Laymen's Report in 1932, a controversy arose concerning portions of that report which suggested that possibility of salvation for those outside the Christian faith. Since the PCUSA was one of the sponsors of the Laymen's Report, the General Assembly of 1933 issued the following statement:

> The General Assembly reaffirms its loyal and complete adherence to the doctrinal standards of the Presbyterian Church. We declare our belief that while certain truths may be found in other religions, complete and final truth is to be found in Jesus Christ alone through the religion of which he is the center. We recognize the necessity laid upon the church as his visible representative upon the earth to bring his full gospel to the whole world as the final hope of men.[16]

Speaking specifically to the text of *Re-Thinking Missions*, the General Assembly repudiated "any and all theological statements and implications in that volume which are not in essential agreement with the doctrinal position of the church."[17]

1936 was the jubilee year for the PCUS and was the occasion for a reaffirmation of the 1861 missionary declaration:

> The General Assembly desires distinctly and deliberately to inscribe on our church's banner as she now unfurls it to the world, in immediate connection with the Headship of the Lord, His last command: "Go ye into all the world and preach the Gospel to every creature;" regarding this as the great end of her organization, and obedience to it as the indispensable condition of her Lord's presence.[18]

1936 was also the year in which the PCUSA acted finally and decisively in the Machen case, thus rejecting the concept of an independent mission board and placing its stamp of approval upon a broadened theological perspective within the church.

Clearly both the PCUS and the PCUSA were searching for a new hermeneutic to match the changes that were taking place in mission. Although the main emphasis was upon foreign missions in a continued sending and receiving relationship, there was the beginning of a social and ecumenical consciousness with the result that preaching the Gospel to the whole creation began to take on a new meaning.

IV. The Period of Ecumenical Mission

"I do not pray for these only, but also for those who believe in me through their word, that they may all be one; even as thou, Father, art in me, and I in thee, that they may also be in us, so that the world may believe that thou hast sent me" (John 17:20-21). The end of the 1940s and the aftermath of World War II brought about an unprecedented internationalization of the world. The United States came under the influence of European theology and there was a growing awareness of the strengths of churches in other lands. Much of the relief effort following the war was carried out jointly with these national churches. At the same time the international ecumenical movement was growing, and all of this had an impact on the mission policies of American Presbyterian churches. Increasingly mission came to be understood in terms of unity with other Christians.

In 1952 the PCUS appointed an Ad-Interim Committee on World Missions "for the purpose of studying the whole missionary obligation and strategy of the church in today's world."[19] The committee's report was presented to the 1954 General Assembly. Of particular interest was the assertion that there was a vitality of biblical and theological studies in the church and that these needed to be related to mission. The influence of Karl Barth and Neo-Orthodoxy brought about a new interest in the Bible and a christological emphasis in mission statements. The Blue Book of the 1954 General Assembly contained a well thought-out christological foundation for the mission of the church.[20] No distinction was made between the church and mission and a theological framework for church-to-church ecumenical mission was proposed. Biblical references cited include Mk. 1:15, 13:10; Jn. 3:16; 1 Cor. 15:24; 2 Cor. 5:14; Gal. 4:4-5; Col. 1:19-20; and of course a reaffirmation of Mk. 16:15, the Great Commission. Indeed, the 1954 PCUS General Assembly cited Mk. 16:15 in connection with a statement on evangelism:

> "The great end of missionary life and service is the preaching of Christ and Him crucified to the non-evangelized peoples." This is no random statement. It represents the deep conviction of our church, based upon its understanding of the Scriptures and the fundamental obligation explicitly set forth in our Lord's command: "Go ye into all the world and preach the gospel to every creature."[21]

Evangelism was now conceived, however, within the context of the worldwide church.

The 1956 PCUS General Assembly recommended that all ministers stress the biblical and theological basis for world missions, including the fact of mankind's lost condition apart from Christ. This was in part a reaction to the theology of Karl Barth with its implied universalism, and to the changed view of mission in the PCUS which recognized the need for applying the Gospel to areas of social concern.[22] The 1958 Board of World Missions Report makes specific references to "the safeguarding of those basic beliefs and convictions of our Church that underlie the missionary enterprise" and points out "that despite the clear Biblical teaching on the subject there are evidences here and there of a tacit universalism which would question the urgency, or even the need, of our missionary efforts."[23]

In 1956 the PCUSA held a mission consultation at Lake Mohonk, New York with the express purpose of redefining mission from the ecumenical standpoint. The reports of the consultation, summarized in William Hogg's *New Day Dawning*, stressed the importance of biblical studies as they were related to the various areas of mission.[24] Most significant, however, was the consultation's definition of mission: "A mission and some of its functions would disappear, but *the* mission would be seen in its enlarged and true perspective. This is the rationale behind 'Ecumenical Mission.' It implies that a church in its entirety—not one segment of it, its boards of missions—affirms its mission."[25] The members of the consultation found a biblical basis for their ecumenical stance in the term *oikoumene*—the inhabited world—which appears fourteen times in the New Testament. Concerning the classic text of the ecumenical movement, Hogg wrote:

> "That they all may be one; as Thou Father, art in me, and I in Thee, that they may also be one in us; that the world may believe that Thou hast sent me" (John 17:21). Christ prayed for the oneness of His followers in order that the world could believe. Here is unity for the sake of mission. Increasingly, men are recognizing that the word ecumenical as it is used today has 2 foci—mission and unity.[26]

In keeping with this ecumenical stance, the PCUSA moved toward integration of their overseas missions into the national churches so that the relationship was changed from that of mission-to-church to one of church-to-church. Missionaries serving in countries where this integration had already taken place were called fraternal workers, for mission was to be carried out by the one church to the whole inhabited world.

The 1958 merger of the PCUSA with the United Presbyterian Church in North America to form the United Presbyterian Church in the USA (UPCUSA) brought about a reorganization of the old boards of world missions. The term foreign missions was abolished as being inadequate "since the historic organized missions are being merged into the churches they helped to establish in many nations."[27] A new agency known as the Commission on Ecumenical Mission and Relations (COEMAR) was formed to continue the integration of overseas mission work into the total mission of the church.

Shortly after its formation, COEMAR issued an introductory booklet explaining the rationale of this new agency to the denomination and providing a biblical and theological basis for this new ecumenical thrust in mission. A number of biblical texts were

Lake Mohonk Conference, 1956

referred to, among them being Mt. 24:14, 28:18-20; 1 Cor. 14:26; 2 Cor. 5:18-19; Gal. 6:10; Eph. 2:19; Phil. 2:10-11; and Mk. 16:15. The Great Commission was affirmed but with a difference— foreign missions was now global mission. Said COEMAR: "We are speaking biblically, and in line with the usage of the New Testament when we say that 'Ecumenical' is a scriptural term."[28]

Although fears of universalism continued to persist, the ecumenical perspective in mission tended to emphasize the positive—Christ's lordship over the whole inhabited earth, whereas the traditional viewpoint of foreign missions stressed the negative—the lost condition of those who were without Christ. As the churches began to work together in mission, however, it became apparent that the unity sought was sometimes more real than the unity obtained, and once again the Presbyterian churches turned their attention to the task of searching for a new hermeneutic of mission.

V. The Period of Ecumenical Relations

"All this is from God, who through Christ reconciled us to himself and gave us the ministry of reconciliation" (2 Corinthians 5:18). As mission came more and more to be understood in a global context, two important factors came to the fore. First, overseas churches began to raise questions concerning the often overbearing policies of the American churches, and they demanded equality when it came to financial matters and the decision-making process. Second, the concept of a truly ecumenical mission meant that the United States was not only a sending nation but also a receiving nation—in other words a mission field. To cite but one example, more than one African convert found that he or she was not welcome in American Presbyterian churches even though converted to Christianity through the efforts of Presbyterian missionaries. A careful consideration of these factors led American Presbyterians to focus their attention upon the ministry of reconciliation.

In keeping with this theme the 1961 PCUS General Assembly accepted a recommendation "that pastors present anew the command to 'Go into all the world and preach the Gospel to every creature,' calling their people to find their particular places in the Church's worldwide mission, in obedience to our Lord's orders."[29] Not only was the global nature of mission emphasized, but the local parish was singled out as an area for mission.

In 1962 the PCUS held a mission consultation in Montreat, North Carolina in response to a call from the 1960 and 1961 General Assemblies for a reexamination of the philosophy and strategy of mission in the rapidly changing world situation. In many ways the concerns of this consultation mirrored those of the Monhonk Consultation of 1956; many of the same issues were discussed, among them being mission and church relations. The consultation concluded that "this relationship should move in the following direction: the missionary should be willing to work in the framework of the national church. Work assignments should be made by the proper court of the national church."[30]

In addition to its reaffirmation of the missionary declaration of 1861, the consultation issued a statement entitled "The Theological Basis for Mission" with the major theme being that of reconciliation. Although no direct quotes from Scripture were used, an appeal was made to the New Testament: "The New Testament shows us the dark background of a world lost without Christ, but in the foreground the love, the hope and the obedience which are the gifts of the Spirit."[31] An appeal was also made for the "church to expand, in the saving name of the Lord of love, our ministry of service to the needs of all peoples."[32]

Many in the PCUS were concerned about universalism and the consultation responded as follows: "How can the Presbyterian Church in the United States strengthen these convictions and meet the challenge of 'practical universalism'? the Consultation affirmation in answer to the question is found in the theological statement preceding the committee reports."[33] Although the theological statement cited no biblical passages to counter the charges of universalism, it did affirm that there is no other king, hope, or life apart from Jesus Christ and that "we who hope in the Lord Jesus alone for salvation stand under the inescapable imperative to carry the Gospel to all those who do not know him as Saviour and Lord."[34] Indeed, the PCUS already accepted this view when they adopted the amendments on "The Gospel of the Love of God and Missions" to the *Westminster Confession of Faith* in 1942.[35] Both the amendments to the *Westminster Confession* and the consultation's theological statement emphasized the positive aspects of Christian mission.

In 1960-61 COEMAR carried out an *Advisory Study* a major thrust of which was the unfinished task of integration and "how ecumenical mission could now proceed through ecumenical relations."[36] There were frequent references to Scripture: Jn. 1:1-3, 12:24; 1 Cor. 1:11-14, 26-28; Eph. 1:23; Phil. 2:9; and 1 Tim. 2:4. John's comments on love in Jn. 13:34-35 were used to reinforce the commitment of COEMAR to ecumenical mission and relations.[37] Following COEMAR's study and the Montreat Consultation, there was a renewed attempt to coordinate UPCUSA and PCUS study and planning. This in itself was a sign of reconciliation between the two denominations, divided since 1861.

1967 was the year in which the UPCUSA adopted both a *Book of Confessions* and a new confession of faith known as the *Confession of 1967*. Its major theme was reconciliation, and although no biblical texts were cited by reference the tone was clearly biblical. 2 Cor. 5:18-20 provided the theme of reconciliation and other biblical passages alluded to supported this theme. The *Confession of 1967* asserted that it was "subject to the authority of Jesus Christ, the Word of God, as the Scriptures bear witness to him."[38] Furthermore it stressed the importance of biblical interpretation and pointed out that the words of Scripture are the words of men and are thus conditioned by culture and history. One task of the church in its mission is to approach Scripture from a literary and historical perspective so that God "will continue to speak through the Scriptures in a changing world and in every form of human culture."[39] The hermeneutical principal was clearly stated: "The Bible is to be interpreted in the light of its witness to God's work of reconciliation in Christ."[40]

Significantly the section on the mission of the church immediately follows the section on the Bible. The influence of Barth can be seen in the assertion that Christianity as a religion is distinct from God's revelation of himself and that God's judgment is upon all religions—including Christianity.[41] The gift of God in

Christ is understood to be for all people and the task of the church is to make this revelation known. Once again, a positive stance is taken toward those outside the Christian church. At the same time, however, the ministry of reconciliation is seen to include not only evangelism, but social action in the areas of race relations, war and peace, poverty, and human sexuality.

VI. The Period of One Mission

"And there was given to him the book of the prophet Isaiah. He opened the book and found the place where it was written, 'The Spirit of the Lord is upon me, because he has anointed me to preach good news to the poor. He has sent me to proclaim release to the captives and recovering of sight to the blind, to set at liberty those who are oppressed, to proclaim the acceptable year of the Lord'" (Luke 4:17-19). As American Presbyterians moved into the 1970s it became increasingly evident that national and international mission concerns were directly related. Furthermore, it became more difficult to separate evangelism from social action, for to be reconciled to Christ also meant to be reconciled to one's neighbor. As a result the churches began to speak of one mission.

Such an emphasis was not new, for from 1706 to 1809 "no distinction was drawn between 'domestic' and 'foreign' missions."[42] In 1975 the UPCUSA returned to this policy when COEMAR and the Board of National Missions were merged into the Program Agency. During the reorganization process several mission statements were issued, and one of these—"Theological Perspective and Priority Determination"—begins with the biblical imperative: "Let your bearing towards one another arise out of your life in Christ Jesus" (Phil. 2:5). The statement shows how this "bearing towards one another" has been highlighted in the *Confession of 1967* and a dialogical methodology of mission is proposed whereby the church seeks to put the biblical text into practice.[43]

In 1975 the UPCUSA General Assembly received a document entitled "A Declaration and Call" from a group within the church, the Presbyterians United for Biblical Concerns. The declaration stated that the root cause of the decline in mission personnel and funds was a deficient theology of mission. Specifically the declaration was critical of the emphasis upon social justice and political liberation, interpretations of Scripture that appeared to be unhistorical, and the tendency towards universalism in various mission statements. Six theological affirmations were proposed, the first of which was "faith in the divine inspiration and unique authority of the Bible as the written Word of God. . . ."[44] The declaration called upon the UPCUSA to accept its six-point theological affirmation as the theological foundation for the church's mission and to set up an independent international mission agency that would be separate from the other agencies of the church.

The General Assembly's response to "A Declaration and Call" centered on two points. First, the General Assembly rejected the imposition of another theological statement upon the church other than those already found in the *Book of Confessions*. Second, it rejected the concept of an independent mission board citing the General Assembly actions of 1934 dealing with Machen and the Independent Board for Presbyterian Missions. A brief history of the development of mission theory and policy in the UPCUSA was presented in which special reference was made to the statement of mission drafted by the Joint Committee on Presbyterian Union (UPCUSA/PCUS) and to the *Confession of 1967*.

The joint UPCUSA/PCUS statement of mission has no direct quotes from Scripture, but it does begin with the affirmation that "the mission of the Church is given form and content by God's activity in the world as told in the biblical story and understood by faith."[45] The statement contains many allusions to Scripture and is biblical in its basis, however, mission is definitely understood as one mission of the church in the whole world.

In 1977, after much study and debate, the PCUS General Assembly adopted the document *A Declaration of Faith* "as a contemporary statement of faith, a reliable aid for Christian study, liturgy, and inspiration, with the clear understanding that only the Westminster Standards are constitutional."[46] *A Declaration of Faith*, much like the UPCUSA *Confession of 1967*, does not quote directly from Scripture, but rather alludes to Scripture in an attempt to restate the faith in contemporary language.

In chapter 1, lines 34-39 *A Declaration of Faith* states that "God is at work beyond our story. We know that God is not confined to the story we can tell. The story itself tells us God works his sovereign will among all peoples of the earth. We believe God works beyond our imagining throughout the universe." Biblical references cited to support this statement are Isa. 45; Amos 9:7; Mk. 9:38-41; and Rom. 2:1-16. The Declaration goes on in chapter 7, lines 54-66 to speak of the church's encounter with other faiths: "We do not fully comprehend God's way with other faiths. We need to listen to them with openness and respect" for "we are confident that God judges all faiths, including our own." Here Mt. 2:1-12, 8:15-13; Mk. 7:24-30; Lk. 4:16-30; and Acts 17:22-34 are cited. It should be noted that these two passages which deal specifically with the question of universalism are not included in the chapter on mission, but rather in the chapters on "The Living God" and "The Christian Church." A Declaration of Faith understands the salvation of unbelievers not as a missionary problem, but as a problem related to the nature of God, revelation, and the church.

Chapter 8 of the Declaration—"The Christian Mission"—includes sections on the proclamation of the Gospel, the striving for justice, the exercise of compassion, and the working for peace. Although over ninety biblical passages are listed as forming the biblical basis for mission, it is interesting to note how closely the definition of mission follows the outline of Luke 4:13-19.[47]

In 1978 the PCUS held a second Montreat Mission Consultation with the theme "One Mission Under God" for the purpose of examining future possibilities for mission and setting mission priorities in the PCUS for the next decade. It was a representative consultation involving Christians from all levels of the church, from different denominations, and from many nations. The significance of the consultation is found in its title, for the one mission concept was affirmed in every possible way.

Only one Scripture passage is cited directly in the consultation's final report—Mt. 28:19-20: "Go and make disciples of all nations, baptizing them in the name of the Father and of the Son and of the Holy Spirit, teaching them to observe all that I have commanded you; and lo, I am with you always, to the close of the age." A Declaration of Faith served as the theological foundation for the consultation's report which neither quoted nor referred to the missionary declaration of 1861.[48] However, the 1978 General Assembly directed that a reference to the 1861 declaration and a quote from the Westminster Confession of Faith (X.2, 4) be included in a preface appended to the original report. This was an obvious response to a continuing concern over both universalism and the role of evangelism in mission.

The consultation officially went on record as moving the PCUS away from the doctrine of the spirituality of the church: "The biblical understanding of human rights and obligations embraces the civil, political, social and cultural dimensions of the whole human community."[49] An ecumenical stance was also taken: "The scriptural mandate for one church is clear, but we confess that we are divided within our own denomination and separated from other Christian churches."[50] As the UPCUSA and the PCUS look toward the possibility of reunion during the 1980s this latter concern will undoubtedly take on increasing significance as the search for a hermeneutic of mission continues.

VII. Conclusions

Speaking of the mission of the church being the mission of Jesus Christ, the 1974 UPCUSA General Assembly stated that "the goal of this mission is constant even though its shape and focus differ according to time and place."[51] An examination of the role of biblical authority for mission in the Presbyterian churches since 1930 shows a similar dynamic at work. There can be no doubt that the Bible is viewed as the authority for mission even though the hermeneutic used for interpretation differs according to time and place. Both the UPCUSA and the PCUS have made selective use of Scripture to support the current emphases in mission. Since 1930 one can discern four such emphases: foreign missions, ecumenical mission, ecumenical relations, and one mission. During each period of emphasis biblical texts are selected and interpreted accordingly. In later years both denominations have also made use of the *Confession of 1967* and *A Declaration of Faith* to support their understanding of mission.

In each period, however, several concerns reappear with regularity. One of these is the tension between orthodox theology and church polity that was present in the Machen case. The 1975 Declaration and Call in the UPCUSA and recent movements within the PCUS to form a foundation for evangelism bear this out. Another concern is the question of the salvation of unbelievers and the fear of universalism. With each new mission statement objections are raised because of this fear. The tension between evangelism and social action can be seen in the numbers of Presbyterians who support independent mission boards financially. Still another concern is the apparent movement away from what some perceive to be a biblical theology of mission. Recent mission statements tend to rely more on the *Confession of 1967* and *A Declaration of Faith*, whereas in the past they contained numerous direct quotes from Scripture.

The pluralism in both the UPCUSA and the PCUS presents

still another problem, for there are groups within each denomination who perceive mission from each of the four periods simultaneously. Many national staff persons refer to the one mission concept in their understanding of mission. Overseas national churches, however, emphasize ecumenical relations while some of the missionaries may be thinking in terms of ecumenical mission. Others in the church, both pastors and laity, may see mission primarily in terms of evangelism and foreign missions. Each group tends to be highly selective in choosing biblical texts to support their position with the result that misunderstanding and even conflict may occur. The fact that biblical texts can be found to support all four concepts of mission leads one to suspect that the way out of this hermeneutical dilemma is found in Scripture itself, for the writers of Scripture were no less pluralistic in their understanding of mission than present-day Presbyterians.

NOTES

[1] We shall use PCUSA to refer to the Presbyterian Church in the USA. In 1958 it merged with the United Presbyterian Church of North America to become the UPCUSA, which we shall use for post-1958 dates. Although the PCUS was originally known as the Presbyterian Church in the Confederate States of America, we shall use PCUS throughout.

[2] Morton Howison Smith, *Studies in Southern Presbyterian Theology* (Amsterdam: Drukkerij en Eitgeverij Jacob van Campen, 1962), p. 183.

[3] Ernest Trice Thompson, *The Spirituality of the Church: A Distinctive Doctrine of the Presbyterian Church in the United States* (Richmond: John Knox Press, 1961), p. 40.

[4] Edwin Harold Rian, *The Presbyterian Conflict* (Grand Rapids: Eerdmans, 1940), p. 41 and J. Gresham Machen, *The Attack Upon Princeton Seminary: A Plea for Fair Play* (Philadelphia: privately printed by the author, 1927), p. 6.

[5] For the view of those opposed to Machen see John Vant Stephans, compiler, *An Affirmation (The Auburn Affirmation)* (Cincinnati: privately printed, 1939), p. 22.

[6] See Rian, *op. cit.*, and Lefferts A. Loetscher, *The Broadening Church: A Study of Theological Issues in the Presbyterian Church Since 1869* (Philadelphia: University of Pennsylvania Press, 1954) for two different views of the Machen case and the conflict over Princeton Seminary. For a discussion of the Princeton and Westminster theologies see John C. Vander Stelt, *Philosophy and Scripture: A Study in Old Princeton and Westminster Theology* (Marlton, NJ: Mack Publishing Co., 1978) and Jack B. Rogers and Donald K. McKim, *The Authority and Interpretation of the Bible: An Historical Approach* (San Francisco: Harper & Row, 1979).

[7] Rian, *op. cit.*, p. 146.

[8] The Commission of Appraisal, *Re-Thinking Missions: A Laymen's Inquiry After One Hundred Years* (New York & London: Harper, 1932), p. 325f.

[9] *Ibid.*, pp. 7, 37, 40, 44f., 58.

[10] By 1934 financial contributions to foreign missions in the PCUS had dropped by one-half and the number of missionaires in active service was down to 365.

[11] *Reports of the Commissions, Congress on World Missions* (Nashville: Executive Committee on Foreign Missions, 1931), pp. 3-8.

[12] *Ibid.,* p. 24.

[13] *Ibid.,* p. 25.

[14] *Report of the Decennial Conference on Missionary Policies and Methods of the Board of Foreign Missions of the Presbyterian Church in the USA* (New York: Board of Foreign Missions, PCUSA, [1931]), p. 25.

[15] *Ibid.,* p. 114.

[16] *Minutes of the General Assembly of the Presbyterian Church in the USA* (Philadelphia: Office of the General Assembly, 1933), p. 158. Hereafter referred to as PCUSA or UPCUSA *G.A., Minutes.*

[17] *Ibid.,* p. 159.

[18] *Minutes of the General Assembly of the Presbyterian Church in the Confederate States of America,* 1861, p. 17. PCUS General Assemblies have reaffirmed this 1861 declaration many times, including 1908, 1916, 1935, 1962, and 1978.

[19] *Annual Report* (Nashville: Board of World Missions, PCUS, 1954), p. 24.

[20] *Minutes of the General Assembly of the Presbyterian Church in the US* (Atlanta: Office of the General Assembly, 1954), *Blue Book,* pp. 13ff. Hereafter referred to as PCUS *G.A., Minutes.*

[21] *Ibid.,* p. 5.

[22] William Davidson Blanks, "The Southern Presbyterian View of the Mission of the Church: 1932-1957: A Study in Historical Development" (Th.M. thesis, Union Theological Seminary in Virginia, 1958), p. iii.

[23] PCUS *G.A., Minutes, Blue Book,* 1958, p. 5.

[24] *Report of the World Consultation of the Board of Foreign Missions of the Presbyterian Church in the USA Held at Mountain House, Lake Mohonk, New York—22 April-1, May 1956* (mimeographed), pp. 24f., 38, 73ff. See also William Richey Hogg, *New Day Dawning* (New York: World Horizons, 1957).

[25] Hogg, *New Day Dawning,* pp. 56f.

[26] *Ibid.,* p. 11.

[27] *Introductory Information on the Commission on Ecumenical Mission and Relations* (New York: COEMAR of the UPCUSA, 1958), p. 7.

[28] *Ibid.,* p. 9.

[29] PCUS *G.A., Minutes,* 1961, p. 74.

[30] Ernest Trice Thompson, *Presbyterians in the South,* Vol. 3: 1890-1972 (Richmond: John Knox Press, 1973), p. 440.

[31] *Consultation Workbook* (Nashville: Board of World Missions, 1962), p. 31.

[32] *Ibid.,* p. 8.

[33] *Ibid.,* p. 31.

[34] *Ibid.,* p. 7.

[35] The *Westminster Confession of Faith,* Chapter XXXV, "Of the Gospel of the Love of God and Missions." These amendments were adopted by the PCUSA in 1903 and by the PCUS in 1942.

[36] *An Advisory Study, 1961-1966: A Report on the Study Process* (New York: COEMAR of the UPCUSA, 1966), p. 1.

[37] *An Advisory Study* (New York: COEMAR of the UPCUSA, [1966]), p. 91.

[38] *Confession of 1967, Book of Confessions,* second edition (Philadelphia: Office of the General Assembly, 1970), sec. 9.03.

[39] *Ibid.*, sec. 9.29.

[40] *Ibid.*

[41] *Ibid.*, sec. 9.41f.

[42] Andrew T. Roy, "Overseas Mission Policies—an Historical Overview," *Journal of Presbyterian History* 57:3 (Fall 1979), 187.

[43] *Theological Perspective and Priority Determination* (New York: The Program Agency, UPCUSA, 1975), pp. 3f.

[44] UPCUSA *G.A., Minutes*, 1975, p. 335.

[45] *Ibid.* This statement is included as Appendix A to the General Assembly's response to A Declaration and Call.

[46] *A Declaration of Faith* (Atlanta: Presbyterian Church in the US, 1977), taken from inside the front cover.

[47] *Ibid.*, p. 28, from the cross-index of biblical passages upon which *A Declaration of Faith* is based.

[48] The 1978 Montreat Consultation strongly emphasized the place of social justice in mission. The 1861 missionary declaration was made by the same General Assembly that put forth an impassioned theological defense of slavery. See *A Digest of the Acts and Proceedings of the General Assembly of the PCUS, 1861-1965* (Atlanta: Office of the General Assembly, 1966), pp. 26-35. No doubt the 1978 Montreat Consultation thought it inappropriate to include a mission declaration that had arisen from a context of social injustice.

[49] *One Mission Under God: Report of the 1978 Mission Consultation of the Presbyterian Church in the Unites States* (Atlanta: Office of the Stated Clerk, 1978), p. 10.

[50] *Ibid.*, p. 11.

[51] UPCUSA *G.A., Minutes*, 1974, p. 130.

For Discussion

This study examines the mission statements of the United Presbyterian Church in the USA and of the Presbyterian Church in the US and their antecedent denominations, in an attempt to identify the manner in which differing interpretations of the biblical message have influenced their concept of mission. The author examines factors which have contributed to differences in interpretation and which of these factors may be sources of conflict in the future.

The following statements and questions provide a basis for discussion of the sections of the study.

I. Introduction

The understanding of biblical authority for mission has been influenced by three historical developments in American Presbyterianism. Identify these elements and keep them in mind as you trace the changes that have taken place in the concepts of mission since 1930.

II. The Point of Change

Identify and discuss the theological shifts that took place in the churches beginning in 1930. What is the biblical basis for pluralism? What challenge does pluralism offer to mission endeavor? How did the social gospel movement affect the church's view of mission?

III. The Period of Foreign Missions

What was the impact on mission policy of the Chattanooga Conference in 1931? How did the Lakeville Conference try to reconcile the voice of Scripture and the social gospel? Do these conflicting views of the biblical basis for mission affect our understanding of mission today? How? Why would some in the church object to the concept of comity agreements? What is your understanding of "ecumenical" mission? How does this concept differ from previous mission policy? What do you think Jesus meant by preaching the Gospel to the whole creation?

IV. The Period of Ecumenical Mission

Read: Mark 1;15, 13;10; John 3:16; I Corinthians 15:24; II Corinthians 5:14; Galatians 4:4-5. Using the biblical statements, how would you define the nature of mission? How does John 17:21 relate to your definitions? What was the significance of the change of name of the UPCUSA's Board of Foreign Missions to the Commission on Ecumenical Mission and Relations?

V. The Period of Ecumenical Relations

II Corinthians 5:18-20 speaks of a ministry of reconciliation. How does this concept affect one's view of the nature of the church's mission enterprise? How do you define "global mission?" How does the call to evangelism relate to the concept of global mission? How do you relate the theme of reconciliation to the Christian view of those outside the faith? What areas of life does reconciliation include?

VI. The Period of One Mission

Read Luke 4:17-19. How does this speak to national and international mission? To social concerns of the church? What does the term "one mission" mean to you? How does the formation of The Program Agency in the UPCUSA reflect these concerns?

Does the concept "one mission" pose a theological universalism? Chapters one and eight of *A Declaration of Faith* understand the salvation of unbelievers to be a problem related to the nature and work of God, not as a mission problem. Do you agree? Why? Does the concept of "one mission" negate evangelistic mission endeavor?

VII. Conclusions

There seems to be in the church tension between evangelism and social action, pluralism and particularism in our view of mission. This tension is reflected in Scripture. Read the Scripture references in this chapter again. What viewpoint does each seem to support: evangelism, pluralism, "foreign" mission, "one" mission, social concerns, etc. List those things you feel the Scripture seems to be mandating in regard to our mission enterprise.

Charles A. Briggs and the
Organic Reunion of Christendom

John J. Feeney, Jr.

I t is common practice for historians of American religion to characterize Charles A. Briggs as one of America's most gifted, German-trained Old Testament scholars whose uncommon ability in the higher critical study of biblical theology made him the central figure in one of the most sensational and highly publicized heresy trials in nineteenth-century America. Both Clifton Olmstead and Sydney Ahlstrom view Briggs as a clergyman who departed from a strict view of inerrancy and verbal inspiration in his biblical scholarship and by so doing stimulated his Presbyterian brethren to try him in one of America's most "sensational heresy cases." Moreover, Ahlstrom and Lefferts Loetscher suggests that Briggs was "America's leading Old Testament scholar." Loetscher in particular found Briggs' view of Scripture to be "dynamic and progressive" even as Briggs "thought of ultimate Christian truths in terms of historic orthodoxy strongly tinged with Calvinism." This view of Briggs as a theologically conservative heretic informed the one sustained attempt to write an intellectual biography of him, Max G. Rogers' 1964 Columbia University doctoral dissertation, "Charles Augustus Briggs: Conservative Heretic." Devoting nearly three-fourths of his dissertation to Briggs' biblical scholarship, and the heresy trials, Rogers argues convincingly that Briggs attempted to implement a "moderate form" of the higher critical method. By seeking to "steer a mediating course" between ultraconservative biblical scholarship and the conclusions of Kuenen and Wellhausen, Briggs alienated his fellow Presbyterians and brought his trial and ultimate conviction for heresy.[1]

    John J. Feeney, Jr., is a research assistant for a law firm in Flagstaff, Arizona.
—*Editor's note.*
    [1]Clifton E. Olmstead, *History of Religion in the United States* (Englewood Cliffs: Prentice Hall, 1960), p. 470. Sydney E. Ahlstrom, *A Religious History of the American People* (New Haven: Yale University Press, 1972), pp. 814, 777. Lefferts A. Loetscher, "Charles A. Briggs in the Retrospect of Half a Century,"

There can be no doubt that these various views of Briggs are well supported by the evidence. However, it is important to complement them with
another view of him, one that has never been fully analyzed—that of Briggs,
the committed Christian ecumenist. Briggs' ecumenical concern has com-
monly been associated with the final twenty years of his life, although at
least one student of him has noted that it "first appeared quite early."[2] An
analysis of Briggs' ecumenical thinking contained in his published writings
indicates that his interest in Christian unity not only emerged when he first
began to engage in serious theological studies but was also as much a controlling factor in his theological and biblical studies during the 1870's and
1880's as it was in his later years. Briggs' theological studies during the
late 1860's enabled him to derive a central idea that informed both his
subsequent ecumenical thinking and his scriptural studies. Convinced that
God's best works in creation exhibited the same organic unity that animated
His trinitarian being, Briggs believed that both the Church of God and
Holy Scripture must manifest this same type of unity. In the 1870's and
1880's Briggs naively felt that the dynamic spirit of unity was so power-
fully at work in the Christian churches that it was sufficient for him to aid
it through a biblical theology that exhibited the organic unity of scripture
and its image of the Church as a mystical body consisting in various members.

Discovering that the solution to church unity was not this simple when his
own Presbyterian denomination splintered apart under the pressure of higher criticism and confessional revision, Briggs set out to define a more practical plan for church unity. In advocating federal union as a means to a more
solid organic union of Christendom, Briggs conceived in the late 1880's an
embryonic vision of the reunited church. Prevented by the ordeal of his
heresy trial from fully exploring this vision, Briggs returned to it after the
proceedings. The heresy proceedings and the Catholic modernist controversy sharpened Briggs' early concern for limiting ecclesiastical authority in
order to achieve unity while his association with Anglicanism and his renewed interest in New Testament exegesis firmly convinced him of the
necessity for apostolic succession and the papacy in the Church of Christ, a
belief he had cultivated as early as the late 1880's. Stimulated by these
concerns and events, Briggs fully explored and constructively expanded
what he had considered at the time of the revision controversy to be the
main problems confronting the organic union of Christendom. By the end

---

Theology Today, XII (April, 1955), p. 41. Max G. Rogers, "Charles Augustus
Briggs: Conservative Heretic," Ph.D. Dissertation, Columbia University, 1964, ii.
William R. Hutchison, *The Modernist Impulse* (Harvard University Press, 1976),
Chapters 3 and 5.

[2]Rogers, *ibid.*, pp. 383, 488. See also Arthur Cushman McGiffert's biographical
sketch of Briggs in the *Dictionary of American Biography* (II, pp. 40–41) for a
good statement of the view that Briggs' ecumenical interests were primarily confined to his later years.

of his life he had developed both an ecclesiastical and a doctrinal plan for organic church unity that still made room for the particular characteristics of the various members of Christ's Mystical Body.

The origin of Charles A. Briggs' ecumenical persuasion can be traced back to the time of his conversion experience. In the fall of 1858, Briggs experienced a religious conversion; and at the suggestion of his uncle, Marvin, he joined the Christian Association at the University of Virginia where he was then enrolled. The question of denominational affiliation immediately arose. Having reared his son in the Methodist communion, it was not surprising that Briggs' father, Alanson T. Briggs, should urge his son to join the Methodist Church. "I suppose that you know that I am strongly in favor of the Methodists and I think you would like to make yourself abundantly useful in the world," his father wrote in December, 1858. "Your father's advice is to unite with the Methodists for they are the safest."[3] While Charles Briggs later admitted that "early life among the Methodists gave me sympathy with Arminianism," the influence of his uncle, Marvin, who was then studying at Princeton Theological Seminary, impelled him "deliberately" to follow Calvinism.[4] While at first undecided whether to join the Episcopal or the Presbyterian Church, Charles eventually joined the church of which Marvin Briggs had been a member, the First Presbyterian Church of Charlottesville. Briggs' Christian ecstasy grew steadily and found expression in numerous letters to his sister. In them he scarcely mentioned ecclesiastical affiliation but instead urged her "to be a Christian" simply by acknowledging Christ to be her savior. Briggs' indecision about denominational affiliation and his belief, expressed in letters to his sister, that the essence of Christianity was union with Christ, make it clear that denominational boundaries were of small importance in his early Christian experience.

Briggs' persuasion to minimize the importance of denominational structures was strengthened by his experience as a student in Germany following the Civil War. While there, Briggs became acutely aware of the ecclesiastical party structure in Germany.[5] Though generally sympatheic to Lutheranism, Briggs could not identify himself with its efforts to become the national church of Germany. Nor could he identify himself with the Protestant Association; for while it sought unity among the churches of Germany, it insisted "on perfect freedom in doctrine and preaching without any confessional restrictions." On the other hand, Briggs was not only sympathetic with but enthusiastic about the Evangelical Union party since its advocates (among whom was one of his principal German mentors, Isaac A.

[3]Alanson Briggs to Charles A. Briggs, December 7, 1858, Briggs Transcripts, III, pp. 180–181, #41 quoted in Rogers, p. 7.
[4]Charles A. Briggs, *Church Unity* (New York: Charles Scribner's Sons, 1909), p. 16.
[5]Charles A. Briggs, "Theological and Literary Intelligence: Germany," *American Presbyterian Review*, New Series, I, 1869, p. 420.

Dorner of Berlin) were struggling not only against rationalism and Protestant scholasticism but "for *Union* of the fundamental principles of the Reformation." Briggs was confident about their ultimate success both because of their adherence to the "fundamental principles of the Reformation" and "for their sympathy with the spirit of the times, which is for Union." Their success, Briggs believed, was virtually certain because of their "stress to evangelize the people and give them a place in the church." Briggs' association with members of the Evangelical Union party had convinced him that the "period of disintegration has passed," and "the period of integration is in progress in church and state."[6]

In addition to his association with Germany's Evangelical Union party, Briggs' biblical studies in Germany were equally important in molding his conviction that Christian union was a vital part of the spirit of his age. As a result of his biblical studies, Briggs became acutely aware of the variety in Holy Scripture. Engaging in the higher critical study of the Old Testament under Heinrich G. A. Ewald, Briggs investgiated the literary character of the four documents of the Hexateuch and was persuaded beyond a reasonable doubt that Moses could not have written the entire Pentateuch. In addition, Briggs became aware of the work of German New Testament Scholars such as F. C. Baur and D. F. Strauss. While he found their conclusions unacceptable, he was nevertheless forced to concede that each Gospel presented a different conception of Jesus Christ and that there existed in the New Testament epistles a great theological variety. In view of this, Briggs' problem, as he confided it to Henry Boynton Smith in 1868, was to find "a truer and higher harmony—a unity all the more striking than the diversity of the elements" in Holy Scripture.[7] In this manner Briggs could maintain that the higher critical method actually confirmed the Bible to be the unified and inspired Word of God.

Briggs' solution, which he called the "evangelical position," amounted to an orthodox version of the transience and permanence in the Judeo-Christian tradition. Distinguishing between the form and the substance of Holy Scripture, Briggs maintained that the scriptures were "vessels of the most holy character" that "have come into contact with the forces of this world, with human weakness, ignorance, prejudice, and folly; their forms have been modified in the course of generations, but their divine content remains unchanged."[8] As a result the Holy Scriptures consist in a great variety of expressions, but underlying all of the variety is a unity that runs through both the Old and the New Testaments. "The true evangelical position is that the Bible is a vast organism in which the unity springs from

[6]*Ibid.*, pp. 420–421.

[7]Charles A. Briggs to Henry B. Smith, May 6, 1866, quoted in Loetscher, *op. cit.*, p. 28.

[8]Charles A. Briggs, *Biblical Study* (New York: Charles Scribner's Sons, 1883), p. 160.

an amazing variety . . . It is the unity that one finds in the best works of God." God's best work in creation had been his incarnation in Jesus Christ which manifested the perfect organic union of the divine and human. Just as the divine and human natures achieved a perfect organic unity in Christ, so too were the Father, Son, and Holy Spirit organically united in trinitarian variety. Affirming the organic unity of God's trinitarian being, Briggs believed that all of God's "best works" in creation partook of this same kind of variety. While His inspired Word resulted from the work of numerous writers and redactors in various periods of biblical history, its substance was inspired and unified by the energy of God's Holy Spirit such that it was "an organism, complete and symmetrical, one as God is one, and thus only divine and human as the complete revelation of the God-man."[9]

Historians who have studied Briggs' biblical theology have generally centered their discussion on his attempts to fathom the higher unity within the variety of the Old Testament. Nevertheless, it is important to note that just as Briggs sought a higher unity in the Old Testament's variety, so he sought a higher unity in that of the New. The central figure who aided him in this quest was Johann A. W. Neander. "The noble Neander," Briggs declared, "sought to distinguish the individualities of the various sacred writers in their conceptions of Christianity and to unite them into a higher unity."[10] In his *History of the Planting and Training of the Christian Church by the Apostles* (1832), Neander claimed that the doctrine of Christ was given as the Word of the Spirit of God to a variety of men. Enlightened by the Holy Spirit, men appropriated the doctrine "according to their respective differences in education and manner." These differences in turn manifested themselves in the "living unity . . . of the Christian spirit according to the various modes of human conceptions, unconsciously complementing and explaining each other." In this way God insured that Christianity was meant for all men in that it adapted itself to the needs of the most varied human characters. While he remained critical of some aspects of Neander's work, Briggs accepted Neander's contention that the unity of the New Testament writers' conception of Christ "will appear the more remarkable as the theology of Jesus, in its organic unity, shines forth through the variety of their conceptions."[11]

Briggs believed firmly that Neander's approach to biblical theology was vitally important to his own age. For one thing, an awareness of the unity in the variety of scriptural doctrine would easily "enable the skillful pastor to apply to each soul the precise tendencies of doctrine that he needed to speak to men through minds kindred to their own." But more importantly,

---

[9]*Ibid.*, pp. 359, 38.
[10]Charles A. Briggs, "Biblical Theology with Especial Reference to the New Testament," *American Presbyterian Review*, New Series, II, 1870, p. 111.
[11]*Ibid.*, pp. 130, 301.

Briggs believed that such an approach was essential to the reunion of Christendom. "Biblical Theology may also have an important influence upon the union tendencies of our time," Briggs asserted, "for, in exhibiting the diversities of view in the apostolic church, it will enable churches, representing different phases of human nature, corresponding more or less with the scripture differences, to come closer together in the spirit of Christian charity, according to the example given in biblical theology."[12] As early as 1870, therefore, Briggs believed that church unity and modern biblical theology reinforced one another. Both the church and the scriptures were organic wholes consisting in a variety of different parts. By demonstrating the organic unity of scripture, biblical theology would make it clear to all Christians that the Church of Christ was one body consisting in diverse members. "The spirit of Christian union," Briggs proclaimed confidently in 1870, "is presented on the very face of Biblical Theology."[13]

Confident that Christian unity was a vital part of the spirit of his age and convinced that biblical theology in the best German sense of the discipline could best further the cause of union, it is not surprising that Briggs devoted most of his energy to biblical scholarship in the decade and a half after his return from Germany. For at least the first fifteen years following his return, Briggs' pronouncements about church unity were subordinated to the activity that was necessary to pave the way to union, biblical theology. While the absence of explicit pronouncements about church unity by Briggs during the 1870's and early 1880's was in part due to this, the ecclesiastical situation of his own Presbyterian denomination was also a contributing factor. The Old and the New Schools of the Presbyterian Church had agreed to a compact of union in 1870, and according to Lefferts Loetscher, the "honeymoon" following their marriage lasted for a good decade and a half.[14] In this atmosphere it is not surprising that Briggs should become even more firmly convinced that God's spirit was working for church unity in his own age. During the 1870's and early 1880's, Briggs regarded his work in the discipline of biblical theology and his co-editorship of the *Presbyterian Review*, a journal which manifested visibly the spirit of Old and New School union, as a vital contribution to his own denomination's unity and to the cause of the organic union of all Christendom.

In addition to his work in biblical theology, Briggs "desired to promote unity by instructing the reunited church in the historic sense of its own standards." This desire informed Briggs' volume, *American Presbyterianism* (1885). "We desire the organic union of all of the branches of the Presbyterian family in a broad, comprehensive, generous, catholic Presbyteri-

---

[12]*Ibid.*, p. 306.
[13]*Ibid.*
[14]Lefferts Loetscher, *The Broadening Church* (Philadelphia: University of Pennsylvania Press, 1954), pp. 1–150, *passim.*

anism," Briggs asserted.[15] Since Briggs was primarily concerned with fostering union in his own denomination, his focus in this volume was denominationally limited. He was primarily concerned with showing how all of the churches of the Reformation could be bound together by the "organic principle of Puritanism," the Westminister Confession of Faith. Notwithstanding his interest in purely Protestant union, Briggs noted that he was also interested in "the Ultimate reunion of Christendom." Even at this point in his irenic thinking, Briggs felt that Presbyterianism was "not a finality" and that it would be foolish for anyone truly interested in the organic union of all Christendom to think so. Rather, both Protestantism in general and Presbyterianism in particular must be viewed as "a stepping-stone" to a higher form of Christianity "which will transcend the Protestant Reformation by its omnipotent energy and world-wide sweep."

Briggs' attempt to use denominational history as a vehicle by which to strengthen the unity of his own church may very well have been generated by his sense that Presbyterian union was beginning to crumble. The harmonious relationship between the Old and New Schools began to wane in the early 1880's, and by the end of the decade it had been rent asunder. Two significant factors that contributed to this breakdown have an important bearing on Briggs' ecumenical thinking. One of these was the issue of biblical criticism. The Old School had traditionally been committed to a theory of inspiration rooted in the verbal inerrancy of the original autographs of Holy Scripture, and it viewed higher critical scholarship like that practiced by Briggs as a threat to a theory that it believed to be an essential foundation of Christianity. Briggs became personally involved in this aspect of the Old and New School controversy when he publicly attacked William Henry Green, general editor of the American edition of the Revised Version of the Old Testament, for objecting to the inclusion in the American edition of any findings derived from higher criticism. In addition, the issue of confessional revision exacerbated tensions created by the issue of higher criticism. In 1889 the General Assembly of the Presbyterian Church confronted the individual presbyteries with the issue of revising the Westminister Confession of Faith. Reaction to the issue generally divided along traditional party lines, with the Old School members disapproving revision and the New School members favoring it. At first Briggs opposed confessional revision, "but subsequently, seeing that the movement was an earnest and powerful one" and sensing that it was necessary to take sides, he "could not refrain from joining the party of progress." As Max G. Rogers has pointed out, "the strain of higher criticism together with the added burden of the revision controversy proved too great for the two parties."[16]

---

[15]Charles A. Briggs, *American Presbyterianism* (New York: Charles Scribner's Sons, 1885), xii–xiii.
[16]Rogers, *op. cit.*, pp. 75–84.

Hence, the bond between Old and New School Presbyterians had been effectively dissolved by 1889.

Because the issue of higher criticism had been central to the distintegration of Presbyterian union, Briggs sensed that church unity could no longer flow naturally from an awareness of the unity in scriptural variety. Briggs, however, never abandoned his conviction that organic Christian union was rooted in the idea of the organic unity of all God's created works. In fact, Briggs summoned all of his exegetical powers in order to argue that the predominance of organic metaphors used by scriptural writers to depict Christ's Church made it imperative for Christians to mend their divisions and respond to the spirit of union. All of the conceptions of the New Testament evangelists proclaim the unity of the Church "in Christ the head," Briggs argued.[17] While they "set forth in various forms and from different points of view the unique relation of Christ and his disciples," they all spoke of this relation as an organically united whole through such images as "body," "head," "flock," and "family."[18] This highly sustained understanding of the ideal of organic union was directly related to Briggs' higher critical exegesis of the New Testament which he began in the mid-1880's and which he hoped would yield two volumes dealing with the messianic conceptions of the Gospel writers and of the apostles. While his involvement in the revision controversy prevented the immediate publication of these volumes, the work on them had been substantially completed prior to it.[19] Briggs was thus able to bring the fruits of his higher critical analysis of the New Testament to bear on the problems of revision and church unity.

The revision controversy not only led Briggs to think out more systematically the biblical roots of his initial conception of organic church unity; it also impelled him to consider the practical problems confronting Christian union in his own time. In *Whither?* (1889) Briggs enumerated a series of barriers to Christian unity. The first of these which he characterized as the "great sin of the Roman Catholic Church" was "the theory of submission to a central ecclesiastical authority claiming divine right of government." Another, of which the Lutheran and reformed Churches were

[17]Charles A. Briggs, *Whither? A Theological Question for the Times* (New York: Charles Scribner's Sons, 1889), p. 290.

[18]*Ibid.*, p. 292.

[19]Charles A. Briggs, *The Messiah of the Gospels* (New York: Charles Scribner's Sons, 1894), vi–vii. "In the autumn of 1886 the volume entitled *Messianic Prophecy* was published as the first volume of a series of volumes on the Messianic Ideal," Briggs stated in the Preface to this volume. "It was my intention at that time to publish the second volume of the series a short time after the first. The material had already been gathered and it was put in the form of a volume in the summer of 1888. But the Revision movement in the Presbyterian Church, U.S.A., made it a duty to take my share in that great ecclesiastical struggle. Some of the fruits of these labors appeared in the volume, *Whither?*, 1889, and *How Shall We Revise*, 1890." vii.

guilty, involved "the subscription to elaborate creeds." A third barrier to Christian union which Briggs found most evident in the Church of England was the insistence "upon uniformity of worship." Finally, Briggs was distressed that the reformed churches had become so obsessed with creeds and confessional affirmation that they had neglected the place of the sacraments in Christian life.[20] By focusing on these four barriers to church unity, Briggs made it clear that the issues of ecclesiastical jurisdiction and authority, creedal subscription, the nature of Christian worship, and the sacraments were important aspects of his ecumenical thought at this point in his life even though the fury of the revision controversy prevented him from formulating positive ways of dealing with them.

During the revision controversy, Briggs came to believe that the Chicago-Lambeth Quadrilateral offered a constructive and workable framework for church unity. Originally conceived in 1865 by the American Anglican ecumenist William R. Huntington and widely propounded in his book, *The Church-Idea, An Essay toward Unity*, first published in 1870, the Quadrilateral was adopted in 1886 by the General Convention of the Episcopal Church and by the Lambeth Conference in 1888.[21] The Quadrilateral consisted in four essential points. The first point of the Quadrilateral asserted that the Old and the New Testaments were the revealed word of God while the second point proclaimed the primitive creeds, such as the Nicene Creed, to be a sufficient statement of the Christian faith. The third point acknowledged the necessity of the two sacraments of Baptism and the Lord's Supper ordained by Christ and administered with His words of institution. Finally, the fourth point called for the adoption of the historic Episcopate as the central feature of church government.

Asserting that the proposals were "entirely satisfactory" to him "provided nothing more is meant by their authors than their language expressly conveys," Briggs argued that no right-thinking Presbyterian could possibly object to the first and third propositions for union.[22] The second, which held the Nicene Creed to be the sufficient statement of the Christian faith, could be viewed by some Presbyterians as insufficient when compared to the Westminister Confession, Briggs felt. Yet he quickly added that Presbyterians who were truly interested in Christian union simply could not "exact from other religious bodies the maximum of the Westminister standards." At this point Briggs felt the Presbyterians should be conciliatory. "If Episcopalians are willing to waive their own doctrinal standards in order to unify, I do not see with what propriety other denominations can refuse to meet them on this common platform," Briggs contended. "It is

[20]Charles A. Briggs, *Whither?*, p. 295.

[21]John F. Woolverton, "Huntington's Quadrilateral—A Critical Study," *Church History* Vol. 39 (June, 1970), pp. 198–211.

[22]Charles A. Briggs, "The Historic Episcopate as a Basis of Reunion" in *Church Union on the Basis of the Lambeth Conference Propositions of 1888* (New York: Church Review Co.), p. 48–49.

not proposed that the denominations should abandon their own symbols of faith, but that they should find a common ground for unity."

The issue of the historic episcopate as a basis for church unity was a far more prickly proposition. Sensing this, Briggs devoted much intellectual energy to the problem of how it could be made acceptable to his Presbyterian brethren. His solution centered on an analogy between church and civil government. Just as civil government contained an executive and legislative component, so too should church government. While the legislative component of church government found its ideal embodiment in the New Testament concept of the presbytery, the executive component was embodied in the evolution of the historic episcopate. "The Presbytery needs an executive head who shall be relieved from the cares of a local church and be consecrated to the superintendency of the whole church in the limits of the Presbytery," Briggs maintained. "Why not call him a bishop? The tendency in the Presbyterian Church is toward such a bishop, who will give the presbytery an executive head and make it more efficient."[23] Briggs believed that modern biblical scholarship had vanquished "*jure divino* theories" about the New Testament origins of the diocesan bishop. Although he did not believe that episcopacy was essential to the well being of the church, Briggs believed that it was important. In trying to convince his Presbyterian brethren of this Briggs noted that by combining the executive function of the episcopate and the legislative function of the presbytery, the reunited church could "enter into the inheritance of both."[24]

While Briggs spoke of the need for the historic episcopate primarily in practical terms, he was not willing merely to accept it on the basis of expediency. Even though he did not find its origins in the New Testament, Briggs felt that it resulted from a divinely informed evolution of the New Testament presbytery. "Although there were no other bishops in New Testament times than presbyteries," the historic episcopate still "was a legitimate and inevitable result of a bench or body of presbyteries that one should have the management of affairs, be the executive head, and preside over the government of the local church," Briggs asserted. In so doing he was firmly convinced that the "Church, guided by the *Divine Spirit*, did not err in its Episcopal government through all these centuries."[25] Implicit in this view is a theory of history that undergirded all of Briggs' thinking about church unity. At Pentecost, God gave his Holy Spirit to the Church to watch over it and guide it through all succeeding centuries. The presence of the spirit injected a sacred component into the church's temporal development. It was that sacred energy that informed the evolution of the presbytery "until the archbishop, patriarch, and pope, one after the

[23]*Ibid.*, p. 49.
[24]Charles A. Briggs, "Federation," *The Churchman*, June 21, 1890, p. 821.
[25]Charles A. Briggs, "The Historic Episcopate as a Basis of Reunion," pp. 58–59.

other gave expression to the higher unities of the growing Church of CHRIST."

Affirming the dynamic character of the church, Briggs speculated that "Christendom might unite with an ascending series of superintending bishops that would culminate in a universal bishop, provided that the pyramid would be willing to rest firmly on its base, the solid order of the presbyter-bishop of the New Testament."[26] Such a vision suggests that Briggs' exegesis of the New Testament was even now deepening his sense of the validity of the apostolic commission given to Peter in Matthew XVI: 17–20. Yet as his phrasing suggests, Briggs' vision of Christendom reunited on the foundation of the New Testament presbyter-bishop with an ascending hierarchy culminating in a universal bishop (or pope) was couched in very tentative terms. This hesitancy may be due in part to Briggs' sense that neither Presbyterians nor other Protestants were ready to think of church union in terms of an episcopal structure. It is also quite possible that the pressure of the revision controversy did not allow Briggs sufficient time to think out completely the theoretical and practical implications of the apostolic commission.

At the time of the revision controversy Briggs was admittedly more concerned with the practical and pressing need to forge unity than he was with the systematic foundations of his theory or organic Christian union. In addition to advocating the proposal of the Lambeth Conference, Briggs centered much of his attention on a number of efforts in the late nineteenth century to create "alliances of kindred churches." Since the 1870's Briggs had been aware of efforts by the reformed church to define a consensus and unite behind it. Noting that all denominations held general conferences, Briggs saw no reason why they could not send representatives to a more general conference whose purpose was to define a consensus for unity. Briggs believed that such denominational federation was an important step to organic church unity and could be easily accepted by his Presbyterian brethren who thought of church organization in the form of assemblies and councils and who would, therefore, naturally "look for church unity through the principle of federation."[27]

However, Briggs was firmly convinced that federation was "only preparatory to closer union." Federation by its very nature was transient since the unity resulting from it stemmed from a particular purpose common to all parties concerned at a particular point in time. With the passing of time the purpose which brought diverse denominations together would pass away; and with its passing, unity would crumble. In order to prevent this, Briggs believed that denominational confederation with a view toward ultimate consolidation was the only way that the organic union of Christen-

[26]Charles A. Briggs, *Whither?*, p. 238. Quoted also in "The Historic Episcopate," p. 60.
    [27]Charles A. Briggs, "Federation," p. 821.

dom could be achieved at the time of the revision controversy. Organic union could come about "by way of federation in the constitution of a council representing the supreme courts of all the denominations" whose specific purpose would be "to arrange for the mutual recognition of the ministry and work of the several branches of the reunited church." By asserting that he saw "no other way of overcoming the separation" of Christian churches "than by organic unity, by confederation first and consolidation afterward," Briggs was attempting to channel the movement toward federation which he still believed to be a vital one into a movement that would launch a new era of progress in Christian history.[28]

Briggs' vision of an organically united Christendom was so powerful that he found all existing denominations wanting by comparison. As a spokesman for Christian union Briggs felt it to be his duty to make Protestants, as well as Catholics, aware of this so that they might reconcile their differences and strive together for unity. An opportunity arose in 1889 when Briggs was transferred to the newly created Edward Robinson Professorship of Biblical Theology in Union Theological Seminary. His inaugural address, "The Authority of the Holy Scriptures", has so frequently been viewed in light of the heresy trial it provoked that it is seldom noted that the address was penned in the heat of the revision controversy when Briggs was applying his intellectual energies to the problem of church unity. While there can be little question that the tone of the address was warlike and polemical, it is important to realize that much of the content and spirit of the address was directed toward the problem of church unity.[29]

The central thesis of Briggs' inaugural address—that there are "historically three great fountains of divine authority: The Bible, the Church, and the Reason"—is a familiar one.[30] Briggs argued that God speaks to men through the Bible, the church, and the reason. While the Bible contains God's revealed word, the church is Christ's kingdom; and because it is inhabited by the Holy Spirit, it provides men with access to God. The reason, which Briggs termed "the Holy of Holies of human nature," is the center of man's conscience and religious feelings; and God works through it in order to convince men of the truths of Christianity. "If God really speaks to men in these centers, there ought to be no contradiction between them," Briggs argued. "They ought to be complementary, and they should combine in a higher unity for the guidance and comfort of men." In view of this ideal, all branches of Christendom were found wanting. "Protestant Chris-

---

[28]Charles A. Briggs, *Whither?*, p. 7–8.

[29]Henry Preserved Smith, "Charles A. Briggs," *The American Theological Review*, XVII, No. 4 (October, 1913), p. 507. Smith is one of the few scholars to note the extent to which Briggs' writing at the time of his heresy trial was directed to the problem of church unity.

[30]Charles A. Briggs, *The Authority of the Holy Scriptures*, 2nd edition, (New York: Charles Scribner's Sons, 1891), p. 24.

tianity builds its faith and life on the divine authority" of the Bible "and too often deprecates the Church and the Reason" while Roman Catholicism exalts the Church by placing its tradition on an equal footing with God's revealed Word. Moreover, the mystics whose reason makes them "conscious of the divine presence within them," have "deprecated the Bible and the Church as merely external modes of finding God." In order to strive for the ideal of an organic unity, all branches of Christendom must admit the harmony of the Bible, the church, and the reason as sources of divine authority and cease to exalt one over the other, Briggs contended. By so doing they would "cut down everything that is dead and harmful, every kind of dead orthodoxy, every species of effete ecclesiasticism, all merely formal moralities, all those dry and brittle fences that constitute denominationalism, and are the barriers of Church Unity."[31]

Briggs' unconciliatory tone clearly obscured his plea for unity. His warlike images and his insistence on sources of divine authority other than the Bible were sufficient to anger a faction of the Presbyterian church which believed that the ultimate authority of a verbally inerrant Bible was essential to the validity of Christian faith. Turning the wheels of ecclesiastical machinery against Briggs, this faction initiated heresy proceedings against him. The story of these proceedings is a familiar chapter in the history of American religion. It is important to remember that apart from the substantive issues of scriptural and doctrinal interpretation, Briggs maintained that the procedural issues were of central importance to the proceedings against him.[32] A large portion of his own defense centered on whether or not the appeal of his 1891 acquittal by the New York City presbytery could be legally entertained by the General Assembly. This aspect of his defense indicates clearly Briggs' interest in the relationship between inferior and superior ecclesiastical judicial bodies and has an important bearing on his subsequent ecumenical thinking. Believing, whether correctly or not, that the General Assembly had exceeded its authority by entertaining the appeal of his 1891 acquittal, Briggs became acutely sensitive to the need to limit significantly the power of supreme ecclesiastical judicatories.

Even before the heresy trial Briggs had claimed that the issue of ecclesiastical jurisdiction and authority was a barrier to Christian union. His own experience between 1890 and 1893 had intensified and sharpened this conviction. Hence, four years after the 1893 trial Briggs attempted to define ways that would limit supreme ecclesiastical jurisdiction and authority in order to pave the way for organic Christian union. Writing in 1897, Briggs maintained that "no one can survey the history of Christ's Church without seeing very plainly that the disruption of the church has been due in the main to the intolerable tyranny of the appellate judicatories in the Church."[33]

[31]*Ibid.*, pp. 64, 28, 26, 67.
[32]Rogers, *op. cit.*, pp. 383, 293.
[33]Charles A. Briggs, "Ecclesiastical Jurisdiction and Church Unity," *The New World*, VI (March, 1897), p. 122.

While he felt that church unity could not exist unless there was a unified appellate judicatory, Briggs believed that "there can be no unity in appellate jurisdiction unless that appellate jurisdiction can be so limited as to make it impracticable that there shall be a recurrence of the intolerable injustice and tyranny under which our fathers suffered, and which still threatens us in all existing religious organizations which have appellate judicatories." In practical terms Briggs believed that the supreme judiciary of the reunited church should not only be ecumenical but also should be so limited in matters of doctrine that its province would consist primarily in creedal interpretation. Such interpretation, he believed, must be limited to "the express statements of the creeds" and "the historic interpretation" of their authors "to be ascertained by historical scholars."[34] Not only did Briggs want to make the supreme judicatory of the reunited church more dependent on the best modern theological scholarship; he also wanted to place jurisdiction over the behavior of laymen and ministers exclusively in the hands of inferior bodies such as congregations, presyteries and dioceses.

In addition to his deepened concern for the problem of ecclesiastical authority, Briggs' renewed interest in New Testament exegesis in the years following his heresy trial sharpened his belief in the validity of apostolic succession. Though evident to some degree in his writings at the time of the revision controversy, this awareness was most clearly distilled while Briggs was revising his earlier higher critical examination of the gospels for publication under the title, *The Messiah of the Gospels* (1894). In that book Briggs asserted "that Peter is the rock upon which the Church is built, as the Roman Catholic and the best modern Protestant interpreters, following the ancient church, teach."[35] Briggs' "scientific exegesis" of Matthew XVI: 17–20 led him to believe that Peter was the foundation of the universal church both because he was the first to acknowledge Christ to be the Messiah and because at Pentecost he was the first to speak "the word of the Holy Spirit constituting the Church." Because he concluded that Peter was "the rock upon which all the other members of the kingdom rest," Briggs asserted that all who belonged to Christ's Church were "his successors, built upon him, his teachings, and his example."

Briggs' belief in the legitimacy of apostolic succession along with his earlier affirmation of the validity of the historic episcopate explains in part why he found it easy to enter the Anglican communion to which he was ordained a priest in 1899. His association with the Church of England also resulted in part from his belief that if offered him the most strategic position from which to work for the realization of organic Christian union. In view of this Briggs was understandably distressed by the English bishops' decision in 1900 to enforce rigid uniformity in worship by prohibiting the

[34]*Ibid.*, pp. 134, 136.
[35]Charles A. Briggs, *The Messiah of the Gospels*, pp. 190–192.

use of ornaments such as incense and processional candles.[36] Expanding in a sustained and positive fashion his belief, first articulated during the revision controversy, that uniformity in worship was a great barrier to Christian union, Briggs reminded his Anglican brethren that their own Chicago-Lambeth Quadrilateral implicitly held that worship was a thing of human ordering and choice and, therefore, was not subject to uniformity. Briggs believed that Anglicans must not only live up to their ideal but set an example for other churches to follow by allowing high and low churchmen to employ whatever ceremonies and liturgies they saw fit in order to worship God.

Briggs' preoccupation with the concept of apostolic succession also impelled him to take a greater interest in Roman Catholicism's place in the reunion of Christendom. Late in 1901 Briggs traveled to Rome and met with a number of Roman Catholic scholars, among them Baron Friedrich von Hügel.[37] That visit made a profound and lasting impression on Briggs. "The Roman church has its foundation in martyrs' blood, and this more than anything else makes her preeminent and perpetuates her preeminence," Briggs asserted in 1903. "In Rome one feels close to the martyrs, in touch with original Christianity. If only the Roman church had maintained her preeminence in love, no one would have denied her primacy."[38] By the spring of 1904 Briggs' attraction to Rome became strong enough so that he sought and was granted an audience with the newly enthroned pontiff, Pius X. In what he termed "a delightful interview with the Pope," Briggs frankly discussed such matters as "infallibility, liberty of opinion, Reunion, etc."[39] Although it is not known exactly what the Pope told Briggs, it is clear that Briggs' audience with Pius X convinced him that the spirit of reform was at work in the Vatican. "Leo XIII was certainly a reforming Pope," Briggs proclaimed, but "the present Pope, Pius X, promises to be a still greater reformer."[40] Briggs believed that Pius X's motto, "to restore all things in Christ," indicated the pontiff's desire to make Christ the central figure in Catholic doctrine and worship. Moreover, the creation of a committee to revise canon law and the talk of curial reform seemed also to be important indications of constructive change.[41]

The subsequent events of the pontificate of Pius X, however, dashed

[36]Charles A. Briggs, "The Present Crisis in the Church of England and its Bearing on Church Unity," *North American Review*, Vol. 170, No. 1 (1900), pp. 97–98.

[37]Rogers, *op. cit.*, p. 414, citing Briggs Transcripts, IX, pp. 123–125.

[38]Charles A. Briggs, "Catholic—the Name and the Thing," *American Journal of Theology*, VII (July, 1903), pp. 433, 420.

[39]Rogers, *op. cit.*, p. 430, citing Briggs Transcripts, X, p. 301, Charles A. Briggs to Emily G. Briggs, March 3, 1904.

[40]Charles A. Briggs, "Reform in the Roman Catholic Church," *North American Review*, Vol. 181, no. 1 (1905), p. 80.

[41]*Ibid.*, p. 89.

many of Briggs' hopes for reform in the Roman Catholic Church. The harassment of modernists, particularly Alfred Loisy, greatly disturbed Briggs; and the verbal gymnastics of the Pontifical Biblical Commission infuriated him.[42] While dismayed and confused by such actions, Briggs did not hold the Pope personally responsible, for he truly believed him to be a generous and well meaning soul. The nemesis was clearly the curia whose members, Briggs believed, were exerting their influence on the Pope in order to use his juridical power to thwart any reform.

The modernist purge provoked Briggs to focus his attention on the problem of curial and papal reform and led him to explore fully the implications of the idea of a "universal Bishop" which he had broached tentatively at the time of the revision controversy.[43] Writing in 1906, Briggs called the papacy "one of the greatest institutions that has ever existed in the world," pointing out that it has "a much firmer basis in a number of texts of the New Testament and in Christian history than most Protestants have been willing to recognize":

> It is evident that Jesus, in speaking to St. Peter, had the whole history of His kingdom in view. He sees conflict with the evil powers and victory over them. It is, therefore, vain to suppose that we must limit the commission to Peter. . . . The commission of the primate, no less than the commission of the Twelve, includes their successors to the end of the world. . . . Therefore, we must admit that there is a sense in which the successors of St. Peter are the rock of the Church, and have the authority of the keys in ecclesiastical government, discipline, and determination of faith and morals. Inasmuch, however, as the commission is given to the Twelve and their successors also as to the power of the keys, it is necessary to take the passages together and conclude that the authority was given by our Lord to the apostles in a body, and that it was given to St. Peter as the executive head of the body.[44]

Briggs' study of the New Testament had convinced him that the Pope was the executive head of Christ's Church by virtue of being the successor of St. Peter. The unity of the church is not in the person of the Pope, but "in his office, as the Universal Bishop, as such, the head of all the bishops as these are of the ministry and the People."

Asserting that the primacy of the Pope does not depend on any particular theory as to the subject matter or extent of his jurisdiction, Briggs claimed that there was hope for papal reform. That hope centered on the need to "define and limit by a constitution" the "jurisdiction of the Pope." Such a limitation could be effected, Briggs believed, through "a representative

[42]Charles A. Briggs and Friedrich von Hügel, *The Papal Commission and the Pentateuch* (London: Longmans, Green and Co., 1906), p. 6.

[43]Charles A. Briggs, "The Real and the Ideal in the Papacy," *North American Review*, Vol. 184, No. 4 (1907), pp. 347–363.

[44]*Ibid.*, pp. 348, 350.

council of Bishops, giving to such a body the legislative function and the right of initiative and veto in legislative matters as in all modern civil government."[45] One advantage of this scheme would be to restrain not only the Pope's power but that of his curial cabinet. In addition, Briggs hoped that limiting papal power would permit the restoration of an harmoniously working "threefold cord" of unity in Christ's Church. This cord consisted in the unity of the Pope, the ministry, and the people. Briggs felt that it was particularly important to harmonize the Pope and the ministry with the great mass of Christian church-goers since the "future Papacy in the modern world depended upon the reinvigoration of the latent principle of the consent of the people through their representatives in some form of ecclesiastical council." Briggs hoped that the great ecumenical councils of the early church would serve as models for such councils because they exemplified to him how representatives of the people could be introduced into the presbyterial and synodical system of the Church.

Briggs' interest in the reunion of Christendom was not merely confined to matters of ecclesiastical jurisdiction, for he was also deeply interested in doctrinal matters. Briggs' concern for locating a doctrinal consensus on which the reunion of Christendom could be built informed his work in the field of theological symbolics during the five final years of his life. His study of the creedal symbols of Christianity convinced him "that there is a fundamental Christian faith expressed in the Ecumenical Creeds upon which the three great divisions of Christianity do actually agree" and which "constitutes a sufficient plan for reunion."[46] Common to the Apostles', Nicene, and Athanasian Creeds is a profession of the fundamental Christian faith, "Jesus Christ, God's Son, Savior." This is the "sacred deposit of teaching which cannot be increased nor diminished, but which can only be interpreted and explained," Briggs contended.[47] While he believed that the essence of Christianity contained in these three great ecumenical creeds provided a firm doctrinal basis for union, Briggs was aware that each of the three divisions of Christendom "has its own particular symbols that are dear to it,

[45]Ibid., pp. 352–353, 359, 361–363. Briggs' model for a unified ecclesiastical government was closely based on American republican government. Just as each American state "has its own special constitution and jurisdiction, all under the supreme jurisdiction of the U.S." constitution, so each division of the reunited church would retain its own particular creedal symbols and jurisdiction even as it became attached to the creedal symbols and juridical range of the supreme authority in the Church. Briggs even went so far as to suggest that the Pope's judicial function "may be separated by the organism of a supreme court of Christendom" (363). Briggs clearly believed that the external ecclesiastical government of a unified church must draw on the best available models of government in modern secular culture.

[46]Charles A. Briggs, *Theological Symbolics* (New York: Charles Scribner's Sons, 1914), p. 412.

[47]Charles A. Briggs, *The Fundamental Christian Faith* (New York: Charles Scribner's Sons, 1913), pp. 6–7.

and which it will not readily abandon."[48] To preserve them, Briggs suggested that "unity may be arranged in a supreme jurisdiction on the basis of the fundamental Faith and Institutions of the Church" while "the subordinate jurisdictions representing each of the three divisions, and the particular jurisdictions into which each of these are divided, may still retain their particular symbols" and institutions without fear of infringement by the supreme body.

In 1909 Briggs summarized his thinking on the problem of the organic union of Christendom in *Church Unity*. The book consists mainly in Briggs' major published articles on ecumenism, but it also contains some previously unpublished material, the most important of which deals with the sacramental system. In the late 1880's Briggs had affirmed that the sacraments were of vital importance to the life of the Church of Christ. Not until he rounded out his ecumenical thinking in *Church Unity* did Briggs explore systematically the question of sacraments. In probing this question Briggs focused on the number of the sacraments and the presence of the divine and material elements in the Eucharist. So far as the former is concerned, Briggs asserted that since "Greeks and Romans agree in the seven sacraments," Protestants "should abandon their opposition," insisting only that Baptism and the Lord's Supper "stand alone by themselves as Sacraments of Sacraments."[49] The question of the presence of the divine and material elements in the Eucharist was a more prickly proposition. Realizing that this had been a divisive issue since the Reformation, Briggs did not presume to have resolved the problem. In exhorting Christians to resolve their differences over the matter, Briggs did, however, propose that they return to the ancient Christian term, "conversion," since it suggested that the "presence of Christ in the elements is . . . a spiritual presence . . . entirely independent of the laws of matter."[50]

Church Unity, however, is much more than a summary of Briggs' ecumenical thinking; for in a very real sense it is the apologia of a man who wanted posterity to remember him as a Christian peacemaker, not a heretic. In defining the "irenic spirit" Briggs used his own experience as a controlling metaphor. Proclaiming that Christian irenics demanded "*a courageous quest for truth,*" Briggs contended that the Christian peacemaker must battle against all obstacles to Christian union even at the cost of great pain to himself.[51] By so doing he was engaged in a task that required "the courage of martyrdom." Nevertheless, his bravery must always be sustained by the conviction that "the divine spirit will eventually" decompose the "dissensus of Christianity" by convincing truly Christian men and women that they are all organically united in Christ. Moreover, Briggs believed that the

[48]Charles A. Briggs, *Theological Symbolics*, p. 412.
[49]Charles A. Briggs, *Church Unity*, p. 249.
[50]*Ibid.*, p. 288.
[51]*Ibid.*, pp. 11–14.

Christian irenicist must acquire a deep sympathy for all branches of Christendom and be open to the truths which each can teach. "Such has been my experience," Briggs asserted as he related his ecumenical odyssey:

> Early life among the Methodists gave me a sympathy with Arminianism, although I deliberately followed Calvinism. Four years of study in Germany enabled me to sympathise with Lutheranism. Many years of labour as a Presbyterian minister and Professor of Theology enabled me to understand thoroughly the doctrine, polity and worship of the Presbyterian and other Reformed churches. Many vacations in England enabled me to overcome early prejudices against liturgy and ceremony in public worship. Several residences in Rome gave me the opportunity to enter into sympathy with Roman Catholic doctrine and worship. And so God's Holy Spirit has guided me through sympathetic study of all these divisions of Christendom to lose hostility to them, and to regard them with an irenic spirit, and with a determination to do all in my power to remove prejudices, misstatements and misinterpretations and to labour for the reunion of them all in one organic whole, the one Church of Christ.[52]

Believing that his own spiritual life has been one of "sympathetic union" with all branches of Christendom, Briggs wanted posterity to remember him not as a cause of division but as a man who lived, thought, and worshipped with a variety of Christian denominations. He firmly believed that a person cannot know a denomination by looking only at its exterior, for there it "always presents to the enemy its warlike, offensive side." Only when he penetrates in sincere friendship its interior can he sense "the peace and unity in the home life."[53] Likewise, Briggs believed that posterity must not know him by the exterior veneer of newspaper clipping portraying him as a warlike and heretical innovator; for to know him as a peaceful and sincere ecumenist, it too must penetrate the interior of his thought.

"The learned doctor's book is a strange mixture of Irenics and Polemics," commented Allen D. Severence of Western Reserve University in his review of Briggs' *Church Unity*. "What he considers error he condemns with no uncertain sound, but the irenic spirit prevails."[54] A book inevitably manifests its author's personality, and Briggs' *Church Unity* is no exception. Just as his book exhibited a strange mixture of irenics and polemics, so too did Briggs' own personality; for his irenic and peaceful character was held in a curious tension with his polemical and combative streak. Briggs' heresy trials bore witness to the fact that the more he became personally involved in a controversy, the more warlike and polemical he became. The publicity that attended his heresy proceedings forged in the minds of his own and

---

[52]*Ibid.*, p. 16.
[53]*Ibid.*
[54]Allen D. Severance, *"Church Unity* by Charles A. Briggs," *Biblioteca Sacra*, LXVII (January, 1910), p. 164.

future generations the image of Briggs as a self-styled warrior of God's Spirit engaged in a tenacious and polemical battle against all who had not come to see the truth which years of diligent and careful study had revealed to him. This image, correct as it is, portrays only one side of Briggs' character; and it is important for students of American religious history to remember Briggs as a committed Christian ecumenist just as did his own contemporaries.[55] Deriving in the late 1860's a belief that God's best works in creation manifested the same kind of organic unity that animated His trinitarian being, Briggs became convinced that the "one Church of Christ" must also be organically united. When a theological student in Germany Briggs came to believe that ecumenism was intimately connected with biblical theology, and his interest in irenics was as much a controlling factor in his life and thought during the 1870's and 1880's as it was in his later years. Having defined well before his heresy trial the essential outline of his vision of the reunited Church, Briggs in the years following the trial explored systematically the points of that outline until he had worked out a doctrinal and juridical plan for the organic union of Christendom.

[55]Severance was not the only reviewer to respond positively to Briggs' irenic spirit. Edward H. Eppens, who reviewed *Church Unity* in the July, 1909 issue of *The Homiletic Review*, noted that it would be "profitable to be reminded of the distance we have traveled since the *cause celebre* of which Briggs was the center." To him Briggs' book was such a reminder since it, along with Briggs' other writings, helped him "get out of the woods."

Ecclesiastical Politics and the Founding of the Federal Council of Churches

JOHN ABERNATHY SMITH

In an influential book of thirty years ago, *The Rise of the Social Gospel in American Protestantism, 1865-1915,* Charles Howard Hopkins interpreted the founding in 1908 of the Federal Council of the Churches of Christ in America, the forerunner of the present National Council, as a stage in the flowering of the social gospel in American Christianity.[1] His interpretation was soon confirmed by John Alexander Hutchison. In *We Are Not Divided,* a study of the pronouncements of the Federal Council, Hutchison wrote that the Federal Council was born of the marriage between "the idea of social service and the idea of interdenominational cooperation".[2] By "the idea of interdenominational cooperation", however, Hutchison meant little more than what Hopkins had already defined as the impulse for social Christianity, and there the matter has rested for subsequent historians, including two former secretaries of the Federal Council.[3]

Hopkins owed his story of the founding of the interdenominational federation to *The Origin and History of the Federal Council of the Churches of Christ in America,* published in 1916 by Elias Benjamin Sanford, the first secretary of the organization. Although Sanford acknowledged that denominational assemblies had earlier been involved in overtures for interdenominational federation, he traced the real impetus for the movement to the Open or Institutional Church League, founded in New York in 1894 to campaign against pew rents and to promote community ministries among urban churches whose congregations had migrated uptown or to outlying suburbs.[4] According to Sanford, who was inclined to place himself in the vanguard of the movement, the impulse for federation began in the Open Church League, of which he was secretary, and after 1901 coursed through the National Federation of Churches and Christian Workers, of which he was also secretary, on its way toward the Federal Council. Because Sanford's account fitted the paradigm of individual and voluntary espousal followed by official endorsement which Hopkins discerned in social Christianity, he appears not to have questioned the story. Neither he nor Hutchison seems to

1. Charles Howard Hopkins, *The Rise of the Social Gospel in American Protestantism, 1865-1915* (New Haven: Yale University Press, 1940), pp. 302-317.
2. John Alexander Hutchinson, *We Are Not Divided: A Critical and Historical Study of the Federal Council of the Churches of Christ in America* (New York: Round Table Press, 1941), p. 25.
3. See, for example, Charles Steadman Macfarland, *Christian Unity in the Making: The First Twenty-five Years of the Federal Council of the Churches of Christ in America* (New York: Federal Council of Churches, 1948), pp. 24, 27; H. Shelton Smith, Robert T. Handy and Lefferts A. Loetscher, *American Christianity: An Historical Interpretation with Representative Documents,* 2 vols. (New York: Scribner's, 1960-1963) 2:394: Sidney Earl Mead, *The Lively Experiment: The Shaping of Christianity in America* (New York: Harper and Row, 1963), p. 182; Sydney E. Ahlstrom, *A Religious History of the American People* (New Haven: Yale University Press, 1972), pp. 802-804; Samuel McCrea Cavert, *The American Churches in the Ecumenical Movements, 1900-1968* (New York: Association Press, 1968), pp. 29-31. Macfarland and Cavert were secretaries of the Federal Council.
4. Elias Benjamin Sanford, *The Origin and History of the Federal Council of the Churches of Christ in America* (Hartford, Connecticut: S. S. Scranton, 1916), p. iv.

Mr. Smith is assistant professor of education in the American University, District of Columbia.

have been puzzled by such obvious problems with Sanford's version as why the Open Church League became diverted into the movement for federation, why the organization of the abortive National Federation of Churches and Christian Workers preceded that of the Federal Council, how the idea of a Federal Council evolved or how denominational assemblies were induced to enter an interdenominational council. Readily accepting Sanford's dismissal of the efforts of denominational assembles, neither Hopkins nor Hutchison investigated the place of federative proposals in the remarkable movement for Christian unity which swept through the denominational assemblies themselves in the 1880s and 1890s despite the potential significance of such inquiry for understanding the Federal Council as well as the progress of social Christianity.

Denominational assemblies were near the zenith of their influence in the 1880s. Such bodies dated from the period of constitution-making when, in preparation for life in the new nation, Presbyterians established their annual General Assembly and Episcopalians their triennial General Convention, which were subsequently copied by other denominations like the Methodists, who instituted a quadrennial General Conference. Eclipsed often by missionary and benevolent societies and by lower judicatories and wracked by schism and dissension in the second quarter of the nineteenth century, these assemblies, nonetheless, gradually became the chief agencies of denominational advance, following what had been Old School policy among the Presbyterians in locating various denominational enterprises directly under the authority of the general body. Each wing of divided denominations evolved its own periodic and delegated assembly of clergy and laity, and in a moment of national enthusiasm after the Civil War, Congregationalists compromised their principles and created a triennial National Council. Entering the era of their greatest power and prestige, which lasted until they were overshadowed by bureaucracies of their own making, these assemblies attracted as delegates the best known ministers and laymen in the denominations. Improved transportation allowed them to space their meetings across the country, and their proceedings were watched by their own journals as well as the papers of other denominations and the secular press, with debates among their illustrious members often reported in the manner of those in the Congress of the United States.

Denominational assemblies were in a unique position to promote American Protestant unity when the movement first began among Presbyterians. In 1881 the General Assembly of the Presbyterian Church in the United States, the southern wing of American Presbyterianism, unexpectedly initiated a telegraphic exchange of fraternal greetings with the General Assembly of the Presbyterian Church in the United States of America. Seizing the opportunity to resolve past differences and improve relationships, the two assemblies engaged in a discussion of grievances, agreed according to the evangelical custom to exchange fraternal delegations in 1883 and established a joint commission to produce a plan for friendly cooperation between them. Although southern opponents of détente dealt a temporary blow to these activities in 1883-1884,[5] the movement was re-

5. *Minutes of the General Assembly of the Presbyterian Church in the United States* (hereafter PCUS) 5 (Wilmington, North Carolina: Jackson and Bell, 1881) : 353, 356, 391-392; 5 (Wilmington, North Carolina: Jackson and Bell, 1882): 523, 526, 530-531, 541, 542, 552-553; 6 (Wilmington, North Carolina: Jackson and Bell, 1883): 19, 20-23, 49-50, 54, 57-58; 6 (Wilmington, North Carolina: Jackson and Bell, 1884): 219-221, 243, 248, 249, 251; *Minutes of the General Assembly of the Presbyterian Church in the United States of America* (hereafter PCUSA, n. s., 7 (New York: Presbyterian Board of Publication, 1882): 50-66, 83-84, 102-103; n. s., 7 (New York: Presbyterian

vived in time to prepare for a celebration of the centennial of their once-united General Assembly in the same spirit of cooperation that had marked the approval by the Methodists' general bodies of a common observance of the centenary of American Methodism in 1884.[6] The joint recognition of their common heritage smoothed the way to adoption of a plan of cooperation between northern and southern Presbyterians in 1889 amid talk of a broader alliance of Presbyterian and Reformed bodies.[7]

In 1886 the movement expanded to include approaches by churches of dissimilar history and polity. By coincidence, the Episcopalians' General Convention and the Congregationalists' National Council met simultaneously in Chicago during the fall. Their agendas included memorials from both individuals and lower ecclesiastical bodies asking for improved relations among American denominations. Lest the unusual opportunity be wasted, Phillips Brooks rallied sentiment in the House of Deputies of the bicameral General Convention for an exchange of fraternal greetings with the National Council. Although Brooks' motion failed to win concurrence from the House of Bishops due to party issues and concern for episcopal prerogatives, the House of Bishops itself subsequently dispatched an invitation to "brotherly conference with all or any Christian bodies seeking the restoration of the organic unity of the Church" and agreed to a commission of the General Convention to carry out such negotiations.[8] Across town the Congregationalists also took action, authorizing a committee to court Free Baptists in hopes of a merger between the denominations and, in a move to rival the bishops' invitation, appointing a second committee to convene a "congress" of American churches.[9]

Congregationalists later reaffirmed their project of a congress of denominations with direct influence on the organization of the Federal Council, but their proposal was momentarily overshadowed by the Episcopalians' reversal of their policy of official aloofness from interdenominational affairs in the United States. The Congregationalist committee decided to leave the matter of a congress to the Evangelical Alliance, which had been revitalized earlier in the decade with the

Board of Publication, 1883): 569, 576, 591, 596, 630, 636, 646, 687; n. s., 8 (Philadelphia: Presbyterian Board of Publication, 1884): 27, 67-70, 101.
6. Dow Kirkpatrick, "Early Efforts at Reunion," in *The History of American Methodism*, ed. Emory Stevens Bucke et al., 3 vols. (Nashville, Tennessee: Abingdon Press, 1964). 2:689-694.
7. PCUSA, n.s., 9 (Philadelphia: By the Stated Clerk, 1886): 25-26, 57-58; n.s., 10 (Philadelphia: By the Stated Clerk, 1887): 26, 35, 57, 116-117, 128; n. s., 11 (Philadelphia: By the Stated Clerk, 1888): 85, 923-102; n. s., 12 Philadelphia: By the Sttaed Clerk, 1889): 64, 68-74, 79-80; PCUS 7 (Columbia, South Carolina: Presbyterian Publishing House, 1886): 20, 22; 7 (Columbia, South Carolina: Presbyterian Publishing House, 1887): 188, 191-192, 193-195, 200-201, 203, 205-206, 207-210, 211, 216-219, 220, 224; 7 (Richmond, Virginia: Presbyterian Committee of Publication, 1888): 420-423, 431-432, 456-463; 7 (Richmond, Virginia: Presbyterian Committee of Publication, 1889): 570-573, 576, 577, 582, 594-598; "The Prospects of Presbyterian Union," *Independent* 40 (1888): 362; Charles Augustus Briggs, "Union of Northern and Southern Presbyterians," ibid., p. 316; Charles Augustus Briggs. "A Plea for an American Alliance," *Presbyterian Review* 9 (1888): 306-309.
8. *Journal of the Proceedings of the Bishops, Clergy, and Laity of the Protestant Episcopal Church . . . Assembled in a General Convention, Held in Chicago, from October 6 to October 28 . . . 1886* (hereafter PEC with year) (n.p.: Printed for the Convention, 1887), pp. 79-80, 199-200, 212, 256-257, 302, 800-844; "The General Convention," *Churchman* 54 (1886): 497-498, 539-540; "Reports on Church Unity," ibid., pp. 560-562; " A Memorial on the Reunion of Christians," ibid., pp. 225, 229 et passim.
9. *Minutes of the National Council of the Congregational Churches . . . in Chicago, Ill., October 5-20, 1886* (hereafter NCCC with year) (Boston: Congregational Publishing Society, 1887), pp. 16, 17, 21, 22, 33-35, 36, 349-350, 356-358.

assistance of prominent Episcopalians.[10] The Evangelical Alliance had embarked on a series of national meetings, continuing, in addition to its own conventions of the 1870s, the Interdenominational Congress called by Josiah Strong in 1885 and the American Congress of Churches, which had been inspired and supported by leaders in the Protestant Episcopal Church.[11] Although the National Council never officially responded to the bishops' invitation, Connecticut Congregationalists had been among the first to make a statement of interest, and the Episcopalians' proposal drew other replies from northern branches of Presbyterians, Methodists and Baptists, the Lutherans' General Synod and United Synod of the South, Disciples and Moravians.[12]

The most important response to the bishops' invitation came from the Presbyterian Church in the United States of America. As editor of the journal published jointly in this age of Christian cooperation by Princeton and Union seminaries, Charles Augustus Briggs was in a position to influence his denomination with his favorable notices of the Episcopalians' action in advance of the spring meeting of the General Assembly in 1887.[13] Briggs' presbytery in New York sent up to the General Assembly a proposed response to the Episcopalians, which won concurrence from several other presbyteries. Even the conservative New Brunswick presbytery had a leading advocate of union with the Episcopalians in Charles Woodruff Shields, professor of philosophy at Princeton.[14] Although New

10. George Park Fisher to William E. Dodge, Jr., December 3, 1887, in NCCC, 1889, (Boston: Congregational Publishing Society, 1889), pp. 251-252; Evangelical Alliance for the United States. I. *Action of the United States Evangelical Alliance on the Death of its President, Hon. William E. Dodge*, Document 16 (New York, 1883), pp. 6-7; Arthur Cleveland Coxe, "A Christian Alliance, the Demand of Our Times," *Independent* 36 (1884): 193-194; "Evangelical Alliance: A Notable Reunion," *New York Observer* 64 (1886) :114; *National Perils and Opportunities: The Discussions of the General Christian Conference Held in Washington, D. C., December 7th, 8th, and 9th, 1887, under the Auspices of the Evangelical Alliance for the United States* (New York: Baker and Taylor, 1887), pp. 303 et passim; Julius Hammond Ward, "The Evangelical Alliance in Boston," *Churchman* 60 (1889): 771.
11. Evangelical Alliance for the U.S., *Eighth Annual Report* . . . *1875*, Document 11 (New York, 1875), pp. 7-11, *Tenth and Eleventh Annual Reports* . . . *1877 and 1878*, Document 13 (New York, 1879), pp. 3-5, and *Twelfth Annual Report* . . . *1879*, Document 15 (New York, 1879), pp. 5-7; *Discussions of the Interdenominational Congress in the Interest of City Evangelization, Held in Cincinnati, December 7-11, 1885* (Cincinnati: The Congress, 1886); American Congress of Churches, *Proceedings of the Hartford Meeting, 1885* (Hartford, Connecticut: Case, Lockwood, and Brainerd, Co., 1885) and *Proceedings of the Cleveland Meeting, May, 1886* (Hartford, Connecticut: Case, Lockwood and Brainerd Co., 1886). See also *National Perils and Opportunities; National Needs and Remedies: The Discussions of the General Christian Conference Held in Boston, Massachusetts, December 4th, 5th, and 6th, 1889, under the Auspices of the Evangelical Alliance for the United States* (New York: Baker and Taylor, 1890); and *Christianity Practically Applied: The Discussions of the International Christian Conference Held in Chicago, October 6-14, 1893, in Connection with the World's Congress Auxiliary of the World's Columbian Exposition and under the Auspices and Direction of the Evangelical Alliance for the United States*, 2 vols. (New York: Baker and Taylor, 1894).
12. "First Response to the Bishop's [*sic*] Declaration on Unity," *Churchman* 54 (1886): 629; "The First Response to the Bishops," *Independent* 38 (1886): 1346; PEC 1895 (n.p.: Printed for the Convention, 1896), pp. 613-627.
13. Charles Augustus Briggs, ed., "Letters on the Relations between the Presbyterians and Episcopalians in England by Benedict Pietet, 1708," *Presbyterian Review* 8 (1887): 132-133; Charles Augustus Briggs, "The Work of John Durie in Behalf of Christian Union in the Seventeenth Century," ibid., pp. 297-309; Charles Augustus Briggs, "The Barriers to Christian Union," ibid., pp. 441-471. See also Charles Augustus Briggs, "Terms of Christian Union," *Christian Union* 35 (May 12, 1887) :8-9.
14. Charles Woodruff Shields, "The United Churches of the United States: Their Existing Agreements in Doctrine, Polity, and Worship," *Century* 31 (1885): 74-84, and "The United Churches of the United States, No. II: A Review of the *Century* Letters on Chris-

Brunswick was critical of major aspects of the bishops' invitation, it did petition the General Assembly to seek improved relations with rival denominations. When the General Assembly convened, it adopted a reply to the Episcopalians and appointed a committee to conduct the negotiations in which the two denominations were engaged until 1896.[15]

The General Assembly itself became the center of the growing movement in 1889. On the heels of the adoption of the plan of cooperation with southern Presbyterians, the committee of the General Assembly participated in a promising meeting with the Episcopalians' commission at the seat of the General Convention in the fall. Subsequently, the committee received a proposal from the National Council for exploring cooperation between the two denominations which had ratified the famous Plan of Union in 1801 and had worked together in the American Home Missionary Society. In addition, members of the General Assembly had become the leading publicists of the scheme for an American alliance of Presbyterian and Reformed churches, which had initially surfaced in 1886 during Dutch Reformed exploration of a union with the German Reformed.[16] At this juncture, the Presbyterian committee on church unity recommended combination "of the Christian churches of the country in some form of official Federation", and in 1890 the General Assembly gave permission to its committee to communicate these sentiments to other denominations. This action, pointing unmistakably to the future organization of the Federal Council, was related to two other projects which Presbyterians undertook for the promotion of Protestant unity in America. In 1890 the General Assembly, at the instigation of Charles Lemuel Thompson, created a new, overlapping committee on church cooperation, which worked for a meeting of home missions officials of all denominations and actually negotiated agreements on interdenominational comity with Congregationalists and Dutch Reformed—events connected with the eventual organization of the Home Missions Council in 1908, the same year the Federal Council was consummated.[17] In a related move shortly thereafter, members of the General Assembly, working through the American section of the Alliance of Reformed Churches Holding the Presbyterian System, initiated the calling of the more successful interdenominational meetings of foreign mission officials, which began in 1893 and became the Foreign Missions Conference of North America in 1911.[18]

In the spring of 1890 Presbyterians had reason to believe that Protestant denominations, including the Episcopalians, might be induced to enter a federation, and it is possible that the matter was discussed at the meeting with the Epis-

tian Unity," *Century* 35 (1887): 254-264. See also "Unity and the Prayerbook," *New York Observer* 64 (1886): 2, and William Milligan Sloan, "Charles Woodruff Shields: A Biographical Sketch," in C. W. Shields, *Philosophia Ultima, or Science of the Sciences*, 3 vols. (New York: Scribner's, 1888-1905), 3: viii-lxx.

15. PCUSA, n.s., 10 (Philadelphia: By the Stated Clerk, 1887): 62, 82, 157-158; "The Beginning of a Great Movement," *Christian Union* 35 (May 12, 1887): 3; "Christian Unity," *Church Union* 15 (June 15, 1887): 6.

16. *Acts and Proceedings of the . . . General Synod of the Reformed Church in America, Convened at Catskill, New York, June 1857*, 16 (New York: Board of Publication of the Reformed Church in America, 1887):363-365, 368-369; Briggs, "A Plea for an American Alliance," pp. 306-309.

17. PCUSA, n. s., 13 (Philadelphia: By the Stated Clerk, 1890): 103-104; n. s., 14 (Philadelphia: By the Stated Clerk, 1891):162-166; n. s., 15 (Philadelphia: By the Stated Clerk, 1892): 91-96; "Comity," *Home Missionary* 65 (1893): 470; "Interdenominational Comity," ibid., pp. 562-563.

18. *Interdenominational Conference of Foreign Missionary Boards and Societies in the United States and Canada, Held in the Presbyterian Mission House, January 12, 1893* (New York: E. O. Jenkins' Son's Printing House, 1893), p. iii.

copalian committee in New York in 1889. William Wilberforce Newton's idea of a congress of churches, hearking back to the writings of William Augustus Muhlenberg in 1835, was the earliest Episcopalian expression of interest in American Christian unity in the 1880s,[19] and his American Congress of Churches, though a fair copy of the Episcopalians' Church Congress, looked in some way toward a more official organization. To judge by the favorable vote on Brooks' motion in the House of Deputies, Episcopalian clergy and laity might have indeed led the denomination into a federation, given more leadership than Newton was able to supply with his *The Vine Out of Egypt*, published in 1887 in support of the idea.[20] High churchmen, whose control of the House of Bishops was solidified after the death in 1887 of the evangelical Alfred Lee, the presiding bishop, launched a campaign to insure, however, that the reference to the "historic episcopate" in the bishops' invitation was construed as entailing the high church theory of episcopacy and that federation was excluded as a possible means of achieving organic unity. In 1888 the Lambeth Conference approved the four points, or quadrilateral, proposed for negotiation in the bishops' invitation, giving high churchmen the opportunity to discard the broader entreaties of the Chicago declaration.[21] After the important symposium in the *Church Review* in the autumn of 1890, it was clear that the high church party had gained control of the negotiations and were in the process of eliminating any chances that the Protestant Episcopal Church would enter a federation.[22]

Among Dutch and German Reformed, however, the cause of federation made a notable advance during 1890 and 1891. Seeking unity but fearing the loss of denominational autonomy, committees of the two churches decided to pursue the alternative of federation which the Dutch had contemplated in 1886. Recommending a federal union to the respective synods in the spring of 1890, the committees were charged with drafting a constitution during the ensuing year. The mechanism of a federal synod was chosen and embodied in a document which was to influence directly the constitution of the Federal Council of Churches. With James McCosh as well as leaders of the denominations publicizing the relationship between federalism and presbyterial polity, the two churches agreed that a federal synod was an appropriate means of uniting Calvinistic churches and dispatched the plan to lower judicatories for ratification.[23] Although German Reformed approved the federal union, the constitution did not win concurrence from the Dutch classes partly because of the revival of the scheme for a union of all

19. William Wilberforce Newton, "Beginning at Jerusalem," *Christian Union* 17, (1883) :268, See also [William Augustus Muhlenberg] *Hints on Catholic Union by a Presbyter* (New York, 1835), rpt. in *Evangelical Catholic Papers: A Collection of Essays, Letters, and Tractates from Writings of Rev. William Augustus Muhlenberg, D.D., during the Last Forty Years*, ed. Anne Ayres, 1st ser. (Suffolk Co., New York: St. Johnland Press, 1875), pp. 27-32, and William Wilberforce Newton, *Dr. Muhlenberg* (Boston: Houghton, Mifflin, 1890), pp. viii, 123ff., 149.
20. William Wilberforce Newton, *The Vine Out of Egypt* (New York: Thomas Whittaker, 1887), pp. 128-129.
21. Randall Thomas Davidson, ed., *The Six Lambeth Conferences, 1867-1920* (London: Society for Promoting Christian Knowledge, 1929), pp. 122, 156-161; Frederick S. Jewell, "Church Unity and the Convention," *Church Eclectic* 21 (1892): 24-25.
22. "Church Reunion," *Church Review* 59 (October 1890): iii-iv, 11-221. See "The Historic Episcopate as a Basis of Reunion," *Church Review* 57 (April 1890): 11-144.
23. James McCosh, "Federation of Churches to Secure that the Gospel Be Preached to Every Creature," *Christian Union* 41 (1890): 180-190; James McCosh, "Federation of Evangelical Churches, *Church Review*, 57 (April 1890):132-134; James McCosh, "Federation of Churches," *Homiletic Review* 21 (1891): 398. See also "Federation of Churches for Evangelistic Work," *Independent* 42 (1890): 778-779.

Presbyterian and Reformed bodies in the wake of the discovery that federation was such an eminently Calvinistic means of unity.[24]

Northern Presbyterians had contributed to this development when in the spring of 1891 their committee on church unity decided to pursue the plan for a federation of American denominations, topped by a "National Council", by asking the other Presbyterian and Reformed bodies to join them in a call for an inter-denominational conference on federation. The initial response was disappointing, due in part to confusion with a project for a liberalized consensus creed, which northern Presbyterians had also proposed to sister churches in 1890. Attempts to dispel the doubt coincided with Dutch Reformed suggestions for a larger union, and in 1892 the two projects were consolidated. Before calling an interdenominational conference, Presbyterian and Reformed bodies would seek a federal union, which they hoped might provide the nucleus for a federation of all American Protestant denominations. Building on the Dutch and German Reformed constitution for a federal synod, Presbyterian and Reformed committees—with the notable absence of southern Presbyterians—drafted between 1892 and 1896 a new instrument providing for a "Federal Council of the Reformed Churches in the United States Holding the Presbyterian System", a closer approximation yet of the Federal Council of Churches.[25]

Support for federation as a possible way of uniting churches had meanwhile spread beyond the Presbyterian and Reformed denominations. In 1892 the Congregationalists' National Council threw its weight behind a federation of all churches.[26] Between 1894 and 1898 northern and southern Methodists—with the Methodist Episcopal Church, South in the lead—took steps to heal their differences and negotiated a plan for a federation, which early in the twentieth century was graced with its own federal council.[27] A Baptist agreement on comity was

24. *Acts and Proceedings of the . . . General Synod of the Reformed Church in America, Convened at Asbury Park, N. J., June, 1890* 17 (New York: Board of Publication of the Reformed Church in America, 1890): 124-134; *. . . Convened at Asbury Park, N. J., June, 1891* (New York: Board of Publication of the Reformed Church in America, 1891): 343-359; *. . . Convened at Asbury Park, N. J., June, 1892,* 17 (New York: Board of Publication of the Reformed Church in America, 1892): 577-586; *. . . Convened at Asbury Park, N. J., June 1893,* 17 (New York: Board of Plublication of the Reformed Church in America, 1893) 816-823; *Acts and Proceedings of the General Synod of the Reformed Church in the United States at Lebanon, Pa., May, 1890* (Dayton, Ohio: Reformed Publishing Company 1890), pp. 36-40; *. . . Convened in Special Session at Philadelphia, Pa., June 4-6, 1891* (Dayton, Ohio: Reformed Publishing Company, 1891), passim; *. . . at Reading, Pa., May 24 to June 1, 1893* (Dayton, Ohio: Reformed Publishing Company, 1893), pp. 28, 33, 42-45; Herman Harmelink, III, *Ecumenism and the Reformed Church* (Grand Rapids, Michigan: Eerdmans, 1968), pp. 32-54.
25. PCUSA, n. s., 14 (Philadelphia: By the Stated Clerk, 1891): 206-207; n. s. 15 (Philadelphia: By the Stated Clerk, 1892): 38-41; n. s., 17 (Philadelphia: By the Stated Clerk 1894): 164-166; n. s., 19 (Philadelphia: By the Stated Clerk, 1896): 47, 180-182; *Report of the Special Committee on Church Unity* [PCUSA] (n. p., 1893), pp. 12-14.
26. NCCC, 1892 (Boston: Congregational Sunday School and Publishing Society, 1893), pp. 39-40, 109-113.
27. *Journal of the . . . General Conference of the Methodist Episcopal Church, South, Held in Memphis, Tennessee, May 3-21, 1894* (Nashville, Tennessee: Publishing House, Methodist Episcopal Church, South, 1894), pp. 117, 118, 128, 162, 177, 217-219; *. . . in Baltimore, Maryland, May 5-23, 1898* (Nashville, Tennessee: Publishing House, Methodist Episcopal Church, South, 1898), pp. 72, 85, 171-172, 237-247; *. . . in Dallas, Texas, May 7-26, 1902* (Nashville, Tennessee: Publishing House, Methodist Episcopal Church, South, 1902), pp. 70, 81, 161-62, 171; *. . . in Asheville, N. C., May 4-21, 1910* (Nashville, Tennessee: Publishing House, Methodist Episcopal Church, South, 1910), p. 264; *Journal of the . . . General Conference of the Methodist Episcopal Church, Held in Cleveland, Ohio, May 1-28, 1896* (New York: Eaton and Mains, 1896), p. 178; *. . . in Chicago, Illinois, May 2-29, 1900* (New York: Eaton and Mains, 1900), pp. 323, 329, 367-370, 469-470; *. . . in Baltimore, Maryland, May 6-June 1, 1908* (New York: Eaton

reached between northern and southern denominations in 1894,[28] and a movement took shape among the General Synod, General Council and United Synod of the South which led to the creation of a General Conference of Lutherans in America in 1898.[29] On a statewide basis, the interdenominational Commission of Maine was created as a federation in 1893,[30] and state and local federation of churches were promoted at the meeting of the Evangelical Alliance and the Parliament of Religions held in connection with the Columbian Exposition.[31] The movement for federation seemed certain of success when the Presbyterian Church in the United States of America found it necessary to withdraw from all unitive endeavors to preserve its own internal solidarity.

Since 1889 the General Assembly had been convulsed by issues of creedal revision and subscription and biblical scholarship. Negotiations between Presbyterians and Episcopalians had early been injected into the controversy when James McCosh, ignoring Charles A. Briggs' announced support for federation, had drawn a sharp contrast between Briggs' desire for "incorporation" and his own preference for federation.[32] After Briggs was deposed from the Presbyterian ministry in 1893, Presbyterians, affirming McCosh's position, became as doctrinaire as high church Episcopalians in their demands for a federation as the price of continued negotiations, which were indeed terminated in 1896.[33] Pres-

and Mains, 1908), pp. 417-418, 621-625, 919-928; Frederick E. Moser, "The Story of Unification," in Bucke et al., eds., *History of American Methodism*, 3: 412-414.

28. *Proceedings of the Southern Baptist Convention . . . Held at Dallas, Texas, May 11-15, 1894* (Atlanta, Georgia: Franklin Printing and Publishing Co., 1894), pp. 15-16; . . . *at Washington, D. C., May 10-14, 1895* (Atlanta, Georgia: Franklin Printing and Publishing Co., 1895), pp. 14-16; Robert Andrew Baker, *Relations between Northern and Southern Baptists* (Fort Worth, Texas: Seminary Hill Press, 1948), pp. 184-202; William Wright Barnes, *The Southern Baptist Convention, 1845-1953* (Nashville, Tennessee: Broadman Press, 1954), pp. 80, 263-268.

29. *Proceedings of the . . . Convention of the General Synod of the Evangelical Lutheran Church in Session at Canton, Ohio, May 24-June 1, 1893* (Philadelphia: Lutheran Publication Society, 1893), p. 50; *at Hagerstown, Md., June 5-13, 1895* (Philadelphia: Lutheran Publication Society, 1895), pp. 56, 77-79; *Minutes of the . . . Convention of the General Council of the Evangelical Lutheran Church, Held in Trinity Evangelical Lutheran Church, Ft. Wayne, Indiana, October 5th to October 10th, 1893* (Lancaster, Ohio: Eagle Job Printing House, 1893), pp. 11-13, 88-89; . . . *in St. John's Church, Erie, Pa., October 14-20, 1897* (Philadelphia: General Council Publication Board, 1897), pp. 9-10, 62-63, 129-130; *Minutes of the . . . Convention of the United Synod of the Evangelical Lutheran Church in the South, Held in Christ Church, Staunton, Virginia, September 18-21, 1895* (Asheville, North Carolina: Southern Lutheran Printing Co., 1895), pp. 56-59; . . . *in Luther Chapel Church, Newbury, S. C., May 11-16, 1898* (New Market, Virginia: Henkel and Co.'s Steam Printing House, 1898), pp. 48-49; *The First General Conference of Lutherans in America, Held in Philadelphia, December 27-29, 1898* (Philadelphia: Lutheran Publication Board and General Council Publication Board, 1899), p. 16.

30. William De Witt Hyde, "Religious Cooperation in Maine," *Review of Reviews* [New York] 5 (1892): 51-52; William De Witt Hyde, "Christian Cooperation in Church Extension," in *Christianity Practically Applied*, 1:261-272; William De Witt Hyde, "Church Union a Necessity: The Maine Experiment," *Forum* 14 (1893): 154-162; *The Interdenominational Commission of Maine* (Portland, Maine, 1894), pamphlet in Union Theological Seminary Library, New York.

31. James McCosh, "The Federation of Churches," in *Christianity Practically Applied*, 1: 230-233; John Henry Barrows, ed., *The World's Parliament of Religions*, 2 vols. (Chicago: Parliament Publishing Co., 1893), 2: 1179-1220 et passim; Egal Feldman, "American Ecumenism: Chicago's World's Parliament of Religions of 1893," *Journal of Church and State* 9 (1967): 180-199.

32. James McCosh, *Whither! O Whither! Tell Me Where* (New York: Scribner's, 1889), pp. 43-44; McCosh, "Federation of Churches to Secure that the Gospel Be Preached to Every Creature," p. 190. See Charles Augustus Briggs, "The Barriers to Christian Union," *Presbyterian Review* 8 (1887): 435-436, 470-471 and *Whither! A Theological Question for the Times* (New York: Scribner's, 1889), pp. 237, 244, 261-265.

33. PCUSA, n. s., 17 (Philadelphia: By the Stated Clerk, 1894): 25-29; PEC 1895 (n.p.: Printed for the Convention, 1895): 608-627; *The Correspondence between the Committee*

byterian relations with Congregationalists, which, like creedal revision, attracted support from former members of the New School, also became a matter of controversy and strained the fragile bonds holding together the General Assembly. After the General Assembly refused to hear and then dissolved its committee on church cooperation, the committee on church unity, which had been packed with conservatives during the controversy, recommended that the General Assembly limit its unitive endeavors to churches of the Presbyterian and Reformed family.[34] With no party in a clear majority, these decisions were no more than an invitation to further discord. The scheme for federating Presbyterian and Reformed churches was itself a product of Presbyterian dissensions, and after becoming marked as a substitute for fellowship with other denominations, it was made the focus of debate. Delayed in 1894 by the device of sending it to the presbyteries for comment but not for ratification, the plan was laid aside in 1896.[35] Except for a home missionary agreement among American bodies arranged in 1897 by William Henry Roberts through the Alliance of Reformed Churches Holding the Presbyterian System, Presbyterians were involved in no further negotiations for unity and cooperation among churches in the United States until after the creedal disputes were resolved in 1902.[36]

As early as 1892 Josiah Strong had distinguished between "federation at the top", or federation of denominational assemblies, and "federation at the bottom." Disturbed by controversies in the General Assembly and the Episcopalians' General Convention, Strong predicted that the future of federation lay not with the denominational assemblies but with the congregations of a town or city, although he foresaw that local federations might themselves join together into regional organizations or even a national council.[37] With the slowing of the Presbyterian drive toward national denominational federation and the withdrawal of the General Assembly from its unitive projects, the kind of organization which Strong envisioned did become the most important phase of the federative movement. Strong maneuvered the Evangelical Alliance into at least a half-hearted support of federation, sponsoring addresses on state and local organizations at the meeting in Chicago, campaigning for state commissions of churches and redefining its plan for branch alliances to allow for the membership of churches as well as individuals.[38] Yet the voluntary Evangelical Alliance was no more comfortable with Strong's new organizational schemes than with his social programs. Members of the Evangelical Alliance successfully opposed the invitation extended to a member of the Presbyterian committee to speak on federation in Chicago;[39] the revised plans for state and local organizations were seldom consummated; and the federa-

on Church Unity of the General Assembly of the Presbyterian Church in the U. S. A. and the Commission on Christian Unity of the Protestant Episcopal Church in the U. S. (Philadelphia: By the Stated Clerk, 1896).

34. PCUSA, n. s., 17 (Philadelphia: By the Stated Clerk, 1894): 22, 143-144, 206-209.
35. Ibid., pp. 22, 25, 164-166; n. s., 18 (Philadelphia: By the Stated Clerk, 1895):25, 27; n. s., 19 (Philadelphia: By the Stated Clerk, 1896): 47, 105, 180-183.
36. Ibid., pp. 66-69; n. s., 20 (Philadelphia: By the Stated Clerk, 1897): 156-157.
37. Josiah Strong, "Practical Cooperation in Christian Work," Review of Reviews [New York] 6 (1892): 301. See also Josiah Strong, The New Era, or the Coming Kingdom (New York: Baker and Taylor, 1893), pp. 312-314.
38. Evangelical Alliance, U. S., Manuscript Minutes, 5 vols., 4: 107-108, 126, 149, 176, 213, 223, 255, 278, 301, in Union Theological Seminary Library, New York; Josiah Strong, "Local Alliances," American Journal of Sociology 1 (1895): 170-181.
39. Josiah Strong to Robert M. Patterson, September 16, 1893, in Evangelical Alliance, U.S., Letters, 6 pressbook vols. 3:159, 287-288, in Union Theological Seminary Library, New York.

tions begun in Pittsburgh's East End by George Hodges and Morgan Sheedy, on New York's East Side by John Bancroft Devins and in Chicago seem to have been little influenced by the Evangelical Alliance. A declining organization after 1893 and virtually defunct after 1898, the Evangelical Alliance proved so unreliable in its promotion of state and local federation that friends of the movement turned to the Open or Institutional Church League as the only available organization through which to further their designs.

The Open Church League had profited from the wave of interest in federation which crested in 1893-1894. Organized at the Madison Avenue Presbyterian Church, of which Charles Lemuel Thompson was pastor, the Open Church League attracted as members the proponents of federation, especially those like Josiah Strong who were working in behalf of state and local organizations. Although not, strictly speaking, a federation itself, the Open Church League allowed congregations as well as individuals to enroll as members—a significant departure from the conventions governing voluntary societies in the nineteenth century. During a decade when the faltering Evangelical Alliance stood virtually alone as a national Protestant organization, the Open Church League spread outward to include members in important cities of the Atlantic seaboard and some from the midwest. The Open Church League was, consequently, a likely candidate for leadership in the movement for federation when it was proposed to seek, in the absence of a national federation of denominational assemblies, a national federation of the state and local organizations which had sprung up during the 1890s and constituted at the time the liveliest part of the federative movement.[40]

The decision to seek a national federation of federations, as Strong had earlier suggested, was inspired by the visit to the United States in 1897 of Charles A. Berry, president of the Free Church Council, which had been formed the previous year to link the local councils of churches spreading among British evangelical bodies during the 1890s and which had embarked on a highly successful campaign for local councils throughout Great Britain.[41] Encouraged by Berry's reports, proponents of local federations in the United States induced the Open Church League at its annual meeting in Worcester, Massachusetts in 1897 to devote its energies to the formation of a similar national organization. Shortly thereafter, the Open Church League concluded a working agreement with the New York Federation of Churches and Christian Workers in the interest of organizing a National Federation of Churches and Christian Workers and placed their secretary, Elias B. Sanford, at the disposal of the New York federation for promoting the project.[42] Although the cooperative arrangement subsequently collapsed, apparently over procedures for calling a convention and the basis of mem-

40. Sanford, pp. 34-57; Aaron Ignatius Abell, *The Urban Impact on American Protestantism, 1865-1900* (Cambridge: Harvard University Press, 1943), pp. 161-163; *The Open or Institutional Church League: Preliminary Conference Held in the Madison Avenue Presbyterian Church, March 27, 1894* (Boston, 1894).
41. Charles A. Berry, "Federation of the Churches and Arbitration in America," *Homiletic Review* 26 (1899): 133-138; "Federation of the Churches," *Homiletic Review* 25 (1898): 96-97; Edward Kenneth Henry Jordon, *Free Church Council: History of the Free Church Council Movement, 1896-1941* (London: Lutterworth Press, 1956), pp. 36-76.
42. Sanford, pp. 85, 103-111, 432-436; *A Brief Statement of the Need, Purpose, and Work of a National Federation of Churches and Christian Workers in the United States, with a Sketch of the Work of the Federation of Churches and Christian Workers in New York City* (New York, 1898), pp. 2 et passim, pamphlet in Union Theological Seminary Library, New York.

bership in the National Federation,[43] the Open Church League called a preliminary conference in Philadelphia in 1900. As the result of the conference, a campaign was undertaken for the organization and revitalization of state and local federations, and in 1901 the National Federation of Churches and Christian Workers was born, assuming the staff and assets of the Open Church League.[44] In 1905 the National Federation of Churches and Christian Workers sponsored the Interchurch Conference on Federation, which drafted the constitution for the Federal Council, and by 1908 it had been absorbed into the new organization, allowing Sanford to establish a direct line between the Open Church League and the Federal Council of Churches.

The connection Sanford made in the *Origin and History of the Federal Council* was, however, the product of his need for personal vindication. Although slated for retirement soon after the Federal Council became operative, Sanford was unceremoniously relieved of his duties as secretary in 1911 while seriously ill.[45] Inadequately pensioned by an organization which was itself strapped for funds and embittered by the experience, Sanford campaigned for larger benefits and salved his hurt by complaining that his successor, Charles Steadman Macfarland, came into office through the "back door." Macfarland, who had not been considered for the post until Sanford's health forced the issue, had entered the Federal Council through the Commission on the Church and Social Service, formed after the adoption of the Social Creed of the Churches by the Federal Council in 1908 and a constant rival of the parent body for funds and publicity. Macfarland further strained his relationship with Sanford with his own account of the founding in *The Churches of the Federal Council* in 1916, playing down Sanford's role and attributing prime importance to the Brotherhood of Andrew and Phillip, with which Macfarland himself had earlier been associated.[46] Although Sanford was doubtless correct in his rejoinder that Rufus Miller of the Brotherhood had done no more than attend a meeting or two in the interest of the National Federation, the Brotherhood of Andrew and Phillip had taken a cue from Presbyterian and Reformed negotiations when it was organized in 1893 and had linked its relatively independent denominational units in a federal council, prompting memory of those negotiations and hope that American denominations themselves might be joined in a federation.[47] Into the 1920s Sanford clamored for Macfarland to withdraw or revise his book, and he acknowledged that the *Origin and History of the Federal Council* had been published in an attempt to set the record straight.[48] It is

43. Sanford, pp. 110-111, 116-117; "The Federation," *Outlook* 61 (1899): 565; "Conference in the Interest of Federative Action among Churches and Christian Workers in the United States, Held in Philadelphia, February 5, 6, 1901," in *Federation Chronicle: Published in the Interests of the Work of the National Federation of Churches and Christian Workers* (New York, 1901), pp. 1-2.
44. Sanford, pp. 112-145; *Federation Chronicle*, pp. 2-12.
45. Sanford, pp. 305-306; *Church Federation: First Annual Report of the Executive Committee of the Federal Council* (New York, 1909), p. 14; . . . *Third Annual Report* . . . (New York, 1911), pp. 8 et passim.
46. Elias Benjamin Sanford to Charles Steadman Macfarland, May 14, 1916, and to Samuel McCrea Cavert, August 16, 1922, in Sanford Special Correspondence File, Archives of the National Council of Churches; Charles Steadman Macfarland, *Across the Years* (New York: Macmillan, 1936), pp. 86-96; Charles Steadman Macfarland, *The Churches of the Federal Council: Their History, Organization, and Distinctive Characteristics and a Statement of the Federal Council* (New York: Fleming H. Revell, 1916), p. 246.
47. Frederick de Land Leete, *Christian Brotherhoods* (Cincinnati, Ohio: Jennings and Graham, 1912), pp. 291-296.
48. Elias Benjamin Sanford to Charles Steadman Macfarland, June 30, 1922, and to Samuel McCrea Cavert, February 28, 1923, in Sanford Special Correspondence File, Archives of the National Council of Churches.

unfortunate that his pique at Macfarland and need to establish a case for support from an organization he had served only briefly prevented his doing so.

In spite of Sanford's impression of a natural evolution from the Open Church League to the Federal Council, a national federation of denominations could scarcely have developed out of a national federation of federations, especially since the denominational bodies which had to send delegates to the Interchurch Conference and ratify the constitution for the Federal Council had earlier planned for "federation at the top." Considerable tension was evident between the variant approaches to Protestant organization from the time Josiah Strong proposed a national federation of federations as a definite alternative to a federation of denominational assemblies until the Federal Council was inaugurated with state and local bodies, in effect, denied representation. Leaders of denominations and of less formal institutions who, like Sanford, were often drawn from those failing to rise through denominational structures, were seldom represented by the same individuals, and the gulf between them appears to have been widening at the turn of the century. Men like Sanford, who claimed that little was to be expected from the denominational bodies themselves and regarded voluntary agencies as the creative edge of American Protestantism, could never have persuaded denominational bodies to join in a Federal Council just as it is unlikely that they willfully gave up the influence of their state and local federations in its behalf. Interestingly enough, it is Sanford's *Origin and History of the Federal Council* which gives evidence that the Federal Council was not the creation of the leaders of the National Federation of Churches and Christian Workers, but the child of prominent leaders of the denominational bodies themselves. Although there was general agreement that Sanford was "indefatigable" in attending to arrangements for the Interchurch Conference—whether or not his health was broken by the strain as he claimed—Sanford acknowledged that William Hayes Ward of the Congregationalists' National Council and William Henry Roberts of the Presbyterians' General Assembly towered above the former members of the National Federation and led the way at every critical juncture on the road to the Federal Council.

The Congregationalists' National Council, reiterating its call for a congress of churches by endorsements of federation in 1892 and 1895, took note of Presbyterian withdrawal from the forefront of the movement for unity and cooperation by reorganizing its own committee on Christian unity in 1895 and giving it a broader mandate to seek unity among American denominations. Reporting in 1898, the new committee proposed that the National Council sponsor a convention to explore the question of federation just as the General Assembly had contemplated in 1890, naming May 1900, in Washington, D. C., as the time and place for the meeting.[49] The date was impossible because assent could scarcely have been obtained from the cycle of denominational meetings in time for the convention. Although the adopted schedule was abandoned, the Congregationalist committee remained steadfast in its support for a conference on federation and, after 1901, concluded a bold plan for joining Congregationalists, Methodist Protestants and United Brethren more closely in a General Council, which met twice before reaching an impasse in 1907.[50]

49. NCCC 1895 (Boston: Congregational Sunday School and Publishing Society, 1896), pp. 20-21, 34-37, 282-308; NCCC 1898 (Boston: Congregational Sunday School and Publishing Society, 1898), p. 36.
50. NCCC, 1904 (Boston: Office of the Secretary of the National Council, 1904), pp. 468

The leader for Congregationalist efforts seems to have been William Hayes Ward, editor of the still powerful *Independent*. Ward was named chairman of the reorganized committee of the National Council and played an important role in the development of both the General Council and the Federal Council. Writing in 1894 for a symposium on Charles W. Shields' *The Historic Episcopate*, another contribution to the discussions between Presbyterians and Episcopalians, Ward set forth a thesis which seems to explain many of his actions with regard to the movement for unity and cooperation. In his communication to Amory H. Bradford, who also became a prominent leader in the renewed Congregationalist approaches toward unity, Ward contended that unity among American denominations would be accomplished not by words, but by "practical ecclesiastical politics."[51] Soon Ward appears to have begun to test his thesis in arranging unitive projects. He was masterful in injecting Congregationalists into what began as a discussion between Methodist bodies,[52] and there is every indication he accomplished the same feat in turning the scheme for a National Federation into a plan for achieving a Federal Council. Although it is impossible to follow every move in the game Ward played in behalf of a Federal Council, Sanford's volume and the reports of the Congregationalist committee do give a basis for reconstructing an intriguing sequence of events.

Confronted with the problem of rival proposals from the Open Church League and the National Council, Ward attended the preliminary conference in behalf of the proposed National Federation of Churches and Christian Workers in February 1900. He became a member of the resulting National Committee on Federation, whose organization may have been necessitated by the disagreement between the Open Church League and the New York Federation of Churches, but which also served as a strategem for linking proponents of the divergent approaches to national federation. When he was assigned the task of drafting the call for the meeting in 1901 which constituted the National Federation of Churches and Christian Workers, Ward wrote into the document the hope that the National Committee on Federation might yet "be the forerunner of an official Federation of Churches to which it shall give place."[53] Presbyterians had sensed in 1890 that a convention on federation called by any one denomination might be doomed to failure, and Congregationalists, whose relations with Presbyterians were themselves an issue dividing the General Assembly, faced peculiar problems in acting alone. Ward solved this difficulty by acquiescing in the organization of the National Federation of Churches and Christian Workers. Returning to the Congregationalists' National Council later in 1901, he won a reiteration of the desire for a meeting of American denominations, but proposed that the National Federation serve as agent in calling the conference, adding Sanford, a Congregationalist, to the committee of the National Council to cement the relationship. In 1902, although Sanford may have consulted on the issue as he suggests, Ward convinced the National Federa-

474, 546-548; 1907 (Boston: Office of the Secretary of the National Council, 1907), pp. 284-291; Gaius Glenn Atkins and Frederick Louis Flagley, *History of American Congregationalism* (Boston: Pilgrim Press, 1942), pp. 353-354; Augustus Waldo Drury, *History of the Church of the United Brethren in Christ* (Dayton, Ohio: Otterbein Press, 1924), pp. 528-532.
51. In Amory H. Bradford, ed., *The Question of Unity: Many Voices Concerning the Reunion of Christendom* (New York: Christian Literature Co., 1894), p. 34.
52. Jacob Henry Dorn, *Washington Gladden: Prophet of the Social Gospel* (Columbus, Ohio: Ohio State University Press, 1968), p. 355.
53. Sanford, pp. 119-121.

tion to undertake the interdenominational meeting which would lead to its own demise.[54]

Ward was not the only ecclesiastical politician attached to a denominational assembly to play an important role in the creation of the Federal Council. Although Sanford made early trips to secure the endorsements of the Methodist Episcopal Church, South and the Disciples of Christ, few preparations were made for the meeting until 1904, and the meeting seemed often in doubt until dramatic events brought the Presbyterian Church in the United States of America back into leadership of the movement for federation.[55] Presbyterian difficulties with the Westminster Confession were at least temporarily resolved during 1902-1903 when moderate conservatives like Henry Van Dyke guided a revision through the General Assembly and its ratifying presbyteries, which produced in its wake a bid for reunion from the Cumberland Presbyterians.[56] In 1902 the Presbyterians also approved a new series of discussions with Episcopalians, occasioned by the rising rate of divorce, which came to be known as the Interchurch Conference on Marriage and Divorce and was expanded to include representatives of other denominations.[57] In 1903 the General Assembly authorized a new committee on church union to deal with the range of questions laid aside during the previous decade as well as to negotiate with Cumberland Presbyterians. The timing of the new committee and the systematic development of its agenda can only reflect considerable planning, probably by William Henry Roberts, stated clerk of the General Assembly and chairman of the committee. Aligned with the persecutors of Briggs and Henry Preserved Smith during the 1890s, Roberts had a more distinguished career in the twentieth century as advocate of interdenominational enterprises and administrator of denominational affairs.[58] Like Ward—and quite possibly in collaboration with him—Roberts seems to have engineered the resumption of leadership by his denomination in the movement for federation and then to have played a major role in the organization of the Federal Council. Indeed, Sanford acknowledged that his labors in behalf of federation had indeed been "herculean."[59] In a series of negotiations Roberts' committee moved toward the union with Cumberland Presbyterians, which was consummated in 1906 in spite of the continued existence of a separate Cumberland minority, and revived the scheme—now disentangled from the proposal for a broader federation—for a Council of Reformed Churches in the United States Holding the Presbyterian System, which this time

54. Ibid., p. 174; NCCC 1901 (Boston: By the Publishing Committee of the National Council, 1901), pp. 35-36, 149-151; Amory H. Bradford, William Hayes Ward, and Washington Choate to Nacy M. Waters, March 3, 1902, in Archives of the National Council of Churches.
55. Sanford, pp. 179, 198-200. See "Church Union and Church Federation," *Independent* 55 (1903): 2701-2702, and James Harvey Garrison to Elias Benjamin Sanford, January 21, 1903, in Sanford Special Correspondence File, Archives of the National Council of Churches.
56. Lefferts Augustine Loetscher, *The Broadening Church: A Study of Theological Issues in the Presbyterian Church since 1869* (Philadelphia: Westminster Press, 1954), pp. 64, 66.
57. PCUSA, n. s., 2 (Philadelphia: By the Stated Clerk, 1902): 125; n. s., 3 (Philadelphia: By the Stated Clerk, 1903): 134-140; n. s., 4 (Philadelphia: By the Stated Clerk, 1904): 75, 235; PEC 1901 (n. p.: Printed for the Convention, 1902), pp. 192, 295-296, 301, 308; PEC 1904 (New York: Printed for the Convention, 1905), pp. 21-22; PEC 1907 (New York: Printed for the Convention, 1907), pp. 22, 291, 514-517; "Church Union and Church Federation," p. 2701.
58. PCUSA, n. s., 3 (Philadelphia: By the Stated Clerk, 1903): 91, 147, 169; Loetscher, pp. 83-89.
59. Sanford, p. 210.

won the cooperation of the southern assembly in a close vote and paved the way
for the Presbyterian Church in the United States to enter the Federal Council.
The committee also recommended the participation of the General Assembly in the
organization of the Federal Council, and by 1908 Presbyterians were willing to
enter the Home Missions Council as well.[60]

After Presbyterian support seemed certain, the National Federation of
Churches and Christian Workers became more energetic in promoting what became known as the Interchurch Conference on Federation—an indication of increasing Presbyterian involvement and of the hope that Episcopalians might re-
consider their earlier position on federation. A "letter missive" was addressed to
the denominations active in the movement of the 1880s and 1890s, and as evidence
of the "political" planning involved in the calling of the Interchurch Conference,
it was given to trusted leaders of denominational bodies to bring before their assemblies at the proper time. The assent of most of these denominations was
secured in 1904, although in 1905 numerous smaller denominations swelled the
ranks of those planning to attend. At times it had seemed unclear whether a new
organization would result from the Interchurch Conference or whether the National Federation of Churches and Christian Workers would merely solicit the
support of the denominations for its work, and in rejecting their invitation Episcopalians betrayed their belief that "federation at the top" was not intended.[61] By
the time the Interchurch Conference convened, however, denominational leaders
were securely in control of the movement. Although the elaborate program of addresses often featured the leaders of voluntary agencies and state and local federations, positions of power in organizing the business of the meeting and in
drafting the constitution for the Federal Council were reserved for Ward, Roberts
and others who, like the delegates themselves, were important figures in their
denominational bodies. Sanford admitted that the constitution of the Federal
Council was the joint product of Ward and Roberts, who in accomplishing their
task turned back toward the plan of federation drafted by Presbyterian and Reformed bodies in the 1890s.[62] Although Ward reportedly styled the name of the
organization, his model was clearly the Federal Council of Reformed Churches,
and the constitutional instrument bore equally apparent marks of its origin. Only
a single vote was cast against the document in this convention of denominational
leaders, and except for the intervention of Ward and Roberts to preserve an
obvious compromise then operating, the delegates would have voted immediately
to bar components of the National Federation of Churches and Christian Workers. As it occurred, the issue was left to die between 1905 and 1908 in the
atmosphere of exultation that surrounded the birth of a national denominational
federation.[63] A federal "congress" of churches—a phrase Ward continued to use

60. PCUSA, n. s., 4 (Philadelphia: By the Stated Clerk, 1904): 21, 57, 76, 104-105, 119-
    140, 152 157; n. s., 5 (Philadelphia: By the Stated Clerk, 1905): 68, 77-78, 81, 86,
    109, 110-117, 182; n. s., 6 (Philadelphia: By the Stated Clerk, 1906): 15, 16, 52,
    123-151, 173, 210-211, 233; PCUS 1907 (Richmond, Virginia: Presbyterian Commit-
    tee of Publication, 1907), pp. 43-47, 55-58; Robert Theodore Handy, *We Witness To-
    gether: The Story of Cooperative Home Missions* (New York: Friendship Press, 1956),
    p. 24.
61. *Church Federation: Interchurch Conference on Federation, New York, November 15-21,
    1905*, ed. Elias Benjamin Sanford (New York: Fleming H. Revell, 1906), pp. 43, 637-
    667; Sanford, pp. 196-197; PEC 1904:60.
62. Sanford, p. 210.
63. *Church Federation*, pp. 75-101. See also *Report of the First Meeting of the Federal
    Council, Philadelphia, 1908* (New York: Fleming H. Revell, 1909), p. 77.

—had come to pass.[64]

It is perhaps unfortunate that the Federal Council did not retain its original character as a congress of churches because the most persistent criticism of the organization and its successor has been isolation from constituencies. Soon after the Federal Council was founded, it began to spawn a bureaucracy which, often as not, drew members from the movement from "federation at the bottom" and proved itself relatively independent of the quadrennial assembly of denominational representatives—the source of the endless controversy over who possessed authority to speak for the Federal Council. Yet the great age of assemblies was passing. The General Council, the Council of Reformed Churches, the Methodists' Federal Council, the General Conference of Lutherans in America did not long survive or possess the resilience necessary to change with the times. Even the assemblies of member denominations were increasingly regarded as inefficient organs for transacting denominational business—a reputation gained in part through their handling of phases of the movement for unity and cooperation. Periodic meetings, mounting costs of protracted sessions, and the difficulty of getting busy ministers and laymen to devote their time to the discussion of denominational affairs led to the creation of denominational bureaucracies, which in time eroded the power of denominational assemblies and often became as isolated from congregations and ordinary church members as any interdenominational organization. Although itself a subject deserving analysis, the bureaucratization of religious organizations should be no more allowed to obscure the role of denominational assemblies in forming the Federal Council than suppositions about the place of voluntary organizations. The Federal Council was initially a creation of these assemblies and resulted from their leaders' skill in ecclesiastical politics.

64. William Hayes Ward, "A Federal Congress of Churches," *Independent* 59 (1905): 1135-1141.

E. V. TOY JR.
University of Wyoming

The National Lay Committee and the National Council of Churches: A Case Study of Protestants in Conflict

THE RELIGIOUS PHENOMENON THAT WILLIAM G. MCLOUGHLIN JR. DESCRIBED as the fourth "great awakening" coincided with the revival of conservatism in American politics in the years after 1945.[1] As the memories of depression were diminished and those of war sharpened by the realities of affluence at home and Communism abroad, millions of Americans turned toward organized religion. The churches responded positively with liberal clergymen advocating a social gospel relevant to the post-depression years and the cold war and religious conservatives urging churchgoers to reject materialism and turn to the Bible and true religion. As in politics, militant anti-Communism added a dimension to religious attitudes that overshadowed and sometimes blurred the older theological distinctions between liberals and conservatives. This ideological dilemma erupted during the brief encounter between the National Lay Committee and the General Board of the National Council of Churches of Christ and demonstrated clearly the tensions in religion and in politics during the 1950s.

The rapidly changing social and economic styles of life in the first decade after 1945 strengthened interdenominational cooperation, but social change was also a catalyst of discontent at virtually all levels of

---

[1] *Modern Revivalism: Charles Grandison Finney to Billy Graham* (New York, 1959), pp. 8, 472. See Wesley and Beverly Allinsmith, "Religious Affiliation and Politico-Economic Attitude: a Study of Eight Major U. S. Religious Groups," *Public Opinion Quarterly*, XII (Fall 1948), 377-89, for correlations between political and religious patterns in the immediate postwar period.

religious involvement.[2] The issues that motivated the social action groups fostered counter-movements that strengthened the anti-Communist bonds between conservative Protestants and conservative Roman Catholics. Even before Senator Joseph R. McCarthy of Wisconsin found an issue in Communism and William F. Buckley Jr. discovered that God was not in residence at Yale,[3] a manifesto of the American Roman Catholic bishops on November 20, 1948, echoed the discontent of many Protestants and warned that secularism was "threatening the religious foundations of our national life and preparing the way for the advent of the omnipotent State."[4]

In the more explicit language of *The Road Ahead* (1949), John T. Flynn, the ex-radical and political columnist, accused Protestant leaders of using the Federal Council of Churches to promote socialism, and in the process Flynn set the tone and the theme for more than a decade of political and religious controversy.[5] The publication of *The Road*

---

[2] Samuel McCrea Cavert, *The American Churches in the Ecumenical Movement, 1900-1968* (New York, 1968), describes the fluctuations in the fortunes of the ecumenical movements, and Will Herberg, *Protestant, Catholic, and Jew* (New York, 1955), explains some of the social factors affecting theological beliefs.

[3] *God and Man at Yale: The Superstitions of Academic Freedom* (Chicago, 1951).

[4] Quoted in Herbert W. Schneider, *Religion in 20th Century America* (Cambridge, 1952), pp. 29-30.

[5] *The Road Ahead: America's Creeping Revolution* (New York, 1949). For an unfavorable appraisal of Flynn see Ralph Lord Roy, *Apostles of Discord: A Study of Organized Bigotry and Disruption on the Fringes of Protestantism* (Boston, 1953), pp. 232-33; 401-2, and for favorable comments see Edgar C. Bundy, *Collectivism in the Churches: A Documented Account of the Political Activities of the Federal, National, and World Councils of Churches* (Wheaton, Ill., 1958), p. vii.

The John T. Flynn papers at the University of Oregon contain the manuscript of *The Road Ahead*, communications about the condensed version that appeared in the *Reader's Digest*, and favorable and unfavorable correspondence. Richard C. Frey Jr. is completing work on his dissertation, "John T. Flynn and the United States in Crisis, 1928-1950."

Other significant collections at the University of Oregon bearing on the controversy about *The Road Ahead* and ultraconservatism include the papers of the Committee for Constitutional Government, Willford I. King, Samuel Pettingill and James W. Clise.

Some letters of Edward Rumely, a pivotal figure in the controversy, are found in the University of Oregon collections, the Henry Ford Collection in Dearborn, the Gutzon Borglum Collection in the Library of Congress, the Harrington Emerson Collection in the Industrial Museum of Pennsylvania State University, the Western History Research Center of the University of Wyoming, and, especially, the Edward Rumely Collection at the Lilly Library of Indiana University.

Other contemporary critics of the ecumenical movements included: James DeForest Murch, *The Growing Superchurch: A Critique of the National Council of the Churches of Christ* (n.p., 1952) and *Evanston, 1954—The Coming Great Church: A Critique of the World Council of Churches* (n.p., 1955); Carl McIntire, *Modern Tower of Babel* (Collingswood, N. J., 1955); Marion John Bradshaw, *Free Churches and Christian Unity: A Critical View of the Ecumenical Movement and the World Council of Churches* (Boston, 1954); Edmund A. Opitz, *The Powers That Be: Case Studies of the Church in Politics* (Los Angeles, 1956).

Ahead virtually coincided with the merging of the Federal Council into the new National Council of Churches, and the social action movements of many denominations shared in the reaction that a conservative Unitarian clergyman, the Rev. Edmund A. Opitz, described as against "political or social actions foreign to the basic concepts of our American system, which might be proposed in the name of His church."[6]

Dr. Samuel McCrea Cavert, a Presbyterian and General Secretary of the Federal Council of Churches from 1921 to 1950, Methodist Bishop G. Bromley Oxnam and Dr. Eugene Carson Blake of the Presbyterian Church, U.S.A., were among the leaders of the new ecumenical mood after 1945. They worked with laymen like Charles P. Taft, Episcopalian, Arthur S. Flemming, Methodist, and J. Erwin Miller, Christian Church, to create an atmosphere favorable to social action and interdenominational cooperation within the National Council, which succeeded the progressive-era Federal Council in 1951. Although its membership was not limited to the traditionally liberal churches, the National Council became the principal symbol of old-line Protestant cooperation and unity.

On the other hand, the National Association of Evangelicals, independent churches and sects, and dissenters within the ranks of the National Council challenged its goals and its authority as the voice of organized Protestantism. The challenge by conservatives had both religious and political implications, and the impetus did not come solely from those persons alienated from the old-line churches. Some dissident Protestants like the Rev. Carl McIntire of the Bible Presbyterian Church, who had been identified with fundamentalist causes since the 1920s and who organized the American Council of Christian Churches in 1941 as a fundamentalist counterpart of the Federal Council, vociferously opposed its successor.[7] In addition, the cold war produced other militant opponents of ecumenical activities like Dr. Fred Schwarz, Major Edgar C. Bundy and the Rev. Billy James Hargis who capitalized on the affinity of religious fundamentalists and political conservatives for organized anti-Communism.[8] Nevertheless, in evangelical and conservative circles

[6] "The Religious Foundation of a Free Society," address at annual banquet of the Maine Farm Bureau, Portland, Nov. 16, 1959, p. 1, Clise MSS.

[7] McIntire's conversion to religious fundamentalism, first as protege then as critic of J. Gresham Machen, evolved into the American Council of Christian Churches and the International Council of Christian Churches, both fundamentalist responses to liberal ecumenical movements.

[8] Among the most important studies of the neofundamentalist influence in recent politics are: McLoughlin, *Modern Revivalism*, pp. 400-522; Roy, *Apostles of Discord;* Richard Hofstadter, *Anti-intellectualism in American Life* (New York, 1963), pp. 117-41; "The Paranoid Style in American Politics," *Harper's*, CCXXIX (Nov. 1964), 77-86; *The Paranoid Style in American Politics and Other Essays* (New York, 1965); *The Radical Right: The New American Right Expanded and Updated*, ed. Daniel Bell

the popular Rev. Billy Graham more accurately expressed the dominant religious theme with his proclamation: "If you would be a true patriot, then become a loyal Christian." [9] This appeal to the flag and to the cross made justification by faith alone a virtual national necessity as well as a Protestant tenet, and political conservatives of many religious beliefs cautioned Americans to avoid mixing religion with social welfare programs, which they condemned as socialistic.

The unfavorable reactions to social action were varied and depended as much on political issues and social interests as they did upon religious beliefs. Clergymen like the Rev. James W. Fifield Jr., of the independent First Congregational Church of Los Angeles, and laymen within the National Council like J. Howard Pew, chairman of the board of Sun Oil Company and member of the Presbyterian Church, U.S.A.,[10] B. E. Hutchinson, an Episcopalian and executive of Chrysler Corporation, and Jasper E. Crane, also a member of the Presbyterian Church in the U.S.A. and an executive of the Du Pont Corporation, repeated virtually the same arguments against the National Council and its new social gospel that they had used two decades earlier against the New Deal and an older social gospel.[11]

Ironically, opponents of social action sometimes found themselves ranged for different reasons with the politically liberal Rev. Reinhold

---

(Garden City, 1963); Seymour Martin Lipset, *Revolution and Counter Revolution: Change and Persistence in Social Structures* (New York, 1968); George D. Younger, "Protestant Piety and the Right Wing," *Social Action*, XVII (May 15, 1951), 5-35; David Danzig, "The Radical Right and the Rise of the Fundamentalist Minority," *Commentary*, XXXIII (Apr. 1962), 291-98; Fred J. Cook, "The Ultras: Aims, Affiliations and Finances of the Radical Right," *Nation*, CXCIV (June 30, 1962), 565-606; Philip Horton, "Revivalism on the Far Right," *Reporter*, XXV (July 20, 1961), 25-29.

For a slightly different emphasis on "fundamentalism" see Harry and Bonaro Overstreet, *The Strange Tactics of Extremism* (New York, Norton paperback, 1964), pp. 144-45 and Brooks R. Walker, *The Christian Fright Peddlers* (Garden City, N. Y., 1964).

9 Quoted in McLoughlin, *Modern Revivalism*, p. 511. McLoughlin (p. 482) views Graham as "a product of this realignment in Protestantism and of the postwar tension which transformed the nation's outlook from liberalism to conservatism." Also see McLoughlin, *Billy Graham: Revivalist in a Secular Age* (New York, 1960).

10 The United Presbyterian Church of North America and the Presbyterian Church in the U. S. A. merged as the United Presbyterian Church in the United States of America in 1958.

11 See George Wolfskill, *The Revolt of the Conservatives: A History of the American Liberty League, 1934-1940* (Boston, 1962), for a description of Pew's activities in the Liberty League and of his fight against Prohibition. The Henry Bourne Joy papers in the Michigan Historical Collections of the University of Michigan portray a like ideological bent in the former president of the Packard Motor Company. Joy, also a member of the Liberty League, fought against Prohibition and the Federal Council of Churches before his death in 1936. The "Epilogue" of Donald B. Meyer, *The Protestant Search for Political Realism, 1919-1941* (Berkeley and Los Angeles, 1960), briefly describes the challenge facing the social gospel in the years after 1945.

Niebuhr and the politically conservative Fifield. These two clergymen diverged from one another and from fundamentalists in their social values and theological opinions. While H. Richard and Reinhold Niebuhr shaped neo-orthodoxy during the two decades after the Great Crash, Fifield, in 1935, founded Spiritual Mobilization as a counterweight to the social gospel and the New Deal.[12] Niebuhr's image as a political liberal remained untainted in the years after the Second World War, and Fifield's religious equivalent to the American Liberty League served as a liaison between religious ideals and economic orthodoxy into the 1960s. Nevertheless, both Niebuhr and Fifield questioned the kinship of the social gospel with theological liberalism. Niebuhr wrote in his *Reflections on the End of an Era* (1934) that "adequate spiritual guidance can come only through a more radical political orientation and more conservative religious convictions. . . ."[13] For Fifield, liberal religious beliefs confirmed conservative social and economic beliefs.[14] James C. Ingebretsen, its last president, explained that Spiritual Mobilization was unique with its "liberal" theology and "conservative" economic and

---

[12] Fifield founded Spiritual Mobilization in Chicago, where George Washington Robnett developed a similar organization, the Laymen's Council of the Church League of America, a few years later. In the mid-1950s Robnett sold his brainchild to Major Edgar C. Bundy, who moved its headquarters to Wheaton, Ill.

Another Congregational minister, Albert Hyma, also fumed against the radical 1930s in *Christianity, Capitalism, and Communism: A Historical Analysis* (Ann Arbor, 1937).

[13] (New York, 1934), p. ix.

[14] See Walker, *The Christian Fright Peddlers*, pp. 133-41, for an analysis of Fifield's theology. H. Shelton Smith, Robert T. Handy and Lefferts A. Loetscher, *American Christianity: An Historical Interpretation with Representative Documents, II, 1820-1960* (New York, 1963), p. 507, lends support to this view. Also note the implied criticism of fundamentalism in Fifield, "A Study of Fundamentalism in the Presbyterian Church since 1900" (Master's thesis, University of Chicago, 1925).

To complicate the issue even further, Bruce Barton, viewed by many as the epitome of the businessman in religion in the 1920s, spurned Fifield's pleas for support on several occasions in the 1940s and 1950s. Fifield and Barton had been acquainted in Illinois, where Barton's father had been a Congregational minister, but Barton rebuffed Fifield's efforts to get him on the Advisory Committee of Spiritual Mobilization. See the Bruce Barton Papers in the Mass Communications Center, State Historical Society of Wisconsin, file box 20. Especially pertinent are: Fifield to Barton, Sept. 13, 1944; Barton to Fifield, Sept. 19, 1944 and Fifield to Barton, July 3, 1957.

Between September 1944 and September 1945, the membership of the Advisory Committee of Spiritual Mobilization included: Roger W. Babson, Dr. Paul F. Cadman, Upton Close, Dr. Donald J. Cowling, Ely Culbertson, Dr. Will Durant, Dr. Cary Eggleston, Dr. Edgar J. Goodspeed, the Hon. Albert W. Hawkes, Dr. Douglas Horton, Eric Johnston, the Rev. Harold M. Kingsley ["Negro leader"], Dr. John A. Mackay, Dr. Robert A. Milliken, Dr. Alfred Noyes, Dr. Norman Vincent Peale, Channing Pollock, the Hon. Norris Poulson, Dr. Robert Gordon Sproul, Dr. Ray Lyman Wilbur, Dr. Mary E. Wooley, Dr. Charles R. Brown, Morse A. Cartwright, Silas Strawn, De Witt Emery, Will Irwin, Dr. William Mather Lewis and Dr. John J. Tigert.

political ideals.[15] J. Howard Pew, though often calling himself a fundamentalist, took a similar theological and political stance.[16]

While their defenders regarded the church councils as fulfilling a necessary social as well as spiritual role, their critics protested against bureaucratic centralization, domination of church councils by clergymen, meddling in social and economic affairs, and any association with the World Council of Churches, which was founded in Amsterdam in 1948. This estrangement of the conservatives eroded support for the National Council at a time when the cold war, the Korean War and McCarthyism absorbed public attention. In the summer of 1950, only a few months after Senator McCarthy first made his sensational charges about subversion in the State Department, J. Howard Pew became the chairman of a group of lay sponsors of the National Council. Many clergymen accepted the choice of Pew as a necessary expedient, but he went beyond the role of financial angel and argued that involvement in social issues diverted the fledgling church union from its stated purpose of making religion a more dominant factor in American life. During a dramatic confrontation at the first conference of the National Council in Cleveland in the fall of 1950, Pew informed the delegates that his committee of laymen wanted to help determine policy in areas where its members had "special competence and interest." [17]

Between July 1950, when clergymen and lay sponsors held their first discussions about organizing and financing the National Council, and June 30, 1955, when the Council disbanded the National Lay Committee, Pew and his supporters fought against activities which they condemned as often coinciding with Communist objectives. These laymen and their ministerial allies protested in much the same way as Opitz, who wrote: "In sober truth we are forced to reply that many of our most articulate religious leaders are part of the problem, not part of the remedy." [18] Pew

15 Ingebretsen to Clise, Dec. 12, 1958, Clise MSS.

16 Pew was the principal financial support of the conservative and neofundamentalist *Christian Economics*, but he also supported Spiritual Mobilization's *Faith and Freedom*. Pew often described himself as a fundamentalist, but he was emancipated from the social taboos many fundamentalists insisted upon, and he sometimes disagreed vehemently with Carl McIntire. Conversely, McIntire criticized Pew's understanding of theology. See Edward Cain, *They'd Rather Be Right: Youth and the Conservative Movement* (New York, 1963), pp. 198-99 for a revealing challenge by McIntire to Pew's use of Scriptural authority. McIntire argued that "the church should not remain silent" about social issues and cited the Decalogue as his source of authority. The question, as Cain made clear, was "Whose 'social gospel'"?

17 "What Laity Are to Be Represented?" *Christian Century*, LXVII (Dec. 13, 1950), 1475-76. The constant concern about lay participation in affairs of the National Council can be traced through the *Biennial Reports* of the National Council of the Churches of Christ in the United States of America.

18 Opitz, "The Religious Foundation of a Free Society," p. 6.

explained that "with few exceptions, the members of the Lay Committee had agreed to serve only because they had been assured that the new National Council would avoid the political involvements and controversies which had characterized the activities of the old Federal Council of Churches. . . ."[19]

Pew believed that laymen needed to counteract the misconceptions that many ministers had about businessmen. And when he invited Frank E. Holman, a Congregationalist and a former president of the American Bar Association, to join the National Lay Committee in October 1950, Pew optimistically assured Holman that the Committee would review economic and social statements prior to approval by the General Board.[20]

As chairman of between 80 and 190 prominent industrial and professional leaders, Pew appeared to command a unanimity that was not truly representative of the thinking of many less conservative laymen.[21] And when Pew announced that his Committee would like to continue its efforts to further Christian work by advising the Council about "announcements and statements of policy in fields in which the lay groups have a special competence and interest" and about "speaking in public with a single tongue," many of his fellow committeemen questioned his motives.[22]

The extent of lay participation in affairs of the National Council was constantly discussed, and at the first business meeting of the General Board the Planning Committee, with Dr. Samuel McCrea Cavert speaking on its behalf, recommended the organization of a permanent National Lay Committee with broad powers of participation and review. The Planning Committee, though expressing reservations, agreed with Pew that the Lay Committee's role should be one "overarching" the National

[19] "Clergy Outvoted Us, 10 to 1," *U. S. News and World Report*, XL (Feb. 3, 1956), 47. See the reply, "Mr. Pew and the Clergy," *Christian Century*, LXXIII (Feb. 22, 1956), 229-31. Paul M. Harrison, "Church and the Laity among Protestants," *Annals*, CCCII (Nov. 1960), 37-49, discusses the dilemma about "integrating" laymen into institutionalized churches in which ministers generally set the theological tone and the positive pace. *Goals of Economic Life*, ed. A. Dudley Ward (New York, 1953 and Howard R. Bowen, *Social Responsibilities of the Businessman* (New York, 1953) were produced by the Study Committee of the Federal Council of Churches and were "not a statement or pronouncement of the National Council."

[20] Copy of letter, Pew to Holman, Oct. 31, 1950; copy of telegram of acceptance, Holman to Pew, Dec. 1, 1950; copy of letter of resignation, Holman to Pew, Dec. 5, 1950, Clise MSS. Holman tentatively accepted a position but resigned within a month after expressing his conviction that the Committee would be ineffective. See the *Biennial Report* (1952), pp. 141-42.

[21] Roy, *Apostles of Discord*, p. 302; "For Christ: 31,000,000," *Newsweek*, XXXVI (Dec. 11, 1950), 78-79.

[22] *Christian Century*, LXVII, 1475-76.

Council, but Bishop G. Bromley Oxnam questioned this function and expressed fear of censorship by such an autonomous body.[23]

The General Board appointed a committee to study the issue and belatedly approved the National Lay Committee on March 28, 1951. Although his committee's role was more limited than Pew had desired, he expressed confidence that laymen, working through it, the General Department of United Church Men and the General Department of United Church Women would have considerable influence. Five men and five women from these other departments were consultants to the General Board in addition to seven members of the Lay Committee who served on it. At the same time, the Board made provisions for appointing 35 members of the Lay Committee to the Council's Business and Finance Committee. Moreover, as Pew explained, laymen could more closely supervise declarations by the Council, since proposals were to be reviewed by the members of the General Board before they would be presented officially. This requirement would permit laymen to consider recommendations with members of the Lay Committee in advance of their discussion by the General Board.[24]

Noel Sargent, an Episcopal layman, the Secretary of the National Association of Manufacturers and a member of the Lay Committee, believed that Pew and Jasper E. Crane had modified their demands since the Cleveland meeting.[25] But it was only a short time before disillusioned laymen blamed the General Board for driving a further wedge between them and their clerical leaders.

Chafing under what he considered unfair restrictions, Pew later complained:

> The members of the Lay Committee were often misunderstood in their urgency to keep the churches out of politics and their insistence on the primacy of evangelism. Our premise was that, instead of appealing to government, the church should devote its energies to the work of promoting the attributes of Christianity—truth, honesty, fairness, generosity, justice and charity—in the hearts and minds of men. We attempted to emphasize that Christ stressed not the expanded state but the dignity and responsibility of the individual.[26]

23 "What Happened at Cleveland," *Christian Century,* LXVII (Dec. 13, 1950), 1481-82, 1500-1; "General Board Meets," *Christian Century,* LXVIII (Jan. 31, 1951), 134-56. *Biennial Report* (1952), pp. 86, 146-48. The General Board appointed a committee of five, headed by Bishop Frank W. Sterrett, to meet with the laymen.
24 Copy of letter, Pew to Holman, Dec. 5, 1950; copy of letter, Pew to Noel Sargent, Apr. 18, 1951, Clise MSS. *Biennial Report* (1952), pp. 141-42.
25 Sargent to Clise, May 21, 1951, Clise MSS. Crane, like Pew and Hutchinson, was also a Trustee of the Foundation for Economic Education.
26 *U. S. News and World Report,* XL, 47.

Its defenders exaggerated its impotence, and despite efforts of liberal clergymen to neutralize it, the Lay Committee successfully hampered programs of the Division of Christian Life and Work, which was in the vanguard of the social reform movement. Laymen and clergymen objected to the goals as well as the methods of the Division, and the *Christian Century* explained that this Division was "most suspect by the more conservative denominations and by the conservative lay group newly interested in cooperative endeavors." [27]

The clerical leaders of the National Council, who found social and economic problems increasingly relevant to contemporary Christianity, hesitated to cooperate with what many of them considered a handful of wealthy conservatives obstructing their mission, and the issue of autonomy remained unresolved. Despite seemingly conciliatory statements on both sides, efforts to compromise failed. The 1952 biennial assembly of the National Council reaffirmed the decision to avoid a direct confrontation by working toward the "speedy and complete integration of lay workers into the structural life of the Council. . . ." The assembly set June 30, 1954 as the target date and concluded that there would "be no need for a Lay Committee (as such) because its members [would] be actively working throughout the Council from top to bottom on a variety of policy, managerial, and program committees and boards where their experience and ability [could] be utilized to the fullest degree." [28] Many members of the Committee feared that integration into the separate divisions would weaken their influence, and Pew, who wanted to expand its powers, adamantly demanded that the Committee remain intact.

The political atmosphere of the early 1950s made the shaky armistice between conservative laymen and liberal clergymen even less secure, and both groups seemed inexorably drawn toward opposite sides in the recriminations about Communism and its influence among clergymen.[29] Since the Lay Committee, which eventually totaled 190 members, repre-

27 "Just Who Can Say What?" *Christian Century*, XLIX (Jan. 23, 1952), 92. *Biennial Report* (1954), pp. 51-53. For insights into Pew's other activities at this time see "National Council Problems," *Christian Century*, XLIX (Jan. 2, 1952), 7-9 and the New York *Times* (Sept. 13, 1951), 29:4. The National Council published a series, *A Forum by Correspondence*, which presented differing views of controversial issues.

28 Quoted in Roy, *Apostles of Discord*, p. 305. *Biennial Report* (1952), pp. 147-48.

29 *Ibid.*, p. 383; J. B. Matthews, "Communism and the Colleges," *American Mercury*, (Aug. 1953), 17-25; "Red Infiltration of Theological Seminaries," *American Mercury*, LXXVI (June 1953), 33-40; "Reds and Our Churches," *American Mercury*, LXXVII (July 1953), 3-13; "Communists and the New Deal (Pt. III)," *American Mercury*, LXXVII (Aug. 1953), 17-25; "Red Infiltration of Theological Seminaries," *American Mercury*; LXXVII (Nov. 1953), 31-36. The July article, in which Matthews charged that "the largest single group supporting the Communist apparatus is composed of Protestant clergymen," aroused President Eisenhower to condemn it. Senator Joseph R. McCarthy soon removed Matthews from a position as research assistant to his Senate subcommittee.

sented many fields of endeavor—"20 in education, 15 in banking, 29 in manufacturing, 14 in labor-union executive positions, 15 in law, 10 in medicine, 8 in agriculture"—it was virtually impossible not to offend or frighten someone.[30] As decisions and statements by divisions of the National Council affected an ever-broader spectrum of public opinion, members of the Lay Committee increased their opposition. In order to exploit the prestige of the Committee and to stem dissent among its members, Pew ceased consulting with many of those less conservative than he. To many members of the General Board, Pew appeared to be using the Committee as a personal platform to denounce social change. And it was no surprise to his critics when the Lay Committee vigorously condemned a study conference criticism of the Bricker Amendment, a General Board statement protesting the "procedural abuses" of congressional committees, expressions of support for the United Nations, and a statement by the Department on the Church and Economic Life about the relationship between economic principles and Christian faith.[31]

Such issues widened the gulf between clerical leaders and conservative laymen, and, inevitably, there also were disagreements among the members of the Lay Committee concerning its functions and its policies. Even the conservatives disagreed, and Crane, who made an invidious comparison between liberal clergymen and subversives, clashed with Sargent, who argued that the Lay Committee should be merely a source of opinion rather than an overseeing body. Crane believed that with tact or, if necessary, with coercion laymen could effectively modify what he considered the harmful actions of church organizations of the past. Though confident the disagreements with the liberals and with the clergy would not cause a final rupture, Crane suggested that conservative laymen could precipitate overwhelming opposition to the National Council by submitting a mass resignation.[32]

After the first general meeting of the World Council of Churches in Amsterdam in 1948, many Americans were angered by what they considered a condemnation of capitalism in the "Amsterdam Declaration." At the second plenary assembly of the World Council in Evanston, Illinois, in 1954, American delegates who sought to soften the final statement of principles seemed pleased that "the 'social reform' or 'leftist' group" thought "that the document [was] 'a retreat from Amsterdam.'"

30 "Laymen and Clergy at Odds on Role of Church in Politics," *U. S. News and World Report*, XL (Feb. 3, 1956), 43. Pew explained that editors, publishers, state and federal officials, judges, scientists and many persons in other fields were also members.

31 "Mr. Pew and the Clergy," *Christian Century*, LXXIII (Feb. 22, 1956), 230.

32 Copy of letter, Jasper E. Crane to Holman, Dec. 14, 1950; Sargent to Clise, May 21, 1951; copy of letter, Holman to Crane, Dec. 19, 1950; copy of letter, Holman to Pew, Dec. 16, 1950, Clise MSS.

Sargent, who was a consultant at Evanston, quoted Charles P. Taft, a moderate conservative delegate and an opposition member of Pew's Committee, as saying: "This (Evanston report) represents a change in the real views of many who at Amsterdam criticized the prevailing (capitalist) economic system." Sargent thought the declaration indicated a reversal of church opinion in the years since 1948, but he cautioned "that it would be unwise to publicly make mention about this Evanston 'retreat from Amsterdam' on social-economic questions—unless and until we can quote from articles which appear (as they probably will) in church publications." Fearing that the next World Council Assembly would revise the statement, Sargent "hoped that people who believe in economic freedom [would] have an opportunity to work on social-economic questions within the World Council. . . ."[33]

Whether on the international or the national level, conservatives seemed to be on the defensive in religious circles. Although Ralph Lord Roy, who wrote *Apostles of Discord* in 1953, believed that conservative laymen were gaining new prominence,[34] within a short time the efforts of the Lay Committee were weakened by opposition from the General Board and by conflict within its own ranks and ultraconservatives had to find a new arena for attacking the National Council. Despite the pervasiveness of McCarthyism and the continuing tensions of the cold war, Mrs. Morgan Padelford, a former national president of Pro America who was active in the Council of Churches and Christian Education, lamented in 1954 that she was merely fighting a holding action "trying with a small group to be the still voice in the wilderness opposing the use of governmental force to achieve all their ends."[35]

Many conservatives lost confidence in their ability to reverse the course charted for the National Council by liberal clergymen and laymen. Sargent, who preferred to work from within rather than denounce the National Council from outside, believed that organizations like the Church-Industry Relations Department of the National Association of Manufacturers could "do really significant work by creating understanding within the Churches of the importance of economic freedom, both in and of itself, and of the relationship between economic and religious freedom."[36] But the National Lay Committee, which was the focal point for ultraconservative opposition to the National Council and the World Council, disbanded in 1955.

33 Mimeographed Report, Noel Sargent to H. C. McClellan, Aug. 28, 1954, Clise MSS.
34 Roy, *Apostles of Discord*, pp. 305-6. Of six at-large vice-presidents selected for Council positions in 1952, Crane, Mrs. Olive Ann Beech and Mrs. Norman Vincent Peale represented the conservative positions.
35 Clise to Leonard E. Read, June 10, 1954, Clise MSS.
36 Mimeographed Report, Sargent to McClellan, Aug. 28, 1954, Clise MSS.

Pew considered the meeting of the General Board in Chicago on May 18-19, 1953, as the critical point in his Committee's life. It was only at this meeting, Pew recalled in 1956, that he finally

realized the extent and character of the philosophy held currently by most of the ordained executives and officers directing the work of the several denominational headquarters staffs, and therefore of the National Council.

Their philosophy, it seemed to the lay committee, looked to an everexpanding government. Clergy and laity active in organized Protestantism seemed to have lost the capacity to understand each other.[37]

Pew concluded that the views of these clerical leaders, though dominant in the General Board, would not have the same support at the congregational level. He intimated that a dedicated minority of clergymen denied laymen their proper role in the National Council.

Ultimately, 1954 was probably more decisive than 1953 both for the Committee and for the National Council. The General Board firmly insisted that the members of the Committee integrate with the other divisions of the Council. Faced with this unyielding resistance, the leaders of the Lay Committee wrote to Bishop William C. Martin, president of the National Council in February 1954, reiterating the need for an autonomous Lay Committee: "The over-all view of the Council's work, plus the opportunity to review this composite picture, is essential to the keeping together of this group of 190 lay people. If our primary task is to be the interpretation of the Council's work, then we must know the whole picture collectively, be organized to discuss it and plan its interpretation together."[38]

Faced with the task of reconciling laymen and clergy, the General Board made a final and futile effort to compromise and extended the life of the Lay Committee through June 1955. But in September 1954, when the National Council authorized its officers to write to the United States delegation to the General Assembly of the United Nations about issues

37 *U. S. News and World Report*, XL (Feb. 3, 1956), 43-44. Dora Jane Hamblin, "Crunch in the Churches," *Life*, LXV (Oct. 4, 1968), 79-84, concludes that "Protestant ministers, moving deeper into the struggle for human rights, are increasingly at odds with their flocks." See also Charles Y. Glock and Benjamin B. Ringer, "Church Policy and the Attitudes of Ministers and Parishioners on Social Issues," *American Sociological Review*, XXI (Apr. 1956), 148-56 and Benton Johnson, "Theology and Party Preference among Protestant Clergymen," *American Sociological Review*, XXXI (Apr. 1966), 200-8; "Theology and the Position of Pastors on Public Issues," *American Sociological Review*, XXXII (June 1967), 433-42.

38 *U. S. News and World Report*, XI, 48.

to be discussed, the Lay Committee, by a vote of 115 to 15, adopted a manifesto entitled an "Affirmation of the Members of the National Lay Committee of the National Council of the Churches of Christ in the U.S.A. on the Subject of Corporate Pronouncements of Denominational or Interdenominational Agencies." The basic argument reflected a belief that the Lay Committee knew theological purposes better than did the clergy:

> Our Committee believes that the National Council of the Churches impairs its ability to meet its prime responsibility when, sitting in judgment on current secular affairs, it becomes involved in economic or political controversy having no moral or ethical content, promoting division where unity of purpose should obtain, nor do we believe that the National Council has a mandate to engage in such activities.[39]

The Lay Committee presented this "Affirmation" to the Committee on Policy and Strategy on September 13, 1954, and to the General Board on September 15, 1954. The General Board accepted the report, but it resisted any attempts to change its decision to dissolve the Lay Committee. In the absence of a compromise, the General Department of United Church Men offered to establish the Lay Committee within its jurisdiction, but Pew and his supporters considered this solution undesirable, since they would be less autonomous than formerly.

Although the General Board continued discussions with representatives of the Lay Committee through the fall of 1954, neither side yielded. B. E. Hutchinson was Pew's representative on a mediating subcommittee, and in a meeting with national officers on October 29, 1954, he persisted in asking for even more authority than the Committee previously had. The General Board refused to change its decision, and, on January 26, 1955, Dr. Eugene Carson Blake, then president of the National Council, notified Hutchinson that the Lay Committee would be discontinued as scheduled.[40] Perhaps it was fitting that the life of the National Lay

39 "Affirmation of the Members of the National Lay Committee of the National Council of the Churches of Christ in the U. S. A. on the Subject of Corporate Pronouncements of Denominational or Interdenominational Agencies," p. 3; Pew to Clise, Dec. 9, 1957, Clise MSS. *Biennial Report* (1954), pp. 145, 148, 156-59; Donald C. Bolles, "The General Board at Evanston," National Council *Outlook*, IV (June 1954), 8-9; Fletcher Coates, "To Express the Christian Conscience," National Council *Outlook*, IV (Oct. 1954), 3-4.

40 *U. S. News and World Report*, XL, 46; copy of letter, Hutchinson to members of the General Board of the National Council of Churches, Sept. 10, 1956; Hutchinson to members of the General Board and of the Staff of the National Council of the Churches of Christ, Sept. 20, 1957, Clise MSS. Hutchinson, who was a vice president at large in 1955, resigned from the National Council in 1957, and in January 1959 he introduced James W. Clise to Robert Welch's "The Politician." See the General Board's defense in "Clergy and Laity—A Partnership," National Council *Outlook*, VI (Mar. 1956), 17.

Committee coincided almost exactly with the success and then the failure of Senator McCarthy's anti-Communist crusade.

The dire consequences Crane had predicted for the National Council did not occur with the demise of the Lay Committee. Instead, the National Council exhibited a vitality and a durability that were both cause and consequence of its involvement in social action programs. Hutchinson, who by 1959 was an active supporter of the John Birch Society, reluctantly concluded that organizing opposition to the National Council cost Pew much money and cost his friends much effort—only to fail.[41] Nevertheless, Hutchinson insisted that he and Pew had nearly accomplished their goal. Enough hope remained that when Pew and his allies turned toward other endeavors after 1958, fundamentalist critics of the National Council continued the assault from outside its ranks.[42]

Although Pew failed to shackle the National Council of Churches, he continued his efforts among Presbyterians. The conservative faction seemed dominant at the meeting of the National Council of United Presbyterian Men in Chicago in the spring of 1957,[43] and, in March 1958, Pew, who was then president of the Foundation of the Presbyterian Church in the U.S.A., asked his fellow Presbyterians: "Is our Church competent to determine all relationships in social and economic life? Should it become involved in all other secular areas of our common life?"[44] These questions took on more than rhetorical significance when Pew began to divert much of his financial and moral support from ultra-conservative educational organizations like the Christian Freedom Foundation, Spiritual Mobilization and the Foundation for Economic Education and turned toward the John Birch Society after 1958.[45] Pew's shift

[41] Hutchinson to Clise, Jan. 15, 1959, Clise MSS.

[42] The Rev. Carl McIntire often alienated his less fundamentalist allies. Clise to McIntire, Oct. 11, 1960, Clise MSS. Clise protested McIntire's alleged anti-Roman Catholic statements.

[43] "Presbyterian Men Betray Themselves," *Christian Century*, LXXIV (Apr. 3, 1957), 412. William J. Grede, who was a former president of the National Association of Manufacturers and one of the eleven founders of the John Birch Society in December 1958, was another speaker at this meeting. See Arnold Forster and Benjamin R. Epstein, *Danger on the Right* (New York, 1964), pp. 62, 267-68, 275-76. Pew's shift in emphasis coincided with his establishment of the J. Howard Pew Freedom Trust in 1957.

[44] Quoted in Martin Marty, *The New Shape of American Religion* (New York, 1958, 1959), p. 19. See also Murray S. Stedman Jr., *Religion and Politics in America* (New York, 1964), p. 23 and "The Church Dare Not Be Silent," *Presbyterian Life*, XIII (May 15, 1960), 16-19. Compare these perspectives with Victor Obenhaus, *Ethics for an Industrial Age: A Christian Inquiry [Christian Ethics and Economic Life]* (New York, 1965), a volume in a series sponsored by the National Council of Churches.

[45] Bernard Lefkowitz, Sidney Zion and Marvin Smilon, "Far Right and Far Left: The Birch Society," New York *Post*, Apr. 2, 1964, Magazine Section, p. 25; "Far Right and Far Left: Richer and Poorer," New York *Post*, Apr. 5, 1964, Magazine Section, p. 6.

toward the Birch Society coincided with the increasingly militant stance of the American right wing.

On March 19, 1960, Pew repeated his role as gadfly when he told the National Council of United Presbyterian Men that many wealthy Presbyterians gave only token support to their church because the clergy had failed in its Christian mission:

> They cannot understand how our corporate church could tolerate such statements and pronouncements on social issues as they have seen in the press. They feel that the corporate church should not go into politics; that it has no mandate to meddle in secular affairs. . . . They know, too, that these pronouncements frequently coincide with the Communist objectives.

The issues, as Pew explained them, were not the objectives of social action but the fact that the church had "erred":

> *First,* that many of these statements are contrary to both natural law and the freedoms and rights guaranteed by our Constitution and Bill of Rights.
>
> *Second,* that the corporate church had no mandate from its members to make these statements.
>
> *Third,* and more importantly, that many of these statements clearly violate the constitution of our church and the basic tenets of Protestantism.

Pew argued that the church was the only institution capable of saving "the world from Communism" and he urged clergymen and laymen "to meet in a spirit of brotherly love, and then quietly and prayerfully come to an understanding of the principles clearly enunciated by Jesus Christ and clearly stated in the Holy Bible." [46]

Pew's charges did not go unchallenged. *Presbyterian Life* defended social action and argued that the church was "to be the conscience of the culture." The editor cited a poll indicating that among Presbyterians "overwhelming majorities felt that it was the job of the church to testify on racial questions, gambling, Communism, alcohol, and foreign aid." [47]

46 " 'Social Issues and Politics'—Are Churches Going too Far?" *U. S. News and World Report,* XLVIII (Apr. 25, 1960), 133-35.

47 Quoted in "Presbyterian Thumps," *Newsweek,* LV (May 23, 1960), 101-2. For additional aspects of this issue, see the New York *Times,* Feb. 14, 15: 2, 5; Mar. 20, 53:1; 28, 1:1; 29, 36: 1; Apr. 3, 78: 3; 4, 33: 3; 6, 40: 6, 1960; Presbyterian Lay Committee, Incorporated, "A Call to Presbyterian Laymen," *Presbyterian Life,* XVIII (Dec. 1, 1965), 18-19; "A Call to Every United Presbyterian," Milwaukee *Journal,* Dec. 27, 1966, II, 12.

The founding of the Presbyterian Lay Committee, Inc., was a latent manifestation of the same drive against social action movements; its target was a new confession that United Presbyterians approved in the summer of 1967 as a replacement for the Westminster Confession.

Advocates of church participation in society benefited from increased emphasis on social ethics and civil rights movements in the years after 1960, but their opponents remained a threat. Political reaction and social controversies periodically created tensions that appeals to religious ideals and racial equality could not overcome, and, after 1964, the intensification of the conflict in Viet Nam enlarged the scope of the debate about the limits of religious and secular values.

Political and economic conservatives seemed most comfortable with the theological status quo, but the sources of their arguments lay in the past as well as in the context of the cold war. "The fundamentalism of the cross," according to Richard Hofstadter, "supplemented . . . a fundamentalism of the flag" in the years after 1945,[48] and David Danzig, who overemphasized the rural and regional roots of the Radical Right, agreed that the international ideological conflict, with its emphasis on "atheistic communism," had become "part of the unending struggle between God and the devil."[49] Danzig believed that "the main strength and appeal of fundamentalist conservatism," which had attempted "to wed Protestant zeal" and a "reactionary animus . . . during the New Deal years," lay in its "nativist nationalism."[50]

What should not be overlooked, however, is an older and influential

[48] *Anti-intellectualism in American Life*, p. 131. Hofstadter suggests that since the 1930s this "has been a significant component in the extreme right in American politics. . . ." See Lipset, *Revolution and Counter Revolution*, pp. 159-76, 246, 332.

Barnet Baskerville, "The Cross and the Flag: Evangelists of the Far Right," *Western Speech*, XXVII (Fall 1963), 197-206 and Robert W. Sellen, "Patriotism or Paranoia? Right-Wing Extremism in America," *Dalhousie Review*, XLIII (Autumn 1963), 295-316, arrived at similar conclusions.

[49] Danzig, "The Radical Right and the Rise of the Fundamentalist Minority," *Commentary*, XXXIII (Apr. 1962), 292, called this movement "a growing socio-religious force in America."

Many of the generally accepted interpretations of fundamentalism still follow the definition by H. Richard Niebuhr in *Encyclopaedia of the Social Sciences*, eds. E. R. A. Seligman and Alvin Johnson (New York, 1931), VI, 526-27. Many historians explain the reactions of fundamentalists as a response to an awareness "that their most cherished beliefs differed greatly from those of the city dwellers" (Norman Furniss, *The Fundamentalist Controversy, 1918-1931* [New Haven, 1954], p. 29) or to "the torrent of populism" that united with the fundamentalist spirit "to batter at the sea wall of civility" (Edward A. Shils, *Torment of Secrecy* [Glencoe, Ill., 1956], p. 93). These interpretations fail to explain the ideological and functional aspects of these beliefs that transcend social boundaries and that make their utility more acceptable to those persons Harvey Cox refers to as "Church-going Bourbons" in "The 'New Breed' in American Churches: Sources of Social Activism in American Religion," *Daedalus*, XCVI (Winter 1967), 135-50. One must agree with William G. McLoughlin Jr., "Is There a Third Force in Christendom?" *Daedalus*, XCVI, 43-68, that we need a clearer definition of fundamentalism. Examine the rhetoric of fundamentalists in Allan H. Sager, "The Fundamentalist-Modernist Controversy, 1918-1930, in the History of American Public Address" (Doctoral dissertation, Northwestern University, 1963).

[50] *Commentary*, XXXIII, 294, 296-97.

source of opposition to the social gospel. The 19th century Protestant clergy often gave religious sanction to businessmen's views. As defenders of laissez faire, property and the cult of success, many ministers took a negative view of social reform and state intervention; "they considered reform a matter of individual regeneration rather than of improved social conditions." [51] Whether as Social Darwinism or the Protestant Ethic, institutionalized Protestantism defended and explained worldly success. For different reasons, evangelicals championed social conservatism, and after the turn of the century Billy Sunday, who "rose to fame on the crest of [the] reaction against the social gospel," [52] also benefited from "the successful businessman's conviction that the workings of the society which nourished him were none of the Church's business." [53]

It was this heritage of social conservatism that J. Howard Pew perpetuated in the National Lay Committee and which underlay the conservative libertarianism of Albert J. Nock and other individualists. Although Nock, according to Opitz,

> does not employ the vocabulary of religion, his analysis may be recast in religious terms. In Christian thought this world is fallen; things are awry, off base, incapable of manifesting their original or true nature. This is especially true of man and his works, and political institutions, being power repositories, are peculiarly liable, or sinful. Hence the distrust of the State which recurs regularly in Christian political thought.[54]

Many conservatives who praised the material productivity of their society and measured the rest of the world by its standards used another religious rationale when they spoke of spiritual values as transcending material values.[55] Spiritual values were important to fundamentalists as well, but their utility sometimes outweighed their transcendent worth

---

[51] Sidney Fine, *Laissez Faire and the General-Welfare State: A Study of Conflict in American Thought, 1865-1901* (Ann Arbor, Mich., 1956, 1964), p. 120. See also. Irvin G. Wyllie, *The Self-Made Man in America: The Myth of Rags to Riches* (New Brunswick, N. J., 1954), pp. 55-74.

[52] McLoughlin, *Modern Revivalism*, p. 399.

[53] Paul A. Carter, *The Decline and Revival of the Social Gospel: Social and Political Liberalism in American Protestant Churches, 1920-1940* (Ithaca, N. Y., 1954), p. 61. A similar controversy, if not with all of the fundamentalist orientation, revolved around the welfare policies of Newburgh, N. Y., and the statements of Senator Barry M. Goldwater. The Newburgh issue is described in Fern Marja Eckman, "Crusade Against the Poor," *Redbook*, CXX (Feb. 1963), 58-59, 96-102.

[54] The Remnant, "Memorandum No. XII," Nov. 3, 1960, Clise MSS. Nock, who taught American history at St. Stephens College, had been trained for the Episcopal priesthood.

[55] James Warren Prothro, *The Dollar Decade: Business Ideas in the 1920's* (Baton Rouge, La., 1954), pp. 42, 62; *Anti-intellectualism in American Life*, pp. 253-71; Walter H. Clark, *The Oxford Group: Its History and Significance* (New York, 1951), p. 240.

for many conservatives who identified the welfare state with atheistic materialism and free enterprise with individualism and spiritual freedom. These conservatives often explained material success as a byproduct of spiritual beliefs and advocated a moral ethic resembling the "pseudo-transformationism" that Louis Schneider and Sanford M. Dornbusch described as "the notion of a simple passage from private virtues to public or social excellences." [56] From this ideological perch it was easier to condemn the social action movements not merely as politically dangerous but also as the antithesis of true Christianity. James W. Clise, a businessman of Seattle, an active supporter of Spiritual Mobilization, an Episcopalian who was a member of the Oxford Group, and, by December 1959, a member of the John Birch Society, complained to Pew:

> it doesn't seem to me very likely that Protestantism will speak out with "one great voice" against Marxian Socialism in the near future. I think individual Christians must speak out with many small voices. However, before they will or can do so, they must have a better understanding of the basic principles of freedom and free enterprise and the dignity of the individual—which seems to exist in our country today only among a very, very small portion of the citizens.[57]

Although individualists like Ayn Rand and Max Eastman denied that religion was an issue,[58] religious ideas remained important for most conservatives, and Opitz, who denounced the National Council for losing touch with the past, lamented that the "original American equation . . . no longer balances because the religious factors in it have been discarded or forgotten." He believed that American society formerly had "a built-in religious dimension" that was a foundation for "second stage" ideas of "individual liberty, equal justice before the law, the right to private property, and respect for minorities." [59] Opitz held his fellow clergymen ultimately responsible for the loss of these traditional ideas and values.

---

56 Schneider and Dornbusch, *Popular Religion: Inspirational Books in America* (Chicago, 1958), p. 99. Clark, *The Oxford Group*, p. 27, declares that its members understood their "world mission in terms of changing people rather than in changing political situations, the social structure, or economic systems."

57 Clise to Pew, Dec. 15, 1957, Clise MSS. Clise cited an article by Pew, "We Must Not Appeal from GOD to CAESAR," *American Mercury*, LXXXV (Dec. 1957), 100-4.

58 Max Eastman, "Am I Conservative?" *National Review*, XVI (Jan. 28, 1964), pp. 57-58, challenges the orthodox, if refined, religiosity of the *National Review*. For a candid and controversial, if not so clear, introduction to Ayn Rand see: "Ayn Rand: A Candid Conversation with the Fountainhead of 'Objectivism,' " *Playboy*, XI (Mar. 1964), pp. 35-40, 42-43, 64.

The theme of religion and conservatism is especially evident in the tenth anniversary issue of the *National Review*, XVII (Nov. 30, 1965).

59 Opitz, "The Religious Foundation of a Free Society," pp. 3-4, Clise MSS.

Dissent like that within the National Council also disrupted the Unitarian, Protestant Episcopal, Congregational and Methodist churches during these two decades after the Second World War, but the controversies about anti-Communism, social action and segregation sometimes created contradictions in methods and beliefs that divided the foes of the new social gospel into competing organizations with different tactics. If political ultraconservatism had a special appeal for fundamentalists like commentator Dan Smoot who accepted the label in politics as well as in theology,[60] fundamentalists often failed to reconcile their religious and social beliefs with their more theologically liberal political allies. While a conservative political rationale and a common antipathy to the social gospel united many conservative business executives and professional men with theologically fundamentalist ministers, their often divergent religious views and social activities weakened the union. Billy Graham was generally more successful than other evangelical and fundamentalist leaders in reconciling the good life with God's life.

Yet, no matter how tenuous their ties, the alliance of political conservatives with religious fundamentalists had important consequences. Both groups rejected church participation in economic and social issues: evangelicals considered social involvement irrelevant to true religion,[61] and political conservatives feared any interference with the American way in free enterprise or individual liberty. Like Pew, who identified the American economic system with Christian liberty, the Rev. Mr. Graham identified his religious message with economic individualism and social stability when he deplored unnecessary strikes, "corrupt or power-hungry labor leaders," or government restrictions on business.[62]

James C. Ingebretsen argued that Spiritual Mobilization presented a practical alternative to the centralization of economic and political institutions with its

60 Dan Smoot, "Who Is the Man?" *Dan Smoot Report*, III (Aug. 5, 1957), 8.

61 Will Herberg, "Conservatism, Liberalism, and Religion," *National Review*, XVII (Nov. 30, 1965), 1088. Herberg wrote that the conservative "affirms religion as the moral foundation of civil society; but, *unless he is something more than a conservative*, he will be tempted to turn religion into an exalted public utility serving social and cultural ends; and this true religion will not tolerate. . . . If the secularistic Liberal is always trying to expel religion from the common life, the secular-minded conservative is forever tempted to make of it a mere instrument of social order. The man of faith must protest against both."

Recently, some evangelicals have become interested in social problems. See George W. Cornell, "Evangelicals Receiving Internal Criticism," Denver *Post*, Sept. 14, 1968, for a description of the Rev. Carl H. Henry's position on social problems. Henry, a Baptist, was until recently editor of *Christianity Today*.

62 McLoughlin, *Billy Graham*, pp. 97-99.

unique blending of economic and political considerations with spiritual and moral values. Those who would have us drop one in favor of concentrating on the other are few and far between. Nearly all felt the importance of our originality.[63]

These beliefs explained the material successes of Americans and their spiritual weaknesses, which conservatives often blamed on failure to understand the economic system that many Americans accepted as Natural Law or the will of God. Ultraconservatives like Pew, Hutchinson and Fifield used these economic and religious beliefs as the source and the justification of their libertarian ideals; consequently religious faith became a substitute for social change and a spiritual barrier between economic institutions and the state. Thus, as these ultraconservatives argued, spiritual values rather than economic well-being gave life its true meaning for the poverty-stricken as well as the wealthy.

[63] Memorandum, Ingebretsen to Board of Directors, July 20, 1957, Clise MSS. Richard H. White, "Toward a Theory of Religious Influence," *Pacific Sociological Review*, II (Spring 1968), 23-28 lends some support to this "interactionist perspective wherein religious influence becomes a category of social influence in general."

FROM EVANGELICAL EXCLUSIVISM
TO ECUMENICAL OPENNESS:
BILLY GRAHAM AND SOCIOPOLITICAL ISSUES*

Richard V. Pierard

PRECIS

During his long career evangelist Billy Graham has significantly modified his views on the issues of race relations, communism, America's standing before God, and most recently nuclear war. Although he was nurtured in a fundamentalist environment, and his early stances on public questions clearly reflected a conservative upbringing, his ever-increasing number of ecumenical contacts and the move to a global ministry enabled him to break out of this constriction and even resulted in bridge-building to the Roman Catholic and Jewish communities. Graham first broke with his evangelical background by racially integrating his crusades and cooperating with Presidents Eisenhower and Johnson in fostering civil rights. He remained a hard-line anticommunist much longer but gradually moved away from this in order to minister in the Soviet bloc. At first he uncritically envisioned America as a Christian nation, but eventually he came to regard this stance as civil religion and himself as a world ambassador. His desire to promote peace by scaling down the nuclear arms race and to preach the gospel everywhere in the world lay behind his much-criticized visit to the Soviet Union. Although these actions cost Graham supporters, one may expect to see a continuing flexibility on his part.

In a *McCall's* magazine interview in January, 1978, evangelist Billy Graham conceded frankly: "I've lost some of the rigidity I once had." He went on to say that he no longer considered America a Christian nation, suggested that Christians living in a communist country such as Hungary may have an easier time in coping with the temptations of their society than people in the United States, and insisted that he would have to adapt himself to different conditions. He also regretted the tendency which he once had of equating Christianity with the

---

*An earlier version of this article was presented at the Symposium on the Public Face of Evangelicalism at Huntington [Indiana] College. I wish to thank Professor Jack Barlow and the Indiana Committee for the Humanities for their support.

Richard V. Pierard (American Baptist) has been Professor of History at Indiana State University, Terre Haute, since 1964. His B.A. and M.A. in history are from California State University, Los Angeles; his Ph.D. in history (1964) is from the University of Iowa. He was a Fulbright scholar at the University of Hamburg, 1962-63. His special interests in evangelical Christianity and political developments and in religious aspects of conservatism and the Far Right are reflected in his articles (*Journal of Church and State*, *Christian Scholars Review*, *Choice*, and *Christian Century*) and chapters in books, most recently: "Religion and the New Right in Contemporary American Politics," in J. E. Wood, Jr., ed., *Religion and Politics* (Baylor University Press, 1983). His books are *The Unequal Yoke* (Lippencott, 1970) and *Twilight of the Saints* (with R. D. Lindner, InterVarsity, 1978).

American way of life and communism with the work of the devil.[1] A year later on the "CBS Evening News" he denounced the nuclear arms race as "insanity, madness," declared that a "nuclear holocaust" would be even more horrible than the Holocaust that wiped out most of the European Jews, and endorsed the principle of agreements to reduce the number of atomic weapons.[2] Then, in a speech at Harvard University on April 20, 1982, he spoke of his "pilgrimage" and revealed that he had "come to see in deeper ways some of the implications of the faith and message I've been proclaiming." He insisted that his basic commitment as a Christian and view of the gospel had not changed, but, when it came to his thinking about the Christian's corporate responsibility, "as I traveled and studied the Bible more, I changed."[3]

The obvious implications of these and similar statements which the Rev. Mr. Graham has made in the last five years are that he has significantly modified some of his opinions and that the strong conservatism customarily ascribed to him by commentators in the light of his earlier pronouncements and actions must be reassessed. This study, therefore, will examine his views on the race question, communism, and America's standing before God and identify where he has altered his stance. I will only briefly touch on his change of heart on nuclear war since I have already dealt with this elsewhere.[4] The modifications did not occur easily, and it is reasonable to assume that his conservative background continues to be a source of inner tension for him.

I

Graham's early years and his development from being just another itinerant evangelist to an internationally known and respected preacher have been examined by numerous biographers.[5] These accounts point out that he was the product of a rural Southern environment, underwent a crisis conversion experience, and received a college education in fundamentalist Christian schools. He was profoundly affected by the events swirling around him as he reached adulthood—the hard times of the depression, the enthusiasm of World War II, the

---

[1]James Michael Beam, "I Can't Play God Any More," *McCall's* 105 (January, 1978): 156.

[2]*Christianity and Crisis* 39 (April 30, 1979): 111. A videotape of the program is in the Archives of the Billy Graham Center, Wheaton, IL. He expanded on these ideas in an interview in *Sojourners* 8 (August, 1979): 12-14.

[3]Frye Gaillard, "The Conversion of Billy Graham," *Progressive* 46 (August, 1982): 26.

[4]Richard V. Pierard, "Billy Graham and Vietnam: From Cold Warrior to Peacemaker," *Christian Scholar's Review*, vol. 10, no. 1 (1980), pp. 37-51.

[5]The Graham bibliography is quite extensive. Probably the most significant accounts are: William G. McLoughlin, Jr., *Billy Graham: Revivalist in a Secular Age* (New York: Ronald Press, 1960); Lowell D. Streiker and Gerald S. Strober, *Religion and the New Majority: Billy Graham, Middle America and the Politics of the 70's* (New York: Association Press, 1972); Joe E. Barnhart, *The Billy Graham Religion* (Philadelphia: United Church

emergence of the Cold War, and the evangelical resurgence of the late 1940's. When the thirty-year-old evangelist strode boldly on to the stage of national attention in 1949, he arrived with a set of views which had crystalized out of these formative experiences: a conservative theology which stressed biblical inerrancy, the new birth, an austere lifestyle, and the second coming of Christ, and a conservative political and social philosophy which emphasized the work ethic, American patriotism, law and order, citizen participation in the political process, the central role of religion in public life and the schools, maintenance of traditional sexual mores and family relations, a strong national defense, and firm rejection of the foreign, atheistic ideology of communism. Personally, he remained a simple, modest, and humble man who never forgot his origins or turned against his friends, and even to this day he retains a sense of the country-boy innocence of his youth.

At the same time there was an element of flexibility in Graham that enabled him to change as the times changed, and this helps to explain his astonishing durability in a public ministry which has spanned thirty-five years. Although critics on the left invariably lamented his association with high public figures, these contacts along with his wide travels helped immensely to broaden his understanding of the world. By insisting upon local-level ecumenical support for his various crusades, he broke out of a fundamentalist constriction and gradually developed connections with a wide variety of expressions of Christianity. The progress he had made was revealed in December, 1966, when he appeared (for the first time) before the General Assembly of the National Council of Churches in Miami Beach and extended a conciliatory hand across the chasm that seemed to separate evangelicals and ecumenists. He affirmed the need for two kinds of conversion: one from the world to Christ, and th. ther with Christ back to the world. "The fruit of rebirth is neighbor love, expressed in social service," but "social service without conversion is absurd." He pointed out that "a great section of the church" feels these should go hand in hand and said, "I am one of them."[6]

He went on to build bridges to the Jewish and Roman Catholic worlds. The American Jewish Committee bestowed its first "National Interreligious Award" upon Graham for his support of Israel and for "strengthening mutual respect and understanding between the evangelical and Jewish communities," while some

---

Press, 1972); W. David Lockard, *The Unheard Billy Graham* (Waco, TX: Word Books, 1971); and Marshall Frady, *Billy Graham: A Parable of American Righteousness* (Boston: Little, Brown, 1979). Especially useful sources of biographical data are three in-house works by John Pollock: *Billy Graham: The Authorized Biography* (New York: McGraw-Hill, 1966); *Crusades: 20 Years with Billy Graham* (Minneapolis: World Wide, 1969); and *Billy Graham: Evangelist to the World* (New York: Harper & Row, 1979). To my knowledge, he is the only writer who has had access to the Graham organization's files. I have discussed some aspects of his career in two articles in the *Reformed Journal*, "Can Billy Graham Survive Richard Nixon?" (24 [April, 1974]: 7-13), and "Billy Graham: A Study in Survival," (30 [April, 1980]: 8-12).
    [6]*Chicago Daily News*, December 6, 1966; *Orlando Evening Star*, December 15, 1966.

Catholic priests and bishops even began encouraging their people to attend his crusades.[7] In response to an interviewer's question about what happened to Catholic inquirers at his meetings, Graham said:

> We are concerned with *Christian* faith; not Catholic or Protestant faith. There is only one Christ. There is one God. Whether you're Roman Catholic or Protestant, Jesus said to Nicodemus, "You need to be *born again*." That's what I'm asking everyone to do. How they find their way and settle their lives afterward is up them and God and the Church, or other believers.[8]

In January, 1981, the evangelist, who had already publicly praised John Paul II for his stance on peace and disarmament, was received at his own request by the pontiff at the Vatican.[9] Graham said later that within two minutes he forgot that John Paul was the pope because of their wonderful rapport.

Both in his Harvard speech and an interview with the Southern Baptist Christian Life Commission at about the same time, Graham provided some insights into the theological underpinnings of his move toward greater social involvement.[10] First, he tenaciously affirms the primacy of evangelism which confronts people with their sin and calls upon them to turn to God and receive forgiveness through faith in Jesus Christ. But he insists that this "new birth" must be accompanied by a life of discipleship, and following Christ means serving others. He also sees evil in the world as a spiritual question, the result of sin, but no longer does he view this in purely individualistic terms. The pervasive social ills of the present day are collective symptoms of the sin pervading the human heart, humanity's rebellion against God. Political solutions alone will not resolve the basic issues in the world and only Christ can change the human heart. Yet, Christians are to work for peace and justice because they are to be witnesses to the love and grace of God by both their words and their deeds. Moreover, Graham concedes that he has been "tremendously influenced by the Old Testament prophets."[11] This includes their determination to declare the word of God regardless of personal cost and their basic themes of justice, repentence, and the divine love for God's people and the divine willingness to receive and forgive them. Thus, Graham is as fully committed as ever to his evangelistic mission and is willing to take whatever risks are necessary to gain new opportunities to preach, but at the same time he has a deeper understanding of the power of sin and the flaws in human nature and a greater sense of urgency about suffering in the world and the threat of global destruction.

---

[7]*Newsweek* 95 (November 28, 1977): 126.

[8]"Billy Graham: Man for All People," *Christian Life* 44 (July, 1982): 28-29.

[9]Billy Graham, "The Pilgrim Pope: A Builder of Bridges," *Saturday Evening Post* 252 (January-February, 1980): 74-75.

[10]Gaillard, "Conversion," pp. 26-27.

[11]"An Interview with Billy Graham: Speaking on Ethics," *Light*, March-April, 1982, pp. 1-4.

Interestingly, as time passed, the sharpest criticisms of Graham and his ministry have come increasingly not from the ecumenical and non-Protestant groups but instead from fundamentalists who are theologically much closer to him. Bob Jones, Sr., declared in 1966 that Graham was "doing more harm to the cause of Christ than any other living man,"[12] and a Florida preacher a few years later charged that Graham, "with his finger upon the public pulse, chameleon-like, the champion of compromise and confusion, changes color with the crowd."[13] One noted fundamentalist Baptist, Ernest Pickering, devoted an entire chapter in his book *Biblical Separation* to condemning Graham's "multiplying compromises" and operating principle of "building churches that deny the Word of God,"[14] while another minor luminary, G. Archer Weniger, warned the World Congress of Fundamentalists in 1976 about the "apostate leadership" that Graham "used, fellowshipped [with] , and commended" and expressed horror about the possibilities of an ecumenism flowing out of the Lausanne Congress on World Evangelism.[15] This meant that, whenever Graham adopted a moderate stance on any social issue, he could almost certainly expect to be attacked from the right. There is no evidence, however, that it had any deterring effect upon him.

II

Graham's first significant change on a sociopolitical issue was the race question. To be sure, his early years had been spent in a society which accepted and even championed segregation. The white evangelical world he came to know at Wheaton College and in the Youth for Christ ministry seldom brought him into contact with like-minded Blacks, and he accepted the practice of segregated seating at his evangelistic meetings in the South, starting with the first one at Charlotte in November, 1947.[16] Still, as he intimated at Harvard three decades later, his conscience bothered him and he realized he would have to take a stand:

> I did not know how. But in 1952, I was holding a series of meetings in a southern city. They had ropes so that black people had to sit behind those ropes. I went down and personally and physically pulled the ropes down. That was among my first acts of conscience on the race question.[17]

---

[12]*Time* 87 (March 18, 1966): 103.

[13]*Excerpts from Church Bulletins of Orlando Bible Church: Billy Graham—Champion of Compromise and Confusion*, April, 1974, p. 23 (mimeographed copy in the Billy Graham Center Archives).

[14]Ernest Pickering, *Biblical Separation: The Struggle for a Pure Church* (Schaumburg, IL: Regular Baptist Press, 1979), pp. 141-155.

[15]G. Archer Weniger, *The Fundamentalist and Ecumenicity* (Greenville, SC: Bob Jones University Press, 1979), pp. 24-25.

[16]Streiker and Strober, *Religion and the New Majority*, pp. 48-49.

[17]Gaillard, "Conversion," p. 26.

Exactly where this was done or what the reaction was is uncertain, but Graham's biographer reports that he did decide quietly and without fanfare to implement non-segregated seating at his crusades, beginning in Chattanooga in March, 1953.[18]

Three years later he explained his stance to the American public in a *Life* article: "Where men are standing at the foot of the cross, there are no racial barriers. . . . The whole weight of Scripture is for treating men with neighbor-love, regardless of race or color." God requires not only justice in this matter but also that Christians exercise love and selflessness. There was no color bar in the Golden Rule and no evidence of racial discrimination in the early church. "Racial discrimination, like other social sins, is a product of man's inherent sinfulness," and thus the converted person has at his or her means the power to overcome this.[19]

His change of heart was welcomed by mainline theologians, but some such as Reinhold Niebuhr pointed out that he had not gone far enough. The idea that individual conversion could solve the problem simply fell short of the mark. The reality of structural sin required forceful preaching on the specific sin of racial discrimination. He insisted Graham should link his preaching to social issues and harness the "saved" and "unsaved" alike in the struggle against moral evils and for social justice.[20]

Actually, Graham did involve himself in a way of which the public was unaware and certainly differently from what Niebuhr would have wanted. When the evangelist called upon President Eisenhower on March 29, 1956, to report about his preaching mission in Asia, the chief executive quickly switched the topic to the race question. Member of Congress Frank W. Boykin of Alabama had already alerted him to the possibility of Graham's usefulness. The race issue "is truly very serious," he wrote:

> The Communists are taking advantage of it. I believe our own Billy Graham could do more on this than any other human in this nation; I mean to quiet it down and to go easy and in a Godlike way, instead of trying to cram it down the throats of our people all in one day, which some of our enemies are trying to do. I thought maybe if you and Billy talked, you could talk about this real, real good.[21]

Since Graham was currently taking a hard-line stance against communism and was a boundless admirer of the president, he could easily be persuaded to volun-

---

[18]Pollock, *The Authorized Biography*, p. 98.

[19]"Billy Graham Makes Plea for an End to Intolerance," *Life* 41 (October 1, 1956): 138-151.

[20]Reinhold Niebuhr, "Literalism, Individualism, and Billy Graham," *The Christian Century* 72 (May 23, 1956): 640-642; "Proposal to Billy Graham," ibid. (August 8, 1956): 921-922; "Theologian Says Evangelist Is Oversimplifying the Issues of Life," *Life* 43 (July 1, 1957): 92.

[21]Frank W. Boykin to Dwight D. Eisenhower, March 19, 1956; Eisenhower Library, Abilene, KS, PPF 1052. (Hereafter cited as E. L.)

teer his services. Eisenhower accordingly communicated to Boykin after the meeting that they had "talked over some ideas" about how Graham might "turn his talents to the easing of some of the more serious problems in our country."[22]

In a "personal" memorandum to the evangelist, Eisenhower indicated that ministers had an opportunity to promote tolerance and progress in race relations and suggested "that success through conciliation will be more lasting and stronger than could be obtained through force and conflict." He proposed that electing "a few qualified Negroes" to local offices, removal of racial restrictions in university admissions, and opening all seats on public conveyances to Blacks were things that "could properly be mentioned in a pulpit." Graham might also praise Catholic Archbishop Joseph Rummel's move to desegregate parochial schools in Louisiana and express approval of other advances in the South and border states. This would encourage federal judges "to operate moderately and with complete regard for the sensitivities of the population."[23]

Graham reported to Eisenhower he was taking "immediate steps to call the outstanding leaders of the major Southern denominations" to a conference where he would outline the presidential suggestions for racial understanding and progress. He would also urge ministers to call upon their parishioners for moderation, charity, compassion, and progress toward compliance with the Supreme Court ruling on school desegregation. The meeting never did take place, but Graham conversed privately with church leaders, addressed a number of denominational annual conventions, and spoke at some black colleges where he "laid before them what I consider to be a sensible program for bettering race relations." He also conferred with the governors of North Carolina and Tennessee about looking at the matter "from a spiritual point of view."[24]

In July, 1957, Graham wrote the president that he was praying that God would guide him in matters of civil rights legislation, and in the Little Rock school integration crisis that fall Eisenhower sought his opinion about whether federal troops should be sent in.[25] The next year South Carolina Governor George Timmerman forbade Graham from holding an evangelistic rally on the state capitol grounds because he was a "well-known integrationist."[26] In 1960 the Graham team held integrated meetings throughout Africa, even in white-supremacist Southern Rhodesia, but they refused to enter South Africa. Only in 1973 did he finally go there when the government consented to allow integrated services. In 1957 he added the first Black to his staff of associate evangelists, Howard O. Jones, and a second one in the early 1960's, Ralph Bell. Lyndon Johnson asked Graham for help in promoting public acceptance of civil rights

[22]Eisenhower to Boykin, March 20, 1956; ibid.
[23]Eisenhower to Graham, March 22, 1956; E.L., Names Series, Ann Whitman File.
[24]Graham to Eisenhower, March 27, 1956; ibid. Graham to Eisenhower, June 4, 1956; E.L., PPF 1052.
[25]Graham to Eisenhower, July 4, 1957; E.L., OF 102-B-3. Willmar Thorkelson, "The Billy Grahams at Home," *Christian Herald* 96 (November, 1973): 32.
[26]Pollock, *The Authorized Biography*, pp. 225-226.

legislation, and, when violence erupted in Alabama in the spring of 1965, he cancelled an engagement in England in order to hold meetings around the state. His sincere efforts on behalf of reconciliation between white and black people placed him far ahead of both his constituency and the white evangelical leadership.[27]

Nevertheless, there was some residual tension between Graham's background and his stance on the race issue. For instance, he commented to Eisenhower in June, 1956: "I believe the Lord is helping us, and if the extremists on both sides will quiet down, we can have a peaceful social readjustment over the next ten-year period." He expressed concern about a rumor that the Republican strategy would be to go all out to win the black vote in the North regardless of the South's feelings and said this would jeopardize the confidence which both white and black leaders had in the president.[28] Seven years later Graham revealed considerable unease about the marches and sit-ins in Alabama led by Martin Luther King, Jr. He urged King "to put on the brakes a little bit" and refused to call himself a "thoroughgoing integrationist" in his own racial views. He pleaded for a "period of quietness in which moderation prevails."[29]

Pollock is correct in saying that Graham rejected such direct participation in the civil rights campaign as marching. He felt it was better to speak out on behalf of tolerance, conciliation, and striking at the root of the problem which was sin. "The race question will not be solved by demonstrations in the streets, but in the hearts of both Negro and white. There must be genuine love to replace prejudice and hate. This love can be supplied by Christ and only by Christ."[30] Graham was highly critical of the urban riots which swept the country, and he chided Dr. King for linking the civil rights movement with opposition to the Vietnam War. As a result, the new generation of black evangelicals began nipping at his heels for "tokenism" and offering merely an individualistic gospel as the solution instead of fervently demanding justice. One may properly conclude, therefore, that, in spite of the very real transformation in his attitudes on racial justice, direct action in the form of confrontations and the refusal to support the nation's Vietnam policy exceeded the bounds which his still rather conservative disposition would permit him to countenance.

[27]Streiker and Strober, *Religion and the New Majority*, pp. 58-59; Richard V. Pierard, "Billy Graham and the U.S. Presidency," *Journal of Church and State* 22 (Winter, 1980): 123.

[28]Graham to Eisenhower, June 4, 1957; E.L., PPF 1052.

[29]*New York Times*, April 18, 1963, p. 21.

[30]Pollock, *The Authorized Biography*, p. 227.

III

The young Billy Graham took a hard-line stand on communism that was very much in tune with public attitudes in the Cold War years. He told the audience at his Los Angeles crusade in 1949 that the world was "divided into two camps." On one side was Western culture which had its foundations in the Bible and the great revivals, and on the other was communism which had declared its opposition to God, Christ, the Bible, and all religion. It was "inspired, directed, and motivated by the Devil himself," and the "Fifth Columnists, called Communists, are more rampant in Los Angeles than any other city in America."[31] In a sermon the following year he announced that "there are over eleven hundred social sounding organizations that are communist and communist-operated in this country," and they "control the minds of a great segment of our people [by] the infiltration of the left wing through both pink and red into the intellectual strata of America."[32] He was incensed that some Americans refused to tell congressional investigating committees whether or not they were members of the Communist Party, and he gave thanks to God for those

> who in the face of public denouncement and ridicule, go loyally on in their work of exposing the pinks, the lavenders, and the reds who have sought refuge beneath the wings of the American eagle and from that vantage point, try in every subtle, under-cover way to bring comfort, aid and help to the greatest enemy we have ever known—communism.[33]

Again and again in the early 1950's he lambasted communism in emotional and apocalyptic terms as a monstrous, sinister force which was out to conquer the world.

Nevertheless, as his stature grew, he became more circumspect in his public remarks about communism and discontinued making specific predictions about the imminence of World War III, such as his comment in 1950 that the country had only two years left and then "it's all going to be over."[34] After a serious flap over a statement in the 1954 edition of the Billy Graham Evangelistic Association's calendar that "socialism" had undermined Britain's historic faith, he had to be careful about promiscuously using that term as well.[35] His youthful pronouncements had become sufficiently embarrassing that he confessed in 1956: "There was a time a few years ago when, in an immature fashion, I made political statements and entered into all sorts of controversies. I have learned better

---

[31]*Revival in Our Time: The Story of the Billy Graham Evangelistic Campaigns* (Wheaton, IL: Van Kampen Press, 1950), pp. 54-55.

[32]*America's Hour of Decision* (Wheaton, IL: Van Kampen Press, 1951), p. 144.

[33]"Labor, Christ, and the Cross," sermon published by the Billy Graham Evangelistic Association, 1953, pp. 5-6. (Hereafter sermons are cited by title and year.)

[34]*America's Hour of Decision*, p. 119.

[35]McLoughlin, *Billy Graham*, pp. 102-105. The evangelist claimed this was a misprint; the proper word should have been "secularism."

now and remain completely outside party politics."[36] Although he repeated this on numerous occasions in the next two decades, it did not mean he had now given up anti-communism. In a personal letter to his friend, Vice President Richard Nixon, in October, 1955, the evangelist declared:

> In my opinion, there is so much good will bubbling out of Moscow that the issue of Communism is no longer as potent as it was politically in the United States. In some ways this is unfortunate in the sense that the basic issues between Communism and the West have not changed, and the communists are now beginning to gain ground rapidly. They have learned that a smile means more than a big fist. This, however, makes the political dilemma in America extremely critical, particularly for a man like you with strong convictions.[37]

The Hungarian uprising revealed the depth of his feeling about communism. He wrote Nixon that it was "difficult for me to see how we can morally continue to stand aside while Russian steel crushes the Hungarian people,"[38] and in a sermon he denounced Soviet actions in the "rape of Hungary." Never in modern times had the world seen anything like the "massacre" there, a "throwback to the Middle Ages for its savagery, torture, pillage, and rape." What happened there "would make even Hitler and Mussolini blush." He warned his American listeners that they "cannot ignore the oppressed, suffering, and helpless peoples behind the Iron Curtain without paying for it at the judgment of God."[39]

The condemnatory remarks continued well into the 1960's. Communism was then entering what "it considers its final phase in controlling the entire world" and "using terror tactics and international blackmail on a scale unknown in human history." Our sleeping nation was hurtling "headlong toward a catastrophe of such magnitude that the human mind could not conceive it."[40] "Our entire civilization is faced with the threat of annihilation. . . . The American atheist and agnostic, whether or not he intends it, is conceding the fight to communism." The communists "are deliberately trying—and succeeding—to smuggle heroin and marijuana into this country. It is their way of hastening our downfall."[41] "Subversives are stepping up their activities all over the world" and have the goal of "world domination by 1972," the communist "juggernaut" has "little

---

[36]"Billy Graham Answers His Critics," *Look* 20 (February 7, 1956): 51.

[37]Billy Graham to Richard M. Nixon, October 8, 1955; contained in the Richard M. Nixon Pre-presidential Materials Project, Federal Archives and Records Center, Laguna Nigues, CA. Series 320, Vice-presidential General Correspondence Box 299, folder: Graham, Dr. Billy. (Hereafter cited as N.P.M.P.)

[38]Graham to Nixon, November 10, 1956; N.P.M.P.

[39]"The Signs of the Times," sermon, 1957, pp. 1-3.

[40]"The Ultimate Weapon," sermon, 1961, pp. 1-2. Graham gave a copy of this to Nixon, who by now was again a private citizen; N.P.M.P.

[41]George Carpozi, Jr., "Billy Graham Speaks Out on Love, Abortion, Illegitimacy," *True Story* 87 (August, 1962): 69.

intention of stopping or giving up," and "history will condemn America for failing to aid the Cuban freedom fighters in the Bay of Pigs."[42]

Graham's deep antipathy to communism and loyalty to President Johnson lay behind his ongoing support of the American Vietnam involvement, but his extensive travels and ecumenical contacts were inexorably pushing him in the direction of a broader, more open understanding of world affairs. Moreover, some of his conservatism must have reflected the outlook of advisers who, as former team member Jerry Beavan pointed out, had "lost touch with reality and think only they have the answers to all the problems of our day." Writing in 1966, Beavan claimed that, if Graham "were left to his own resources, [he] would undoubtedly follow a more logical approach to the problem of bringing the Christian solution to the ills of our time."[43] But, in fact, the circle of advisers was beginning to widen from that original band of stalwarts from the early 1950's, as two Blacks and an Indian (Akbar Abdul Haqq) were now associate evangelists, and Graham established contacts with Christian leaders in Africa, Asia, and Latin America who communicated Third World perceptions to him. His brother-in-law Leighton Ford understood the intense interest in social concern animating the new generation of evangelicals (and many older ones as well) and boldly proclaimed it from such forums as the U.S. Congress on Evangelism at Minneapolis in 1969. Graham himself saw this event as a "breakthrough," for it demonstrated that evangelical Christianity was now "where the action is."[44]

Although Graham had not openly repudiated his anti-communist beliefs, his first foray into Eastern Europe in 1967 gave evidence that some sort of shift was in the offing. Josip Horak, president of the Baptist Union of Yugoslavia, persuaded the authorities to allow the evangelist to hold two low-key meetings in Zagreb on a July weekend. In what turned out to be an ecumenical event, he preached to an open-air gathering on the Catholic seminary soccer field and a packed house in a Lutheran church. The good impression produced by this resulted in approval being given three years later to pipe a videotape television relay from Graham's Euro 70 campaign in Germany into a Zagreb church.[45]

He also was coming to respect the ethical side of communism, even if he was repelled by its ideology. He acknowledged in a *Christianity Today* interview in 1970 that communists did a better job of living up to the demands and discipline of their ethic than Christians did.[46] However, the evangelist dismayed some American fundamentalists when he told a reporter in 1973: "I think commu-

[42]"It's Later Than You Think," sermon, 1961, p. 1; "Facing the Anti-God Colossus," *Christianity Today* 7 (December 21, 1962): 266-267; "A Time for Moral Courage," *Reader's Digest* 85 (July, 1964): 50.

[43]Jerry Beavan, "The Billy Graham I Know," *Christian Herald* 89 (September, 1966): 83.

[44]"Billy Graham: Spanning the Decades," *Christianity Today* 14 (November 7, 1969): 136. Ford's address is in ibid. (October 24, 1969): 6-12.

[45]Pollock, *Evangelist to the World*, pp. 74, 81-85.

[46]"Billy Graham and 'Civil Religion,'" *Christianity Today* 15 (November 6, 1970): 154.

nism's appeal to youth is its structure and promise of a future utopia. Mao Tse-tung's Eight Precepts are the same as the Ten Commandments. In fact, if we can't have the Ten Commandments read in schools, I'll settle for Mao's precepts." An outraged American missionary pressed the Graham organization for an explanation, and a top associate, George Wilson, replied that if young people did "not want to accept Almighty God and His Ten Commandments" and believed instead in Chairman Mao, then it would be better for them to listen to his Eight Precepts, "because basically they are taken from the Bible."[47]

In the early 1970's Graham backed away from declaring his support for the Vietnam War and tried to maintain a neutral stance.[48] At the same time pejorative comments on communism disappeared from his sermons and public statements, and he emphasized increasingly the opportunities for spreading the gospel in the communist bloc. Writing in *Christianity Today* he affirmed: "I actually think that the evangelism of the future might come out of the Soviet Union. We're hearing so many stories of young people being converted there and in all of Eastern Europe. This shows the spiritual hunger and the response to the Gospel." He refused to take a stand on U.S. relations with Taiwan ("I don't think I should get into that sensitive, political area right now,") and declared he would go anywhere, even to socialist nations, to preach Christ so long as there were no strings attached to the message.[49] Unlike what he had done on the race issue, Graham quietly and without fanfare shelved his overt anti-communism, and, when the opportunity finally came to go to a Soviet-bloc country, he eagerly seized it.

After five years of delicate negotiations the president of the Council of Free Churches of Hungary, Sándor Palotay, was persuaded to invite Graham to his land. The evangelist said his aims were "to proclaim the Gospel of Christ to as many people as possible" and "to help establish bridges of understanding between the peoples of the world." Arriving on September 3, 1977, he spent eight days there and spoke to large crowds even though the rallies were not widely publicized. He had lengthy conversations with state officials, including Imre Miklós, the Marxist cabinet minister in charge of the Office for Church Affairs, and Deputy Premier György Aczél, the chief theoretician of the Hungarian Communist Party. In various meetings and press conferences he described how his thinking had changed in recent years and that his concerns "now encompass the whole world." He had come with an "open mind" to learn and to get

---

[47]Gerry Johnson, "Billy Graham and Mao Tse Tung," *The Projector* (Milton, FL) 3 (July, 1974): 1, 5.

[48]Pierard, "Billy Graham and Vietnam," pp. 47-50; Billy Graham, "A Clarification," *Christianity Today* 17 (January 19, 1973): 416. Replying to critics who wanted him to speak out against the war, he maintained that he was called to be a New Testament evangelist, not an Old Testament prophet, and he insisted he had "never advocated war" but rather deplored it.

[49]"Taking the World's Temperature: An Interview with Billy Graham," *Christianity Today* 21 (September 23, 1977): 1323-1324.

a perspective about life there, and he confessed that his old anti-communism might be outdated since he had seen Christianity survive under a communist regime. He found freedom to worship and preach, and, although he recognized there were problems: "I can report the church is very much alive in Hungary." And, because hearts and minds were changing as well as the times, "perhaps under God someday we will have one world, where wars will be no more, whether they be hot or cold."[50]

Graham's low-key approach to communism and heightening concern for world peace were evident again in the visit to Poland a year later. Satisfied by the outcome of the Hungarian trip, the State Office for Church Affairs approved an invitation by the Baptists, and ecumenical support quickly gathered steam. The ten-day preaching mission in October, 1978, was even more spectacular than the one the year before. As before, he insisted he had come with an "open mind" to learn about the Polish society and churches and met with top state and ecclesiastical officials. Among the most meaningful events was a call paid to the Nazi death camp at Auschwitz where he laid a wreath and urged world leaders "regardless of their political ideology, to learn the lessons of Auschwitz." Christians must not isolate themselves but be dedicated "to the Lord Jesus Christ, to the cause of peace, to reconciliation among all races and nations."[51]

In January, 1981, he revisited Poland and Hungary and was awarded honorary degrees. Speaking in Warsaw he declared that "you and only you can find solutions to your problems." I will pray that "the voices of conciliation, common sense, and moderation" might prevail.[52] This was a far cry from the fire-eating Cold War pronouncements of the 1950's, and it reflected the realization to which Graham had come that he had to abandon all overt expression of antipathy to communism if he expected to be able to preach in the Soviet bloc.

It is clear that the two trips had a significant impact on the transformation of his social views. As he told *Sojourners*: "I went with many stereotypes in my mind, but I came away with a new understanding especially of how the church exists and in some instances thrives in these societies—and a new awareness of their concerns about peace."[53] In letters to Bishop Károly Tóth of Budapest, president of the Christian Peace Conference—an organization which critics in the West often accuse of having an East-bloc bias—Graham frankly admitted that he, like many other Christians, had given too little attention to the matters of peace and the arms race. During the journey to Hungary "the Christian's responsibility to work for world peace came to me in a new way," and this happened again in

---

[50]Pollock, *Evangelist to the World*, pp. 297-306; *Christianity Today* 21 (September 23, 1977): 1348-1349, and 22 (October 7, 1977): 48-50; "CBS Evening News," September 4, 1977, and September 5, 1977, videotape in the Billy Graham Center Archives.

[51]*Christianity Today* 23 (November 3, 1978): 190-193; Pollock, *Evangelist to the World*, pp. 307-311.

[52]*New York Times*, January 6, 1981, p. B6.

[53]"A Change of Heart: Billy Graham on the Nuclear Arms Race," *Sojourners* 8 (August, 1979): 13.

Poland. Since technology has made humanity almost completely interdependent, Graham said, a reckless arms race affects not only the destiny of the two great nations but also everyone on the earth. Because this competition diverts such massive amounts of human and natural resources, hundreds of millions of people are condemned to a lifetime of suffering from poverty, hunger, sickness, and ignorance. Thus, it was "out of a deepening sense of Christian responsibility" that ever since the 1977 trip he has sought "to make whatever contribution I can to building bridges of understanding and peace in our world." Peace is not a political but a moral and spiritual issue that "demands the attention of every Christian."[54]

Scaling down the arms race, moving toward a "SALT X" agreement where all nuclear weapons would be destroyed, and affirming the unity of humankind irrespective of political differences are now as much a part of Graham's message as the call to repentance and faith in Jesus Christ. Since 1979 he has been saying that almost everywhere he goes because, as he told reporter Frye Gaillard, he believes he has "a total Christian moral responsibility to speak out" on matters such as nuclear arms and nerve gas just as he would on the race question.[55] The mature Billy Graham has dropped the anti-communist rhetoric which pervaded his preaching on social issues during the early years and replaced it with a deep concern for peacemaking and bridgebuilding between East and West. In turn, this provides him with opportunities to preach in places where before he had not been welcome.

IV

The young Billy Graham had a naive view of the United States as a Christian nation, and he uncritically linked God and country as most evangelical preachers of the time tended to do. In his early sermons he regularly portrayed America as the bulwark of Christian civilization which was holding back the Red hordes, and he made what to more perceptive Christians seemed to be utterly outlandish statements. America was "created for a spiritual mission among the nations," but it cannot survive and "cannot carry out her God-appointed mission, without the spiritual emphasis which was hers from the outset" (1956). "Until this nation humbles itself and prays and . . . receives Christ as Savior, there is no hope for preserving the American way of life" (1952). "The Church is the channel through which God sends the streams of blessing down to the nation, and I urge all of you today that love America and who have an appreciation for the blood that was shed in Korea and have a pride when you hear our National Anthem or see the Stars and Stripes wave, to fall upon your knees . . . pray and

---

[54]"Billy Graham: Peace Is a Spiritual Issue," *The Other Side* 17 (January, 1981): 19.
[55]Frye Gaillard, "Righteousness Reconsidered: The Mellowing of Billy Graham," *Tar Heel: The Magazine of North Carolina* 10 (August, 1981): 25.

turn from your wicked ways, that God might send the revival that we so desperately need as a nation" (1953). "If you would be a true patriot, then become a Christian. If you would be a loyal American, then become a loyal Christian" (1955).[56] In a widely publicized sermon, "Satan's Religion," Graham argued that "the best defense against Communism is a citadel of strength through Godliness . . . ," the elements of which are: "old-fashioned Americanism . . . conservative and Evangelical Christianity . . . prayer . . . a genuine spiritual revival," and receiving Christ as Savior. "The greatest and most effective weapon against Communism today is to be born again Christian."[57]

This indicates how closely tied Americanism and anti-communism were in his thinking, and it provides insight into the struggle that must have gone on within Graham as he was endeavoring to extricate one from the other. In these years he fully accepted the cardinal doctrines of what Robert Linder and I have labelled "evangelical civil religion," that is, America was a nation whose founders honored and reverenced God, but in the last few years it has drifted from these moorings. As he declared in 1952 (to an English audience, no less), there was first the "intellectual departure from God," and then a decline set in. Never before were there more gangsterism, crime, immorality, and divorces than today. Finally came the religious departure which produced a nation of empty churches, and America could not take its place in moral leadership "as seemingly Providence had planned." Now the communist "barbarians" were "beating at our gates," and we were facing a spiritual power that could not be defeated on the battlefield. The United States could not escape the judgment of God unless the people turned to God in repentance. The only hope was a revival such as those which in the past diverted America from the path of apostasy.[58]

Even in the 1960's and early 1970's Graham saw national survival as incumbent upon its people turning to God. In 1962 he wrote that America is a "covenant nation" which "draws upon its origins in loyalty and devotion to God for strength," and its political leaders needed to "have faith in God," if they hoped to find a solution to "the present crisis."[59] The secret of the nation's strength was not military might but "faith in God," and America would never be saved unless it were willing to turn to Jesus Christ and know his regenerating power. "When you make your decision for Jesus Christ, it is America making her deci-

---

[56]Quoted in McLoughlin, *Billy Graham*, pp. 142-143.

[57]Billy Graham, "Satan's Religion," *American Mercury* 79 (August, 1954): 45-46.

[58]Billy Graham, *The Work of an Evangelist: An Address Given in the Assembly Hall of the Church House, Westminster, on 20th March 1952* (London: World's Evangelical Alliance, 1953), pp. 7-11. My thinking on this is developed more fully in Robert D. Linder and Richard V. Pierard, *Twilight of the Saints: Biblical Christianity and Civil Religion in America* (Downers Grove, IL: InterVarsity Press, 1978). In all fairness, it should be mentioned that some writers—most notably Robert Bellah in *The Broken Covenant: American Civil Religion in Time of Trial* (New York: Seabury Press, 1975)—view the concept more positively than we do.

[59]Billy Graham, "Our Right to Require Belief," *Saturday Evening Post* 235 (February 17, 1962): 9.

sion through you."[60] At the "Honor America Day" extravaganza on July 4, 1970, Graham called upon "all Americans" to stop the polarization which was occurring and "proudly gather around our flag and all that it stands for." After making the thoroughly unbiblical assertion that the Bible says "honor the nation," he enumerated seven reasons why "we honor America," the last of which was that "there is woven in the warp and woof of our nation faith in God." He urged his listeners "to raise your voices in prayer and dedication to God and in commitment to the ideals and dreams upon which our country was founded."[61] These themes appeared again in a 1973 *Decision* article where he stated categorically: "Our forefathers founded the United States upon faith in God, and our country will survive and be great only as long as it honors God."[62] It is no wonder that Graham came under heavy fire for preaching civil religion, although he denied this was really so.[63]

It was obvious that such true-blue Americanism would never do for one who was rapidly becoming a world figure. The first inkling of a change in outlook was in 1967 when he told the press while in Yugoslavia that he was not "a representative of any government, I am a representative of the kingdom of God."[64] But by July, 1974, his thinking clearly had shifted, as he pointed out in the keynote address to the Lausanne Congress on World Evangelism. He said it was an "error" to:

> Identify the Gospel with any one particular political program or culture. This has been my own danger. When I go to preach the Gospel, I go as an ambassador for the Kingdom of God—not America. To tie the Gospel to any political system, secular program, or society is dangerous and will only serve to divert the Gospel. The Gospel transcends the goals and methods of any political system or any society.[65]

In a *Wittenburg Door* interview that same year he underscored the point that "our Gospel is not Americanism; our Gospel is not America." Rather, the message is Jesus Christ crucified and risen again, and he "can make a great impact on any country whether it's the Soviet Union or the United States."[66] At the Pan-African Christian Leadership Conference in Nairobi in December, 1976, he can-

---

[60]"Changing the Tide of History," sermon, 1966, p. 3; "Rioting or Righteousness," sermon, 1967, p. 11.

[61]"Honor America," sermon, 1970, pp. 3, 10.

[62]Billy Graham, "God and America," *Decision* 14 (July, 1973): 1.

[63]"The Preaching and the Power," *Newsweek* 76 (July 20, 1970): 55; Reinhold Niebuhr, "The King's Chapel and the King's Court," *Christianity and Crisis* 29 (August 4, 1969): 211-212; "Billy Graham and 'Civil Religion,'" p. 152; "Can the Tide Be Turned?" sermon, 1976, p. 10.

[64]*Dallas Morning News*, July 9, 1967, quoted in Lockard, *The Unheard Billy Graham*, p. 140.

[65]J. D. Douglas, ed., *Let the Earth Hear His Voice* (Minneapolis: World Wide, 1975), p. 30.

[66]"Door Interview, Billy Graham," *Wittenburg Door* 19 (June-July, 1974): 6.

didly admitted that some of his early preaching "almost fell into the trap of civil religion. I came close to idolatry. . . . Americanism is not Christianity. I am not an ambassador for America but for the Lord Jesus Christ."[67]

Still, from time to time Graham "backslid," most notably during the Bicentennial observance when evangelicals generally allowed themselves to be carried away in exultation over America's spiritual heritage and calling the nation back to God.[68] In his Bicentennial sermon, "Can the Tide Be Turned?" he alleged that there was "a definite relationship between a vital and vibrant Judeo-Christian faith and the well-being of the nation, politically, socially, economically, and culturally." America was in danger of falling just as Rome did, because it lacked a "moral center," and "spiritual apostasy and moral decay go together." "When people are neither grateful to Almighty God nor to the heroes of yesterday who bought their freedoms at the price of blood, then irresponsibility takes over as the dangers of despotism and national degradation increase." The "three great powers" which believers can utilize to keep America free are repentance of national and individual sins, prayer, and the ballot box.[69] Even though these old views lay just below the surface and emerged on such occasions as patriotic observances, he resisted the pressure to become involved in the abortive scheme of Campus Crusade for Christ leader Bill Bright to "recapture the country for Christ" during 1976.[70]

A *New York Times* editorial in 1980 called Graham's change of heart "appealing." Referring to his statement, "I used in the 50's to make the mistake of almost identifying the Kingdom of God with the American way of life. . . . I have come to see that other cultures have their own way that may be just as good," the newspaper declared it "shows that a person with the most fiery convictions *can* amend them, *can* come to see another point of view and still cling to principles."[71] The evangelist's present stance is that he feels called to a "world ministry" and is a "world ambassador," and in fact he regrets President Eisenhower's characterization of him as "the greatest ambassador that America has." As Graham put it, now that the ministry is a global one, "I think now when I say something, 'How is this going to sound in India? How is it going to sound to my friends in Hungary or Poland?' "[72] Just as he had substantially

---

[67]*Partnership* (Abington, PA), no. 8 (March 4, 1977), p. 3. Interestingly, the sermon text contained in *Decision* (18 [May, 1977] : 1-2) omits these remarks by Graham.

[68]See Richard V. Pierard, "Evangelicals and the Bicentennial," *Reformed Journal* 26 (October, 1976): 19-23.

[69]"Can the Tide Be Turned?"

[70]Bright's Christian Embassy venture collapsed after his rightist ties were exposed by Jim Wallis and Wes Michaelson in "The Plan to Save America," *Sojourners* 5 (April, 1976): 5-12. See also "Politics from the Pulpit," *Newsweek* 88 (September 6, 1976): 49, 51. The principal biography of Bright whitewashes his involvement and does not mention Graham's coolness at all: Richard Quebedeaux, *I Found It! The Story of Bill Bright and Campus Crusade* (San Francisco: Harper & Row, 1979), pp. 188-190.

[71]*New York Times*, February 8, 1980, p. A30.

[72]Marguerite Michaels, "Billy Graham: America Is Not God's Only Kingdom," *Parade*, February 1, 1981, p. 6; Gaillard, "Righteousness Reconsidered," p. 25.

modified his stance on race and communism, so his approach to American nationalism had mellowed, and this, too, helped to increase his level of acceptance elsewhere in the world.

V

The extent of Billy Graham's changes and effort to maintain a genuinely ecumenical outreach could be seen in two developments in 1981 and 1982. One was his attempt to keep the lines open to the evangelical right, even as he was risking his enormous popularity among conservatives and fundamentalists by his advocacy of peace and reconciliation with the communist-bloc nations. The other was his trips to the Soviet Union and the German Democratic Republic, events which even in the late 1970's seemed to lie far beyond the realm of possibility.

His speech to the convention of National Association of Evangelicals and National Religious Broadcasters in January, 1981, was widely interpreted as a criticism of Jerry Falwell and other practitioners of the electronic church who were active in the new Christian right. In it he reiterated his support for the rediscovery of Christian social action and concern about the nuclear arms race, and he criticized the emphasis on the latest technology and the use of "worldly and carnal methods" of "gimmicks and high-pressure professional fund-raising tactics" by broadcasters and other Christian organizations.[73] His feelings about the new right were more evident in a *People* magazine interview:

> I think where political issues invade moral situations, spiritual leaders have to speak out. But I do not intend to use what little influence I may have on secular, non-moral, non-religious issues like the Panama Canal. . . . There is a danger that we can get side-tracked into issues that blur the clear-cut message of the Gospel.[74]

The preacher was perhaps most forthright in speaking to a *Parade* magazine writer:

> It would be unfortunate if people get the impression all evangelists belong to that group. The majority do not. I don't wish to be identified with them.
>
> I'm for morality. But morality goes beyond sex to human freedom and social justice. . . . Evangelists can't be closely identified with any

---

[73]The text of the N.A.E.-N.R.B. address is in *Eternity* 32 (May, 1981): 19-21. One columnist who perceived the speech as critical of Falwell's stance was Colman McCarthy, but he did not foresee a public break between them: "How Some of the Evangelicals Feel about Moral Majority," *Washington Post*, February 12, 1981, p. M2.

[74]"Billy Graham, First of the Big-Time TV Preachers, Warns Falwell & Co. of Danger Ahead," *People Weekly* 15 (February 15, 1981): 32.

particular party or person. We have to stand in the middle in order to preach to all people, right and left. I haven't been faithful to my own advice in the past. I will be in the future. . . .

I told [Jerry Falwell] to preach the Gospel. That's our calling. I want to preserve the purity of the Gospel and the freedom of religion in America. I don't want to see religious bigotry in any form. . . . It would disturb me if there was a wedding between the religious fundamentalists and the political right. The hard right has no interest in religion except to manipulate it.[75]

In these remarks Graham placed himself squarely in the middle, in order that he could have access to as wide a range of people as possible in his preaching ministry. Although obviously uncomfortable with the right, he did not wish to cut himself off completely from that segment of society, so he composed an irenic letter to Falwell which was released to the press. The opening line was: "Dear Jerry: I am deeply disturbed that there seems to be an attempt to drive a wedge between us."[76] Kenneth Kantzer of *Christianity Today* later observed that Falwell "has made his peace with Graham," but it is improbable that the evangelist would be invited to speak from his pulpit.[77] Since Falwell is practicing his own brand of ecumenism through the Moral Majority, it is not unrealistic to assume that the two preachers could arrive at a *modus vivendi* even though they apparently differ widely on sociopolitical issues.

Graham's desire to promote peace and preach the gospel led to his decision to attend (as an observer) the international conference, "Religious Workers for Saving the Sacred Gift of Life from Nuclear Catastrophe," hosted by the Orthodox Patriarch of Moscow, May 10-14, 1982. Fearing that he would be exploited by Soviet propaganda, the White House tried to discourage the trip (Graham insists, however, that President Reagan did not specifically ask him to stay home), but he decided to take the risk anyway. In his speech at the conclave he issued a ringing call for negotiated arms control with the ultimate aim of total disarmament, repentance by the leaders of the nations for their lack of concern about the needs of the poor and their failure to place top priority on peace, actions to increase trust and understanding among the peoples of the world, and finally for "all governments to respect the rights of religious believers" as outlined in the United Nations Declaration of Human Rights and the Final Act of Helsinki.[78] His tightly packed schedule included preaching in two churches,

---

[75]Michaels, "Billy Graham," p. 6.

[76]Gaillard, "Righteousness Reconsidered," p. 26. Referring to the N.A.E.-N.R.B. speech, *Los Angeles Times* reporter Robert Scheer claims that the Virginian "was stung by Graham's remarks," and he "obtained a letter from Graham stating that he was not attempting to single out Falwell for criticism" (March 4, 1981, p. 17).

[77]Kenneth Kantzer, "Reflections: Five Years of Change," *Christianity Today* 26 (November 26, 1982): 15. To a *Christian Life* interviewer Graham said he was not a member of the Moral Majority and had met Falwell only once, "But I do believe in many of the moral goals the Moral Majority espouses" (July, 1982, p. 32).

[78]The text of the speech is in *Christianity Today* 26 (June, 18, 1982): 20-23.

visiting the Siberian Seven in the U.S. Embassy, and talks with the high Soviet officials and with Christian and Jewish religious leaders.

In hindsight, it appears that Graham had not adequately informed himself about the Soviet situation and did not take along as advisers the best available evangelical specialists on Soviet church affairs who could have steered him past the pitfalls there. His bending over backwards to be accommodating to his hosts gave the impression he was being used by them. As a result he made some slip-ups that the press corps quickly seized upon. At the Baptist church he said that God gives a Christian "the power to be a better worker, a more loyal citizen because in Romans 13 we are told to obey the authorities." Unfortunately, a reporter took the phrase out of context from a sermon on Christian conduct and made it into the major point.[79] Also, tongue-in-cheek comments that churches in Moscow were more crowded on Saturday night than in his hometown of Charlotte and that he was served caviar with every meal were portrayed as glaring examples of insensitivity.

The heaviest fire was directed at his observation that more religious freedom existed in the Soviet Union than he had thought, as worship services are being held and there was no state church. Upon his return home he defended himself by saying that this was a relative matter. In the United States he does not have freedom "to go into a public school and preach the Gospel, nor is a student free in a public school to pray, or a teacher free to read the Bible publicly to the students."[80] Experts on religious liberty instantly recognized that this was no rebuttal at all, and it only made him look worse.

Another *faux pas* was his attempt to explain away the arrest of a woman for unfurling a banner during his sermon in the Baptist church, which read in English: "We have more than 150 prisoners for the work of the Gospel." Graham's reply to reporters' queries about this was (other than that he did not see it): "We detain people in the United States if we catch them doing things wrong. I have had people coming to my services in the United States and causing disturbances and they have been taken out by the police."[81] It was *Boston Globe* writer James Franklin who correctly captured the meaning of this. Graham had just compared it "to the way zealous ushers remove dissenters from his rallies in this country—just a matter of good order, he seemed to say."[82] For Graham watchers this evoked painful memories of the Billy Graham Day debacle in 1971 where a large number of demonstrators was expelled from the carefully orchestrated rally in the Charlotte coliseum, and an embarrassing civil suit was brought by those who had been excluded.[83] And there was the incident in Baltimore only

---

[79]Edward E. Plowman, "Moscow: Quiet Diplomacy," *Evangelical Newsletter* 9 (July 2, 1982): 4. A well-known evangelical reporter, he accompanied Graham to Moscow and recorded nearly all his public comments.

[80]Press release by Graham, New York, May 19, 1982.

[81]*Washington Post*, May 13, 1982, p. A22; *Newsweek* 99 (May 24, 1982): 89.

[82]*Boston Globe*, May 23, 1982, p. A2.

[83]Frady, *Billy Graham*, pp. 455-463.

a year earlier when evangelical peace activist Dale Aukerman and several associates were subjected to verbal abuse and pushed around by crusade workers when they tried to pass out peace literature at the Graham meetings there.[84]

In fact, the volume of criticisms was remarkable. Understandably, Graham was denounced in the *Moral Majority Report* and *Human Events* and in the syndicated columns of articulate conservatives such as William F. Buckley, Jr., William Safire, and George F. Will. Moreover, major newspapers such as the *Baltimore Sun* and the *Chicago Tribune*, as well as *Time* and *Newsweek*, were less than kindly disposed, and Methodist evangelist Edmund Robb, chairperson of the Institute on Religion and Democracy, chided the "naive" Graham on ABC's "This Week with David Brinkley" for "serving the propaganda apparatus of the Soviet Union" and bringing "great discouragement" there.[85] Actually, this showed that James Wall of *The Christian Century* was right on target when he pointed out that the real beneficiary of the trip was not Soviet propaganda but rather the Soviet-haters. They seized upon his mistakes as a means of discrediting dialogue and détente with communist countries.[86]

Nevertheless, as sovietologist Frank H. Epp trenchantly shows, Graham's speech, the entire conference itself, and the final communique comprised a momentous event. The Soviet constitution guarantees freedom of religious belief and worship but not its propagation, yet the 590 conferees spoke as "religious people" and on the basis of "religious values." They were saying that religion in the Soviet Union can no longer mean merely belief and liturgy but is profoundly ethical and social and, therefore, political as well. It set in motion what may well be an irreversible redefinition of religion in the U.S.S.R. For Graham it was personally significant because his call for repentance on the arms race implied that the reign of God is not just in the spiritual realm or postponed to some distant point in the future but actually is now, here on earth, for our time. Like most evangelicals he has thought eschatologically, but, whether he realizes it or not, yet another reorientation within himself may be taking place.[87] It is still too early to tell, but this does bear watching.

In some respects the 1982 missions to East Germany, October 14-25, and Czechoslovakia, October 29-November 4, were anti-climactic. To be sure, Graham had long been a watchword in the G.D.R. for Western religious arrogance (one writer called him an "offering-plate Goebbels"), but his change of heart on the peace issue was widely known, and the Moscow experience opened the way for state approval for a visit. Invited by the Baptists, he had strong backing from the Lutheran and other Protestant churches, and in a whirlwind tour of one-night stands he preached in various cities and met with state and church officials.

---

[84]Gaillard, "Righteousness Reconsidered," pp. 26-27; *Newsletter: Brethren Peace Fellowship, Mid-Atlantic District*, July, 1981.

[85]Clippings and videotape in the Graham Center.

[86]James M. Wall, "A Few Kind Words for Billy Graham," *The Christian Century* 99 (May 26, 1982): 619.

[87]Mennonite Central Committee News Service release, May 28, 1982.

The now-familiar themes pervaded his sermons—repent and turn to Christ, the changed person can change the world, peace is desperately needed—and he refused to comment on sensitive political questions either from the pulpit or at press conferences. The situation was identical in Czechoslovakia where the invitation was issued by the Baptist Union with the support of the fourteen-member Council of Churches, and he preached in the three largest cities.

Unlike the Russian venture, this foray into the East attracted little attention back home. Although church leaders in both countries expressed satisfaction with his proclamation of an evangelistic message coupled with a concern for peace and for stimulating more public awareness of the continuing role of the church in Marxist states, the West German press sharply disapproved of his lifestyle and message there, his unwillingness to criticize the communist regimes, and his assertion that religious freedom existed in the Soviet bloc.[88]

Early in 1982, Billy Graham told *Newsweek*'s Kenneth Woodward that "the issue of the '80s is going to be hermeneutics, or how to interpret Scripture properly and apply it to personal and social life."[89] This quote reflects his own "pilgrimage" in that, while he stands firmly by the idea of an inspired, authoritative Bible, he has learned that when the light of Scripture is brought to bear on social views formed under the influence of one's cultural background those views may well require alteration. Surely his ecumenical contacts and openness to new ideas lay behind his growth and development through the years and has produced noteworthy modification of his opinions on sociopolitical matters. These actions have undoubtedly cost him support, and he is no longer number one in the amount of funds attracted to his ministry. But there is no indication that he is ready to back down from the broader course he has chosen, and one may expect to see a continuing flexibility in the remaining years of his public ministry. Christians can ask no more of Graham than this.

---

[88]The most perceptive report was by the Mennonite free-lance writer Bill Yoder in the *United Methodist Reporter*, November 26, 1982.

[89]"The Split-Up Evangelicals," *Newsweek* 99 (April 26, 1982): 91.

The Rhetoric of the Radio Ministry*

WILLIAM M. CLEMENTS

THE RELATIONSHIP BETWEEN FOLKLORE AND THE MASS MEDIA is a topic too infrequently explored by folklorists. When the subject has been treated, the thrust of research has been directed primarily toward proving one of two points. The first is the notion that folklore transmission owes a good deal to the media, perhaps as much as to pure oral tradition. This is one of the ideas emerging from Archie Green's collection of case histories of coal miners' songs. Even the sub-title of Green's book suggests that phonograph records are central to the dissemination of these songs,[1] the point being that the modern media have not destroyed folk tradition but have invigorated it, just as broadsides and chapbooks did in the past. The second primary goal of folklore–mass-media research has been to demonstrate that the messages broadcast through the media are strikingly influenced by folk material. Tom Burns' report of folklore culled from a day's television viewing illustrates the pervasive use of folklore and "folklure."[2] Although Burns has gone beyond "text-hunting" in his research, studies such as his parallel in many ways the folklore-in-literature approach that is an established tributary of American folklore scholarship. The results of studies like those of Green and Burns are indeed significant, but another dimension of the interaction between folklore and the mass media merits discussion. While the mass media have been exploiting the commercial potential of folksiness,[3] folk performers have likewise been exploiting the mass media as fully as possible. The purpose of this paper is to examine one instance of such exploitation, the radio ministry of folk preachers, to isolate the strategy that these preachers employ in their use of the radio medium, and ultimately to suggest that a radio preacher's broadcast

---

* A briefer version of this paper was read at the Fourth National Convention of the Popular Culture Association in Milwaukee on May 3, 1974.

[1] Archie Green, *Only a Miner: Studies in Recorded Coal-Mining Songs* (Urbana, 1972).

[2] "Folklore in the Mass Media: Television," *Folklore Forum*, 2 (1969), 90–105. The term *folklure* was coined by Priscilla Denby, "Folklore in the Mass Media," *Folklore Forum*, 4 (1971), 113–121.

[3] For a discussion of folksiness in media advertising, see Tom E. Sullenberger, "Ajax Meets the Jolly Green Giant: Some Observations on the Use of Folklore and Myth in American Mass Marketing," JOURNAL OF AMERICAN FOLKLORE, 87 (1974), 53–65.

can be comprehended most clearly by viewing it as a folklore event similar to occurrences in the context of the preacher's church.

One of the most firmly established institutions associated with America's folk churches—those religious groups whose beliefs and rituals lack direct contact with the secular power structure in a given community—is the radio ministry. On every day of the week, but especially on Sunday, local radio stations present broadcasts by individual preachers, singing ensembles, and even full congregations. Though such broadcasts in theory are excellent devices for reaching "sinnerfolk," nonchurchgoers who might hear the gospel message over the airwaves, the programs seem to be directed at believers already familiar with the structure and content of a church worship service. The occurrence of the performances of preachers and singers in a natural folk-church context reflects the performers' awareness of audience reaction, and their behavior during radio programs seems to assume that a similar performer-audience relationship is operative. In other words, the "pure" folk context is translated—with changes that normally occur during any translation—to a media context.

The Milieu

The research for this study was carried out in Craighead and Poinsett, two contiguous counties of northeastern Arkansas. Both are predominantly flatland, the eastern halves containing the edge of the Mississippi River Delta and the western halves a part of the flood plains of the Cache and White rivers. The two counties are bisected by Crowley's Ridge, a gentle forested uplift left as residue when portions of the Mississippi River system shifted channels in prehistory. The economy relies heavily upon agriculture. Soybeans, cotton, and rice have brought wealth to many farmers, so that the average income in the area is relatively high. The largest city in the two counties, Jonesboro, county seat of Craighead, has a population in excess of twenty-five thousand. The Poinsett County seat, Harrisburg, has fewer than a thousand residents and is thus second in the county to Trumann, some fifteen miles northeast on the Delta. The vast majority of area population is white; Craighead County is only about twelve percent black. Therefore, white folk-churches in the area are more numerous than black and provide a spiritual home for individuals who feel out of place in mainstream religious institutions centered in Jonesboro, Harrisburg, and Trumann.

The study of the folk religion of these white congregations involved the implementation of a number of field research techniques. Participant observation was the most useful, for the optimal method for gaining information about religion is to attend and observe as many religious events as possible. This must be complemented, though, by formal interviews, both directive and nondirective, in order to obtain explication of the events observed. Casual conversation with folk Christians at religious events may also be useful, for many are quite eager to discuss their beliefs and experiences with one who may not have shared these. Finally, an examination of the media is imperative. Printed tracts from denominational presses and newsletters from local churches comprise a good deal of the reading material of folk Christians. More significantly for this study, radio broadcasts of religious orientation have a special appeal and can be monitored easily by the researcher. Although all of these methods for gathering data were employed during the summers of 1972 and 1973 to provide this study an overview of white American folk religion, only the information gained from monitored radio broadcasts, formal interviews, and participant observation is of present concern. It should be noted that all the broadcast tapes used in the study represent performances by folk preachers who had been observed in the church context and for whom formal interview data were available.

While folk religion has been characterized above in terms of its relationship to the rest of American culture rather than on the basis of particular kinds of belief and behavior, only one category of folk religious groups, the Pentecostal, is treated here. The kind of behavior under examination is more striking among preachers of this theological persuasion than among those of Holiness and Baptist churches, the other primary folk religious groups in northeastern Arkansas. Thus, evidence for the conclusions reached here is particularly apparent among the Pentecostals, though the conclusions apply as well to preachers outside the Pentecostal realm.

Pentecostalism is distinguished from the stances of other Christian groups primarily by the addition of some personal experiences the mature Christian must undergo. Following a crisis conversion that occurs after one has reached the age of "accountability," Pentecostals believe Christians next must seek for "sanctification," or "holiness," and the "baptism of the Holy Ghost," experiences that may occur simultaneously or at different times. These notions are derived in part from the theology of John Wesley, whose ideas about the stages in Christian life have been outlined as "sinfulness in man, his repentance, his justification through faith, his regeneration or new birth, his repentance after justification (should he fall back into sin), his assurance of present salvation, and his sanctification."[4] An emphasis on the last stage, defined in the 1890's as "the holiness of a fallen, but redeemed human being, . . . enjoyed and lived, by one who is subject to human infirmities and surrounded by all the circumstances incident to human life. . . . [with] a heart thoroughly cleansed from all sin, both inherited and acquired, and filled with the Spirit of purity,"[5] brought about the formation of Holiness churches, many of which became Pentecostally oriented during the early twentieth century. Despite the fact that sanctification was a part of Wesley's teachings, American Methodists have generally underplayed its importance. During the denomination's early history primary emphasis was directed toward evangelizing the Ohio Valley frontier; religious energy was to be spent in winning new Christians rather than in leading believers on to higher stages of spiritual experience. A brief flurry of interest in sanctification among Methodists during the decades before the Civil War quickly waned when this "second blessing" came to be scorned as the denomination gained established respectability. However, a number of individuals and groups on the periphery of Methodism continued to believe that sanctification was an experience devoutly to be sought. Although originally not schismatics and interested only in restoring sanctification to its legiti-

[4] Charles J. Koerber, *The Theology of Conversion According to John Wesley* (Neo-Eboraci, 1967), 1.
[5] *The Double Cure or Echoes from National Camp-Meetings* (Boston, 1894), 10.

mate place in Methodist theology, these fringe groups developed into a number of new denominations—usually fairly localized—during the 1880's. Often known as the "Church of God" or "Holiness Church," these groups differed from the Methodist Episcopal Church on the matter of sanctification and occasionally on notions about church polity. It is out of these late nineteenth-century Holiness churches that Pentecostalism as a movement developed.

In order for a group to be properly termed "Pentecostal," it must believe in an individual's receiving the "baptism of the Holy Ghost." This experience may occur before, after, or concurrently with sanctification, and often the only difference among Pentecostal groups is the way they order the experiences. An experience as dramatic as the crisis conversion, the baptism of the Holy Ghost—also called the "infilling of the Holy Ghost," "receiving the Holy Ghost," and "Spirit-baptism"—is always accompanied by a subject's speaking in a language unknown to himself. This glossolalia, for which the primary scriptural authority is the experience of the apostles on the day of Pentecost,[6] is regarded as the "evidence—external evidence of an internal experience—internal transformation that is shown externally—demonstrated externally by speaking with other tongues."[7]

Speaking in tongues at the time of Spirit-baptism is not viewed by Pentecostals as the only manifestation of the Holy Ghost's presence in the mature Christian's life. As long as he is willing, the Spirit-filled person will continue to pray and praise God in languages whose meaning is unknown to him. This continued glossolalia maintains the strength of the believer's conviction, allows him an exclusive channel of communication with God when the language is considered a heavenly rather than an earthly one, and permits the Holy Ghost to make prayer requests that the individual's "carnal" reason would not recognize as being needed. Also, the Spirit-filled believer may be an agent through whom the Holy Ghost can operate one or all of His nine spiritual gifts. St. Paul lists these gifts as the word of wisdom, the word of knowledge, faith, healing, the working of miracles, prophecy, discerning of spirits, diverse kinds of tongues, and interpretation of tongues.[8] These nine, exercised publicly as the Holy Ghost directs, comprise the ideal operation of a Pentecostal congregation. Preachers, having been baptized by the Holy Ghost, are thus channels for these gifts. How their ministry operates in the natural church context and in radio broadcasts will be compared.

The Strategy

In order for an individual to receive Spirit-baptism or to act as an agent through whom the Holy Ghost heals, prophesies, and the like, a dissociation from worldly affairs must take place. It may be accomplished by allowing the emotions complete and unfettered expression. Therefore, Pentecostal preachers have well-defined notions about their responsibilities in regard to the spiritual and emotional conditions of their congregations. The Pentecostal who comes to

---

[6] Acts 2:1–13.
[7] Interview with J. G., Pentecostal minister, in Jonesboro, Arkansas, on August 16, 1973.
[8] I Corinthians 12:8–10.

church to "get a blessing"—spiritually, emotionally, or physically—relies upon the preacher to create an atmosphere wherein such a blessing is readily available and the Holy Ghost is welcome to exercise His baptizing power and nine spiritual gifts. A preacher at an Assembly of God church characterized his role in a natural church context: "I've got to create an atmosphere in here. In my church I've got to create an atmosphere of where men are drawn to Christ. . . . When I crawl in that pulpit, the Holy Ghost knows who's in that service. And He knows what they need. If I'm in tune with God, *every* person in that building will be ministered to."[9] A similar consciousness of role was demonstrated by the pastor of an independent Pentecostal congregation: "I'm a terrible fellow about feelings. . . . Yes sir, I get everybody else to moving and feeling good, and they think I'm enjoying it, and I'm all the time—I'm trying to pull them up, you know. That's why they call it the 'pull-pit.' You pull them from the pit, you know."[10] I have observed this preacher adjust the thermostat in his church even while in a state of apparent ecstasy, waiting for the Holy Ghost to interpret a message in tongues. This does not suggest that he is a charlatan but that he is ever conscious of his responsibility to minister to the people's needs.

Even without the supporting comments from the folk preachers it would be evident that much of their effort in a natural church context is directed toward providing the congregation with an environment in which spiritual emotionalism can be manifested overtly and in which the affairs of the world are allowed to intrude only rarely. The creation of this atmosphere—the fundamental strategy of the Pentecostal folk preacher—is achieved primarily through sermon style and content, direct pleas for congregational responsive expression, and manipulation of miscellaneous aspects of the worship event such as singing and testimony.

Bruce A. Rosenberg has described in detail the sermon style of black Pentecostal folk preachers.[11] Their white counterparts differ only by degree in their use of chanted spiritual sermons, which Rosenberg found to be both barometers of spiritual emotionalism in worship and catalysts for it. It needs to be reiterated here that the chanted sermon is an extremely effective device for arousing congregational excitement. Ideally preaching under the "anointing" of the Holy Ghost, the folk preacher aims to deliver messages that "just *flow* like a river."[12] Significantly, though, the chanted style of sermon presentation is dependent upon reciprocity from the audience. As congregational responses increase, the chant becomes steadier, more vociferous, and thus more likely to elicit further responses.

The content of sermons also contributes to their emotional effect. All folk preachers treated in this study employ the "text-and-context" approach, whereby a particular scripture passage is read and then expounded upon.[13] Any scripture text is a legitimate foundation for a folk sermon, but the ultimate theme of every sermon seems to be the same: sinners must convert and saints must help them.

[9] Interview with D. C., Pentecostal minister, in Harrisburg, Arkansas, on July 20, 1973.
[10] Interview with W. O., Pentecostal minister, in Jonesboro, Arkansas, on June 14, 1973.
[11] *The Art of the American Folk Preacher* (New York, 1970).
[12] Interview with D. C., Pentecostal minister, in Harrisburg, Arkansas, on July 20, 1973.
[13] Rosenberg, 14.

In realistic detail the horrors of hell and the machinations of Satan are depicted as escapable only through accepting the Lord Jesus Christ as one's personal savior. This acceptance must be immediate, for an imminent Apocalypse is indicated by military conflicts in the Mid-East, general moral decay, and the phenomenal spread of Pentecostal experiences throughout Christendom. A fervent invitation urging convinced sinners to approach the altar always climaxes an emotion-charged presentation.

Although the style and content of the sermon itself are usually sufficient to elicit emotional, Spirit-filled responses from the congregation, sometimes the preacher may find that these devices are not completely successful in creating the atmosphere necessary for the operation of the Holy Ghost. To compensate, the preacher may turn to direct pleas for congregational involvement. An admonition to say "Hallelujah" and eschew the wiles of Satan, who is always interested in preventing spiritual emotionalism, may bring a recalcitrant congregation into responsiveness and effect the desired results. I have heard a Pentecostal preacher remind a listless congregation, "This is not a Presbyterian service," in reference to a denomination known for its unemotional formality in worship. Even a standing ovation for Jesus may be called for if congregational exuberance is especially low.

Furthermore, the folk preacher does not limit his attempts to create an emotionally spiritual atmosphere to the sermon portion of the church worship event. Rousing songs like "I Would Not Be Denied" and "Victory in Jesus," loud periods of prayer and praise, and healing rituals may all contribute to the shaping of the proper congregational attitudes. Especially effective are those devices that involve the congregation directly in the proceedings. By emphasizing these, the folk preacher gives certain members of the congregation an additional vested interest in achieving spiritual arousal. Performing special musical selections or testifying about Jesus' activities in their lives provides individuals the opportunity to evince licensed emotionalism before their peers and perhaps to encourage those peers to do likewise. The successful Pentecostal folk preacher affords his congregation every chance for emotional expression as a group and as individuals.

In a natural church context the strategy of a Pentecostal folk preacher clearly involves the creation of an atmosphere wherein the congregation can allow free rein to the emotions, thereby bringing about in themselves a condition suitable for the activity of the Holy Ghost. This strategy is carried over to the radio broadcast, but the basic techniques undergo transformation to meet the exigencies of that medium, perhaps the most crucial of which is the absence of a live, responsive audience. Except in those instances when an entire worship service is presented, the radio preacher operates in a vacuum, speaking live into a studio microphone or using a tape recorder in his home or study. As Rosenberg has observed, audience response—the reciprocity mentioned above—is normally an essential force in molding the style of the folk preacher's presentation, for the congregation influences the degree of emotionalism, the tone, and even the length of the folk preacher's message.[14] The absence of this agent of response would certainly affect the folk preacher's performance.

14 Rosenberg, 12–13.

A second factor that shapes the radio broadcast is the time limit imposed. While a folk preacher may not necessarily be longwinded in a natural church context, the presence of a strict control over the amount of time allowed to him during a broadcast must have an inhibiting effect. Often a given program will last only fifteen minutes, and the preacher must adjust his message to fit that period. Even though the Holy Ghost anoints and blesses the message, the radio preacher must always keep a wary eye on his wrist watch.

Third, the radio preacher must employ a delivery style different from that used in natural church contexts. Gestures, facial expressions, and personal allusions—all valuable aids to the transmission of a sermon message—are useless for a radio audience. Over the airwaves the preacher must rely upon the content of his message and the quality of his voice to accomplish all of his purpose.

These differences in context when the folk preacher shifts from church to mass media necessitate his adjusting his techniques for carrying out the strategy he has brought with him from the church worship event. His intent is still to create a spiritually emotional atmosphere for his audience—in this case a group bound together perhaps only by their having tuned in his radio program—so that they will be in the proper state to welcome the operation of the Holy Ghost in their lives. To accomplish this, the radio preacher uses the techniques he has developed for the church context and adapts them to the broadcast situation.

To begin with, the sermon style approximates that used in church, but because of the lack of a responsive audience the radio preacher is less likely than his pulpit counterpart to employ the emotion-charged chant. However, chanting does occur during radio broadcasts. In a series of about a dozen tape-recorded programs featuring the same preacher, I discovered at least one section of chant in every sermon. For example,

> Brother, it takes the power of the Holy Ghost.
> It takes prayer and fasting and bombarding heaven.
> And I *feel* the answer is this:
> That God's going to send an old-fashioned latter-rain
>   outpouring.
> We're living in the greatest time of all—prosperous
>   times.
> I feel that God *wants* us to have revival.
> I feel it's time the reason why the showers have been
>   withholden.
> God's people don't expect revival.
> They speak in negative terms. Yes sir.
> They have a lot of problems.
> But I feel today as it was in Noah's day.
> There's apostasy, unbelieving, and falling away—
> Not from church membership, but people are falling
>   away from the real faith.[15]

This was part of a message in anticipation of a thirty-day revival period in the

[15] Radio sermon preached by W. O. over KTBM in Jonesboro, Arkansas, on June 24, 1973.

preacher's church. His optimism about the time's being particularly apt for such a marathon undertaking was somewhat unfounded, for the revival lasted only three weeks and even at that often seemed on the verge of fizzling out.

If the style of the radio sermon differs, its content departs little from the familiar gospel message. A climactic call for converts may not be appropriate for the radio context, for the preacher has no precise concept of the nature of his audience and is not in a position actually to welcome them to the altar. Nevertheless, he does put forth a plea for listeners to get right with God through church attendance or private worship. Using the text-and-context approach of the pulpit ministry, the radio preacher too employs any scripture passage as a foundation for his ultimate evangelical goal: salvation of the lost. As the supposed agent of the Holy Ghost, the preacher has some consciousness of the spiritual needs of his listeners and seems to manifest that consciousness through the content of his sermon messages.

It is in the use of direct urging for emotional response that the radio preacher diverges most strikingly from pulpit technique. Of course, with no way of knowing how his listeners are reacting to his broadcast, a specific plea for emotional involvement might be superfluous. Although occasionally I have heard a radio preacher tell his listeners to say "Hallelujah," this is much less common than general indirect encouragement for his listeners to be receptive to the operations of the Holy Ghost. The radio preacher can offer continual reminders of the Pentecostal trait of overtly manifesting spiritual emotionalism, or he can disparage the cold formality that has driven true religion out of many churches. Perhaps no one in the radio audience shouts or sings in response to these indirect suggestions, but the constant reiteration that these responses are vital parts of worship must have some effect.

There are several devices outside the actual sermon message through which the radio preacher attempts to involve his listeners in the broadcast experience just as they would be involved in a natural worship event. He makes himself personally available to them by providing a telephone number they can call at any time when in need of prayer or spiritual guidance. He makes himself dependent upon them by relying on their contributions to pay for air time. Even when the radio preacher does not make a direct call for contributions, he may present a veiled plea by thanking by name the listeners who "sponsor" the broadcast.

The most dramatic way the Pentecostal radio preacher involves his listeners in the broadcast event takes place in the context of healing ritual. Here, if anyone desires the results of healing, he must make a definite commitment to involve himself in the activity. The commitment may take the form of placing a hand on the radio as a "point of contact," raising a hand toward heaven, or merely having faith and trust that God's healing power will be channeled through the radio preacher. An explanation of the nature and necessity of explicit audience commitment was offered during a broadcast by a preacher recording his message from a small Pentecostal church in Apt, an unincorporated community in Craighead County:

I believe last Sunday it was that he [a listener] had her [his wife] lay her hand on the radio, and he said she was feeling better afterwards. So tonight we ask Sister Andrews to place her hand upon the radio as a point of contact. And we'll pray for you at this time. Also you others out in radioland that are sick and afflicted—you place your hand upon your radio as a point of contact. Or if you can't reach the radio, you go to the Lord in prayer where you're at. Place your hands upon your own body. Now some people say, "Well, why? My hands are fastened to my body." Yes, but if you—if you can pick those hands up, lift them toward heaven or put them on your body, that's a sign that you're really sincere with God.[16]

The radio preacher literally expects listener response and involvement, and it is this expectation that causes him to employ the basic strategy he uses in the natural church context. Although he adjusts his techniques to the broadcast situation, his goal is still the creation of a spiritual atmosphere where sinners may be saved, the afflicted may be healed, and saints may get a blessing.

The folk preacher recognizes a twofold purpose for taking his strategy to the airwaves. First, the radio ministry affords an excellent means for getting the gospel message to individuals who cannot attend church due to physical incapacity or some other legitimate cause. Where once these shut-ins received spiritual nourishment by means of visits from fellow Christians, the radio ministry offers them the opportunity to participate in an actual worship experience. Second, folk preachers view the radio ministry as an inexpensive method for spreading Christianity to a vast number of people. For example, during the summer of 1973 an hour-long broadcast over a radio station in Trumann in Poinsett County cost only twenty dollars. And this was for noon on Sunday—prime time! The preacher who directed this broadcast once boasted that he knew of people living as far away as seventy-five miles who listened to the program.[17]

In addition to these patent uses, it must be briefly noted that the radio ministry also functions to reinforce ego satisfaction for the folk preacher. Often low in secular status, folk preachers may adopt their vocations in order to exercise a degree of power and prestige in a society where their lack of education and other worldly commodities renders them powerless. The radio ministry represents a logical extension of the prestige enjoyed in a natural church context. The validity of this contention is evident from the envious disparagement folk preachers direct at such successful manipulators of the mass media for evangelistic ends as Oral Roberts and the late A. A. Allen. When asked about these figures, a folk preacher with a radio ministry immediately responded, "Yes, I believe they really have the goods." However, within ten minutes he had related the story of Allen's death from cirrhosis of the liver due to alcoholism and lamented Roberts' ungallant defection from the Pentecostals to the Methodists.[18] Another radio preacher boasted of his success in healing a woman whose cancerous foot had not responded to the ministrations of Roberts or of William Branham, a mass evangelist who flourished several decades ago.[19] In pointing out their celebrated rivals' shortcomings, the folk preachers reveal their awareness of the prestige attached to their activities.

[16] Radio program broadcast over KTMN in Trumann, Arkansas, on July 15, 1973.
[17] Interview with J. P., Pentecostal minister, in Apt, Arkansas, on July 11, 1973.
[18] Interview with W. O., Pentecostal minister, in Jonesboro, Arkansas, on June 14, 1973.
[19] Interview with J. P., Pentecostal minister, in Apt, Arkansas, on July 11, 1973.

Conclusion

This examination of the strategy of radio preachers is intended to suggest a direction for studies of the relationship between folklore and the mass media. The radio preacher does not merely incorporate folklore "texts" into his media performance; rather, the whole performance is an attempt to transfer a folklore event to the media context. The personal audience-performer relationship or small group environment that some hold to be a necessary constituent of folklore is missing,[20] but the strategy brought over from pulpit ministry remains unchanged.

The Pentecostal radio preacher is not the only folk performer who has done this sort of thing. Perhaps similar discussions could demonstrate how urban bluesmen have taken a strategy from a folklore event into media contexts.[21] Certainly such a perspective is valid for the performances of white folk musicians who have radio or even television programs. At any rate, it is evident that the folk preacher's strategic use of a mass medium as a device for extending the scope of a folklore event suggests that folklore—no matter how one defines the term—is dynamic enough to adjust to any cultural innovation.

Arkansas State University
State University, Arkansas

---

[20] Dan Ben-Amos, "Toward a Definition of Folklore in Context," JOURNAL OF AMERICAN FOLKLORE, 84 (1971), 13.
[21] In *Urban Blues* (Chicago, 1966), Charles Keil has made some suggestions along this line.

Copyright Information

191

Index

Editorial corrections appear in this index in brackets adjacent to the entry as it appears in the text.